# WORKS CORTINA, CORSAIR & CAPRI
## IN DETAIL

# WORKS CORTINA, CORSAIR & CAPRI
## IN DETAIL

By Graham Robson

Photography by Simon Clay

Herridge & Sons

Published in 2016 by
Herridge and Sons Ltd
Lower Forda, Shebbear
Devon EX21 5SY

ISBN 978-1-906133-71-9
Printed in China

# CONTENTS

# INTRODUCTION

*Lotus-Cortinas were the mainstay of the Ford-UK motorsport programme from 1963 to 1968. This particular car was first seen in 1965.*

It is now more than fifty years since the first-ever works Cortina started a motorsport career, more than fifty years since the works team settled in to its new home at Boreham in Essex – and, unhappily, it is now some years since that facility was closed down. Even so, for all Ford motorsport fanatics– and naturally that includes the author – it is important to set down the complete (if possible!) story of these cars and their careers.

In just six years – 1962 to 1968 – the ever-developing pedigree of works Cortinas spearheaded a successful attempt to transform the Ford motorsport effort from one of merely being 'good chaps', into one of the most formidably successful in the world. Not only that, but the cars built, or inspired, by the Boreham team, won all over the world, and were still winning when they gave rise to an even more significant successor – the works Escort. Without the Cortina, for sure, there might

never have been a works Escort, and without both of them, the company's image might never have been what it became.

Although books have been written about some aspects of the most famous Cortinas (and the Capris which evolved from them), and of particular cars, no previous author has ever had the chance, the scope or the space to go into great detail about the individual histories of each car, or especially to explore some of the myths and legends surrounding them. Until now, that is – for this book separately surveys every one of the authentic works cars and their often-complex lives.

I have been digging into the history of Cortinas and Capris for many years, but this is the very first time that I have been able to list every event (International and National status) tackled by every one of the works cars, and to find time to list (and often illustrate) the different paint jobs, sponsors' deals, and programmes gifted to each example. Not only that, but in some now notorious cases I have finally been able to list the ways that certain 'clones' were created, how some cars seamlessly evolved from one identity to another, and how some cars managed to be made ready, often at breakneck speed, to tackle a major event.

I should emphasise, here and now, that this is not just a story about Cortinas in racing and rallying, for I have also gathered together the story of various record attempts, high-speed demonstrations and – yes, let us be frank – stunts in which the cars also took part. It would not have been right to ignore the small but significant involvement which the Corsair added to this story, and in particular the way that the works Capris (whether British or German) evolved from the Cortina's chassis platform and running gear to build their own successful record.

In all humility, I think I can claim that it is all here. To do it, and do it competently, I tried to find as many of the surviving personalities from the 1960s period, and found out exactly what and who did which and what. There is no space here for speculation and rumour, which is why I have always steered clear of so-called re-creations and replicas.

I don't believe that anything like the full story of the Works Cortinas has ever previously been told, but now here it is.

*Works Capris – originally 2300GT, latterly RS3100s – were developed and raced by Ford-Germany from 1969 to 1975. This was one of the formidably successful 3-litre engined RS2600s of the 1972-73 period.*

## Acknowledgements

Over the years – more than fifty years since the original Cortina family was launched – many people have helped me to recollect the Boreham motorsport centre, all the Cortinas, Corsairs and Capris which began their careers there, the saga of their development, and the way in which its people operated, very well indeed. Without them I would never have been able to tap into the character, and charm, of this increasingly successful operation, or understood why the Cortina developed in the manner which it did. As the years passed, too, I managed to interview almost all the important people, whose insight made the compilation of this story so much easier.

These are the people whose personal, face-to-face, interviews and (I am proud to say) friendship have all helped enormously: Peter Ashcroft, Len Bailey, Bill Barnett, Terry (later Sir Terence) Beckett, Terry Bradley, Colin Chapman, Keith Duckworth, Mike Hall, Walter Hayes, Bob Howe, Mick Jones, Alan Mann, Henry Mann, Bill Meade, Andy Middlehurst, Ian Perrett, Jimmy Simpson, David Sutton, Henry Taylor, Stuart Turner, Jeff Uren, Simon Woolley. A special thank you goes to my friend Dave Watkins, who not only owns, or has restored, some of the finest ex-works Ford competition cars in the world, but has an encyclopaedic knowledge of the entire pedigree. Dave cheerfully read what I had to say on this subject, commented on it, found several of the characters and the cars which helped me flesh out the story, and put me right on several points which would otherwise have been wrongly published.

It would also have been impossible to get everything right if, over time, I had not met, talked to, and got to know many of the famous Cortina drivers and co-drivers of that period. There are perhaps too many to be listed here, but in particular I would like to mention: Jim Clark, Roger Clark, John Davenport, Vic Elford, Eric Jackson, Brian Melia, Gunnar Palm, Jim Porter, Peter Procter, Peter Riley, David Seigle-Morris, Phil Simister, Rosemary Smith, John Sprinzel and Sir John Whitmore – all of whom helped me with reminiscences.

Finally, I want to thank all those wonderful people who helped me amass the pictures which do so much to make this book memorable. Over the years, most of the pictures came from Ford's own Photographic Archive, whose staff know just how many hours were needed to dig out the special images. Most recently, therefore, I want to thank Dave Hill for his patience, assistance, and great service. His predecessors, mostly now retired, helped set the whole project in motion.

My grateful thanks, too, for the enthusiasts who have preserved some magnificent Cortinas and Capris to this day, for allowing us to photograph them in all their current glory: Henry Mann (of Alan Mann Racing), Peter Smith, and Michael Webster.

Then, of course, there were the individuals who helped to fill in the gaps that even Ford could not fill – these being highlighted by LAT (and Kathy Ager), and Dave Watkins. Without them it would not have been possible to complete this monumental project, and I am extremely grateful to all of them.

GRAHAM ROBSON
December 2015

# CHAPTER 1:
# BEFORE THE CORTINA: MOTORSPORT WITH ANGLIAS, ZEPHYRS AND ZODIACS

When Ford opened its Motorsport centre at Boreham in Essex it had only recently become serious about motorsport, with a well-organised works team. Victories had come along almost by chance, mainly because a few drivers – many of them Ford dealers – had been clever enough to pick and enter the most suitable events in the best available Ford cars. Although this was not haphazard, it happened in the most informal way.

When Bill Barnett, Boreham's legendary Rally Manager in the 1960s and early 1970s (which covers the Cortina and Capri period) left Motorsport at Boreham in 1973 for a different position at Ford, the company's Public Affairs Chief, Walter Hayes, organised a presentation dinner in his honour, and told this story, which illustrates the way things used to be done:

"When I joined Ford I had to ask 'Edgy' Fabris what he did.

"Publications and competitions," came the reply.

"And what does Competitions consist of?"

"Rallying. Around the end of the year we finish Publications early and go off on the Monte Carlo rally."

"And who organises it all? I mean, surely it takes a lot of planning, all this rallying?"

"Oh," said Fabris, "Bill Barnett does that. Bill does everything!"

That summed up Bill's pre-Boreham job exactly. From the late 1950s to 1973 he was Motorsport's top planner, the one man who knew every car's programme, every service schedule, every driver's private phone number – and he also knew where the best restaurants and hotels in rallying really were. In the beginning, though, he could not have imagined ever working on such programmes:

"I started work at Ford in the advertising department," 'Bill told me, "I had no motorsport ambitions, and there were no connections, none at all."

The motorsport connection finally clicked with Bill in the 1950s. At that time Edgell ('Edgy') Fabris ran the small works rally team, whose cars were prepared in the Lincoln Cars building on the A4 Great West Road on the way out to Heathrow Airport, alongside other Ford cars which were being maintained as press demonstrators. This was a massive white building in the Art Deco style, which in the 1930s had handled the importation of Lincoln motor cars from Canada. Its only advantages were that it was already in existence, was staffed with competent mechanics, and had space available. For Motorsport any move from there to more specialised premises would be an advance.

"Edgy had a triple role," Bill told me, "He was head of administration at Public Relations, head of Publications, and he was also de facto Competitions Manager. He had built up a team around people like Ken Wharton in V8 Pilots, then with Gatsonides in the Zephyr, and Ford dealers like the Harrison family. One day, quite simply, he called me in and said: 'Bill, I've got to go on the Alpine rally, will you please start organising some travel and hotels for me?' It was as casual as that. The next year, 1959, Edgy asked me to do the same thing again. I recall Anne Hall, Gerry Burgess, the Harrison family, Vic Preston and Dennis Scott were all in the team, and on that occasion I actually travelled with the team. It was fascinating, because apart from my wartime service, I hadn't been out of

*Until 1963, Ford's works motor sport effort was modest, and the cars were prepared and maintained at the Lincoln Cars building, on the Great West Road, Brentford, in west London. This building still exists, but is no longer owned by Ford. This particular shot dates from 1958.*

*Immediately after the Second World War, Ford had no competitive rally cars, but careful reading of regulations sometimes allowed unexpected results to be achieved. In 1949, for instance, private-entrant Ken Wharton (he later became a successful race driver) borrowed this 10hp-engined 'Export Anglia' from the Ford press fleet, and used it to win the Dutch Tulip rally outright. The car was mechanically standard, and there was no service support from the factory.*

*Joy Cooke used the same Ford Anglia press demonstrator to compete in the Lisbon rally of 1950.*

Britain before, yet here I was driving Edgy around in France and in Italy!"

From that day on there was more sport and less 'Publications' in Barnett's life, and it wasn't long before the entire works effort relied on his method, his knowledge, and his planning. Rally car specifications were settled by Jack Welch, and team tactics were usually dictated by Cuth, the senior member of the Harrison family. Technical support and some sponsorship came from Castrol.

"I wasn't really interested in rallying, not at first," Bill told me, "but the bug struck on the 1959 Alpine and I came to love it. I organised entries for other events after that, including the RAC and the Monte, before Jeff Uren came in as Team Manager for about a year." Changes then came thick and fast. Uren moved out, Walter Hayes arrived to replace Colonel Buckmaster as the head of Public Affairs, and Syd Henson was hired as Competitions Manager: "But it wasn't a happy time. Syd was always threatening to resign, thumping on the table until he got his way. Walter Hayes didn't like that, so one day he called Syd in, with me listening, smiled sweetly, and told him: 'Syd, I've decided to accept one of your resignations!' – and that was that."

It was at about the same time that Hayes realised he needed to put the entire operation on a more professional footing, and the Boreham project was born. V8-engined Fords had already won the Monte Carlo rally twice in the 1930s, but at the time there was no such thing as a works team at Dagenham to support them. Even in the late 1940s it was individuals like

Jackie Reece and Ken Wharton (both of them Ford dealers) who started to bring home the victories. Although they had enough influence to borrow cars from Ford's press fleet (which explains why their competition cars often had Essex-based registration numbers), these cars were not at all special.

Ken Wharton won the Tulip rally in a burly V8 Pilot, and Jackie Reece achieved brave Monte Carlo rally placings in a side-valve Ford Anglia, but it was not until 1952, after Wharton had won the Tulip rally again, this time in his own Consul, that Ford's publicity chief, Col. Maurice Buckmaster, persuaded Sir Patrick Hennessy to back a limited motorsport programme.

For 1953 a tiny Competitions Department was set up, operated on a strictly part-time basis. Edgy Fabris devoted some of his time to administration, Jack Welch, Alf Belson and Norman Masters maintained the cars, but it was the team of drivers, usually led by Ford dealer T C (Cuth) Harrison of Sheffield, who carried out much of the organisation. Everyone – manager, mechanics and drivers – had other full-time jobs, so strategy and engineering development were extremely sketchy.

First time out, in January 1953, Ford persuaded the Dutch

*The Ford Pilot sometimes performed with honour in European events. This was a driving test on the Zandvoort race circuit at the end of the 1950 Tulip rally, where Joy Cooke won the Ladies' Prize.*

*In 1953, Maurice Gatsonides used this works Ford Zephyr to win the Monte Carlo rally outright - a quite unexpected success, and one which helped Ford get more serious about motorsport.*

rally ace Maurice Gatsonides to drive one of the new Zephyrs, and he rewarded them by winning the Monte Carlo rally outright. Rallying must have looked very straightforward. Class and category wins followed, and when D P Marwaha and Vic Preston won the East African Safari of 1955 it began to look positively easy.

But it wasn't actually that easy. Even when the team added after-market engine conversions (for events where the regulations allowed their use), and chose only the most favourable events, there would be no more outright victories until 1959. Not even racing driver Jeff Uren could make the vital difference. Having started racing at his own expense, Uren contacted Fabris for help but was initially refused.

"Then for 1959," Uren once told me, "the BRSCC announced a much more open set of regulations, which was promising. So I then wrote *another* letter to Ford, and to Raymond Mays at BRM at Bourne. I told them I could win the British Saloon Car Championship, but that I needed their assistance. Would they help me? Fortunately they both said yes." Neither provided money, but Mays built and supplied two Zephyr engines, both with aluminium cylinder heads, triple Weber carburettors and a claimed 168bhp at 5800rpm,

*Famous picture, famous occasion. Maurice Gatsonides (left) and Peter Worledge (right), with VHK 194, the Ford Zephyr in which they won the 1953 Monte Carlo rally outright. The cowl over the extra lamps was a Gatsonides, not Ford, invention.*

*Later in the 1950s, resourceful private owners such as Jeff Uren turned the Mk II Zephyr into a competition saloon car racer – here is Jeff battling for the lead, at Silverstone, against Jack Sears's works Austin A90 Westminster.*

*Four works Zephyr IIs being prepared at Lincoln Cars to compete in the French Alpine rally of 1960. All of them had much-modified 150bhp engines (developed by Raymond Mays in Lincolnshire), and front-wheel disc brakes. Team manager Jeff Uren and team-leader Edward Harrison (both with cigarettes) are standing behind the cars.*

while Ford allowed Jeff to base his car at their Lincoln Cars premises in Brentford, "... where I would have to pay for work done, but at a 'special rate'. Mine was the only race car they supported.'"

The engineers – Jack Welch, Alf Belson and George Cheeseman among them – helped enormously, while some of the rally team's expertise and kit (including the latest in front-wheel disc brakes) was applied to the car. Although the Zephyr wasn't quite fast enough to win races outright, Jeff won his class six times and finished second once. He then received a summons from Ford. "Colonel Buckmaster called me to lunch with him. He told me how grateful Ford was for the way I had raced successfully in the last couple of years – and then invited me to become Competition Manager." At Ford, no one had ever officially held the post of Competition Manager before. The canny Uren turned down the staff job and accepted a one-year consultancy contract instead.

It was a fascinating, high-profile year, in which Gerry Burgess's Zephyr won the 1959 RAC rally (the event was hit by a blizzard in Scotland, but Burgess fought his way around its fringes), while on the 1960 Safari Vic Preston finished third

and the Zephyr team won the much-prized Manufacturers' Team award. "But we couldn't win anything on the Alpine because the time schedule was impossible for the Zephyrs, and the regulations were totally anomalous," recalled Jeff.

After that year, Jeff presented his own ideas for Ford's motor-sport strategy – a 27-page paper which included a recommendation to set up a separate department, with its own budget and the ability to sell parts. On reflection, Jeff reminded me that this paper forecast the need for 'a Boreham', and for an Advanced Vehicle Operation – but it was not accepted at the time. Jeff then returned to run his own plant hire business for the next two years and had little to do with motor racing.

In 1961 and 1962, therefore, the works team was gradually becoming a little more professional, though this was still a publicity-led, rather than an engineering-led, operation. Fabris once again became titular competitions manager, but he still relied heavily on Cuth Harrison's advice, and this was still a period when the drivers were 'Good Chaps' rather than thrusting young heroes.

Although the Zephyrs were still the backbone of the team, underpowered side-valve Anglia 100Es had often been used in

By the early 1960s, the works team was rallying Zephyrs and Anglia 105Es. This was Anne Hall, on a driving test held at the end of the 1961 RAC rally. By that time the Anglia had been rendered obsolescent by the new front-wheel-drive BMC Mini-Cooper.

the 1950s where handicaps and class structures were favourable. Then, from 1960 the much more promising Anglia 105E arrived, complete with its enormously robust and tuneable overhead-valve engine. Keith Duckworth's Cosworth concern produced loads of horsepower, Lotus produced amazingly agile Formula Junior cars, and suddenly Ford began to look like a modern company.

Henry Taylor's experience of being hired by the team was typical. Taylor, a farmer, a one-time bobsleigh ace and a successful racing driver at all levels including F1, had just retired after a serious single-seater accident, but was invited by Ford to drive an Anglia in the 1961 Monte, his co-driver being Dick Bensted-Smith of *The Motor* magazine. Henry, who had never previously rallied, and had not previously driven on studded tyres, found it all very novel. "In practice I was getting this car sideways and really enjoying myself on the ice. I thought I could win the rally, easily. Dick then suddenly cried out 'Stop', so I stopped – and he told me that if I didn't get my finger out I wouldn't even get into the top sixty! That's how much I had to learn."

Before he was introduced to the Cortina, Henry Taylor's

baptism of fire was in a 997cc Anglia which probably had all of 50bhp. Hampered by a handicap formula which favoured overweight French cars like the Panhards, he finished well down the lists but got the rallying bug. Convinced, however, that Ford's Lincoln Cars team did not know enough about preparing rally cars ("they simply couldn't get power from the engines") he started a persistent process of nagging for more specialisation and a dedicated programme. It didn't take long before he became, de facto, rally team leader, especially of the Cortinas, and it seemed almost inevitable that one day he would become Competition Manager.

Soon after this, Ford's chairman, Sir Patrick Hennessy, decided to revive his company's image and hired Walter Hayes, a successful Fleet Street newspaper editor, to do that for him. It was an outstanding appointment, for Hayes would be the guiding genius behind almost every Ford sporting initiative of the next 30 years. "I knew nothing about motorsport when I joined Ford," Walter Hayes once told me, "except that I'd hired Colin Chapman to write about cars for one of my newspapers, I was a complete novice." Maybe, but he certainly learned fast. Who but Hayes could have transformed Ford's

*Peter Hughes (left) was not only an accomplished driver, but the importer of Ford cars to Kenya in the 1960s. Here he is seen celebrating his second place on the 1963 Safari in his works Anglia 1200. Once the Cortina was established in motor sport, Ford rapidly 'retired' the Anglia.*

*John Patten drove this works Anglia 105E on the 1961 Monte Carlo rally of 1961, without success, hampered by a lack of power – only about 45bhp – and it was this sort of short-fall which made Ford look forward so impatiently to the arrival of the Cortina family in 1962-63.*

public and sporting images, could have persuaded its management to back the Lotus-Cortina project, could have eased the company into Formula 1, and got the entire Rallye Sport programme approved?

If not Walter Hayes, you might say, would someone else have done the same? Absolutely not. Not according to Sir Terence Beckett (who became Chairman and Managing Director in that period). Not according to Stuart Turner (later Ford's most famous Director of Motor Sport). And not according to Henry Ford II himself, who made Hayes his closest British confidante.

We must remember just how different a company Ford-UK actually was before Hayes arrived. A big company, sure. A profitable company, definitely. But with a sporting image – certainly not. Although the Zephyr had won the Monte, the RAC and the Safari rallies by that time, even in 1960 Ford-UK's image was still very mundane. Yet by 1970, after a decade in which the Cortinas and Lotus-Cortinas had starred, there was glamour all around. In 1960 Ford was barely involved in motorsport, but by 1970 Ford it winning everywhere. The last sidevalve-engined British Fords were made in 1962, yet the first 16-valve twin-cam-engined Cortinas raced just a year later, in 1963.

In, around, and behind this transformation was the dynamic, dapper and utterly persuasive character of Walter Hayes. These days we would call him a fixer, a wheeler-dealer or a spin-doctor, and he was vital to what followed. He arrived at Ford in the winter of 1961/62, at the same time as Ford-USA embraced its new Total Performance philosophy. Although Ford, along with other car-makers in Detroit, had tacitly agreed to ignore motorsport in the late 1950s, Henry Ford II soon found that his rivals were finding underhand ways to get round that agreement. By the early 1960s, therefore, he was ready to tear up the agreement.

Encouraged by ebullient company personalities like Lee Iacocca (who was gleefully pushing forward the Mustang programme), Henry Ford II finally went public in May 1962. At a stroke, he was to abandon the old AMA (Automobile Manufacturers' Association) and set out on a high-performance strategy aimed at attracting the mass of young drivers, the 'baby boomers' who had grown up in recent years. All of his subsidiary companies – especially those in Europe – were encouraged to embrace a philosophy of 'Total Performance'. Bright ideas, and a new approach to performance motoring, were needed, and came at exactly the right time to inspire Walter Hayes, who recognised a great publicity challenge when he saw one. Hayes already knew some of the right sort of people, in racing if not in rallying. Having employed the brilliant engineer Colin Chapman of Lotus to write in the *Sunday Dispatch* ("but he was hopeless at meeting deadlines..."), he soon turned to Chapman with an exciting proposal, and dined out for years on the story. "Colin, I said, why don't we

join forces? Starting with the Cortina, why don't you design a new saloon we can go racing with — and why don't you make them all for us, too?"

Although it wasn't as simple as that – it is never simple at Ford, where everything is analysed in great detail – the eventual result was the Lotus-Cortina, complete with its Lotus twin-cam engine and lightweight panels and casings, a car

*Walter Hayes was the dynamic ex-newspaperman attracted by Ford to completely rejuvenate their public image. Here seen in contemplative mood, he was already planning to make Ford a world leader in motor sport. He would be the pivotal figure at the head of Ford's motorsport activities for thirty years.*

## WALTER HAYES

Between 1961 and 1989, when he finally retired from Ford, Walter Hayes was one of the most dynamic and enthusiastic supporters of all high-performance Ford programmes, whether they concerned motorsport or road cars. Yet by his own admission he was really a newspaperman and not a motor industry executive, and latterly a publicist rather than a motorsport administrator.

Already famous as an editor in the world of British newspapers, he joined Ford to revolutionise their public face, his first job being to oversee the launch of the new Zephyr/Zodiac Mk III range. Originally in charge of Ford-UK's Public Affairs department, and soon to become the influence behind every one of its motorsport programmes, he helped to modernise Ford's thinking in every way. It was Hayes who found the money to build the Boreham motorsport centre, who originally urged Ford to finance Cosworth's new DFV F1 engine, approved the launch of the Escort Twin-Cam, lobbied hard for the opening of the Advanced Vehicle Operation, hired Stuart Turner as his new Director of Motorsport – and much more.

By the 1980s he had become Vice Chairman, Ford-of-Europe, and brought back Stuart Turner from the Public Affairs operation into Motorsport at Boreham. Later he kept the Sierra RS Cosworth in being when others had 'gone wobbly' on it, and did more than most to make sure that the Escort RS Cosworth finally went into production.

When he reached his 65th birthday he was obliged to retire, for that was a global ruling at Ford, but he was not yet ready to forget about cars. One of his later tasks was to become Aston Martin's chairman, to get the new DB7 project approved, and generally to revive yet another struggling organisation. When the time came to 'retire' the Escort from top-flight motorsport, Walter was one of the most honoured in a glittering array of special guests.

Guru? Of course. Inspiration? Certainly. Influential 'top brass'? Naturally. But also a deep thinker, a visionary, a motoring enthusiast – and a very important man. Without him, in many peoples' opinion, Boreham as a motorsport centre might never have existed and Ford might never had got into Formula 1.

*Boreham airfield, north of Chelmsford, had little in the way of facilities before Motorsport moved in late in 1963.*

*Boreham airfield, north of Chelmsford, had little in the way of facilities before Motorsport moved in late in 1963.*

which won as many races (and, later, rallies) as it infuriated its owners with a lack of reliability, and a car which transformed Ford's motorsport image. Quite inconceivable to Ford's old guard, it was the first of many innovative sporting cars inspired by Hayes.

Even so, it was his decision to build a new motorsport HQ at Boreham, in Essex, with a mainly new workforce, which made such a difference. Up until then, as he put it, "I soon found that the works rally cars had been prepared in the press garage in Brentford, and the team had been for 'gentlemen and our dealers'. Some of our rivals were much more serious, so I had to change all that."

Changing that included hiring Syd Henson to run the team, digging deep to find £32,000 (other authorities later quoted £47,000, but either figure looks ludicrously low today) to build the new Boreham Motorsport centre, which would open in 1963, and making sure that he re-arranged the management succession: Before he joined Ford, Syd Henson had been competitions manager of Ferodo and was really another of the Old Guard, who might have loved motorsport but also seemed to believe in having a good time at the expense of the company whenever he could. He also wanted his own way at all times and was a stubborn, cocksure and abrasive character.

After Henson arrived at Ford he ran Motorsport, which

was still based at Lincoln Cars in the short period that he was in charge, and big changes were made in the works effort. In 1962, for example, the team was running Anglias and Zodiacs, their drivers including Henry Taylor, Gerry Burgess and Anne Hall. In 1963, not only was the Cortina GT being developed and the Lotus-Cortina was in the wings, but newly-hired drivers included David Seigle-Morris, Peter Riley, and that redoubtable lady, Pat Moss.

Told that he was expected to deliver victories, and that the funds would be available, Henson had to go out and find new drivers. Fortunately for him, Stuart Turner had just taken over at the rival BMC works motorsport department and was busily hiring new Scandinavian drivers, thus making some of the established BMC personalities redundant. All three of Henson's new signings came from that source.

Pat Moss, however, was not immediately anxious to leave BMC – but it was Henson's big money offer which persuaded her. Promised that the Lotus-Cortina was about to arrive (a car which everyone at Ford was convinced would obliterate its rivals), she succumbed to an offer reputed to be £7000 a year, which was much the highest that any rally team was paying a driver at the time. To quote Stuart Turner, who was trying to keep Pat at BMC, "I was only authorised to bid £1500, but that was never likely to be enough. Alf Moss [Pat's father] eventually called me, telling me that Ford had made a big offer. I took a deep breath, raised my offer for 1963 to £4000, only to be told that Ford was offering £7000. I didn't attempt to match that. Yet we parted as friends."

As it happened, Pat would only stay at Ford for one season, and only briefly got to know Boreham, but her signing was an indication of just how serious Ford actually was. "Henson hired Pat Moss," Hayes told me, "which was right". Yet following Syd Henson's resignation over a disagreement Hayes appointed Alan Platt in his place.

It was that 1963 season, no question, which was a real turning point for Ford in motorsport. It was not only the year in which the works team started using a fleet of Cortina GTs, but it was also the one in which the Boreham workshops were completed. It was the year in which Ford's entire approach to motorsport was transformed.

Looking back, it's difficult even to compare one team (operating out of Lincoln Cars) with the other (operating from Boreham). Before 1963, the works race and rally cars were simple and rugged, with few modifications. Afterwards, they were faster, more specialised, and much more professionally run. The inspiration for all that was on the edge of a windy airfield in Essex.

*This aerial view was of the fully-developed Boreham complex, which Ford had owned since the 1950s, and which became the home of Motorsport from late 1963. The airfield origins are obvious, and a variety of special circuits and facilities were added over the years.*

*The car build workshops were in the building to the lower right of this shot, the Motorsport Parts warehouse was in the centre, with more workshop, storage and parking space behind it. The administrative offices were to the left, partly screened by trees. The massive marquee in view was not a permanent feature.*

# CHAPTER 2:
# THE ORIGINAL CORTINA: CONCEPT AND EVOLUTION

The Cortina changed the face of Ford – and of British motoring. In the 1950s medium sized British cars had been heavy, technically old-fashioned and relatively expensive. The original Cortina of 1962 was an innovation: it was hundreds of pounds lighter than its direct rivals, and much cheaper too. More than a million Mk Is would be made in the first four years, and sales rarely slackened after that. Well over four million would be built before the last Cortina of all rolled off the track at Dagenham in the summer of 1982.

Before the Cortina was launched, Ford had a thoroughly unbalanced product range, but after its arrival there soon seemed to be something for everyone. When work started on the 'Archbishop'project in 1960, Ford-UK was making small Anglias and big Consuls and Zephyrs, but there was nothing in between. In 1962 the new Cortina not only filled that market gap but also offered a huge variety of variants. By 1963, with the range fully developed, there would be 1.2-litre, 1.5-litre, 1-5 litre GT and Lotus twin-cam engined types, in two-door saloon, four-door saloon and five-door estate-car derivatives. Here was a masterpiece of product planning, Ford-USA style, which squeezed every possible version out of one design.

There were two main influences behind its development. One was that Ford needed a new product to confront the BMC Mini, which was making all the headlines even though it was not making any money for the British Motor Corporation. The other was Ford-UK's quirky decision to compete head-on with Ford-Germany, which was currently developing its own new car, originally coded 'Cardinal' but soon to be marketed as the Taunus 12M. In 1960 Sir Patrick Hennessy, Managing Director of Ford-UK, instructed his product planning chief, Terry Beckett, not only to surpass the still-secret

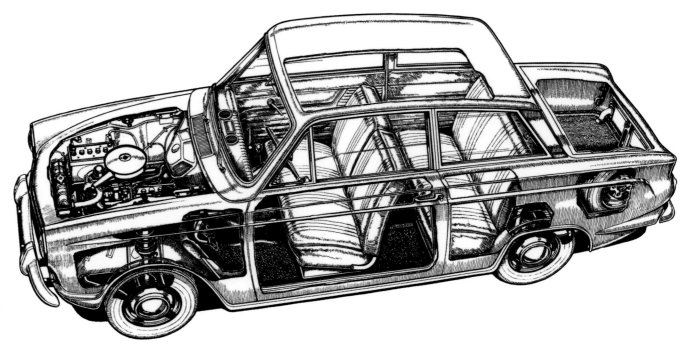

*This 1962 cutaway drawing shows the simple layout of the original Cortina, this being a 1200 De Luxe. GTs and Lotus derivatives would soon follow.*

*The first Cortina GTs of 1963 featured this instrument panel, with a rev-counter mounted on a separate pod behind the steering wheel. The handbrake was an 'umbrella handle', just visible under the steering wheel. It was also the first Cortina to feature a remote gear change.*

Taunus, but to create a new range of medium-sized cars for Ford-UK that would increase its sales, keep showrooms busy, make money and generally modernise the company's image.

Introduced in September 1962, the original Cortina was a front-engine/rear-drive car which had simple styling (and those now famous 'Ban the Bomb' tail-lamp clusters) and a rather stark level of interior trim and equipment. Powered by a simple, high-revving 49bhp 1.2-litre engine, it had an all-synchromesh gearbox (with a choice of steering column or floor change), a beam rear axle, drum brakes all round and narrow tyres.

Even though the new car was almost aggressively simple in technical terms (it would be another decade before Ford saw how it could make commercial sense out of a front-wheel-drive layout) the original Cortina broke new ground in two important ways. It was very light (contemporary aerospace bodyshell stressing techniques helped) and it sold at astonishingly cheap prices. Conscious of what was unique about it in marketing terms, Ford decided to advertise it as 'The Small Car with the Big Difference'. In other words, the new car was larger and more capacious than rivals like the Morris Oxford and the Vauxhall Victor, but it was at once cheaper, delivered better performance and offered better fuel economy.

The pundits at first scoffed at this approach because many were still dazzled by the front-wheel-drive layout and advanced suspension of the then-new Mini (and BMC 1100) models. The public, however, never seemed to have any doubts. When they saw that a new Cortina 1200 cost a mere £639 (compared with £675 for a Morris 1100, and £702 for a Vauxhall Victor) there was a rush to buy. The fact that Ford could deliver from stock (while waiting lists still existed for some other models) helped enormously.

Thousands of cars were built before announcement, deliveries began at once, and the Cortina jumped straight to the top of the list of best-sellers. From the start there were Standard and De Luxe trim packs, along with two-door and four-door saloons, on offer. But there was more to come, for within months Terry Beckett's long-planned range expansion had begun. First came the better-trimmed Super, complete with a 60bhp 1.5-litre engine, then automatic transmission became optional, and an estate-car and the sporty 78bhp Cortina GT saloon soon followed. This was where the new car's likely use as a competition car became clear.

The real glamour followed during 1963 when Lotus, already famous for its successful sports and racing cars, began building the two-door Lotus-Cortina, a saloon that not only used Lotus's own Ford-based 105bhp twin-cam engine but also had a new and more sophisticated rear suspension lo-

## COLIN CHAPMAN

It was Chapman, the founder of Lotus, who conceived the idea of making a twin-cam conversion of a Ford four-cylinder engine (though he hired in experts to do the design work for him), and who later 'sold' himself to Ford as the self-styled genius who could turn the Cortina into a race car. It was Chapman, therefore, who conceived the Twin-Cam engine, first for his company's Elan road car, later for the Lotus-Cortina, and latterly for the Escort Twin-Cam. Not only that, but it was Chapman who linked himself to Ford when it developed F1 ambitions, and it was Chapman who persuaded Ford to let his Lotus concern build the entire production run of Lotus-Cortina Mk I road cars from 1963 to 1966.

Chapman, virtually on his own, was the inspiration, the design genius and the spark behind almost every Lotus development of the 1960s, and although he had little, personally, to do with the works Lotus-Cortinas which were raced by Team Lotus from 1963 to 1967, his ambition was always in evidence behind the team.

Having started his working life as a qualified structural engineer with British Aluminium, he had already built his first Austin 7-based special by the end of the 1940s. Lotus Engineering Ltd was founded in 1952, the first Lotus for sale – the space-frame chassis Lotus Six – followed in 1953, and a meteoric rise followed. He was a brilliant innovator and visionary. His advances embraced chassis design (space frames, monocoques, ground effects, suspension innovations) and always involved running battles with legislators and officials worldwide.

The first Ford links came in 1960, when he started running Cosworth-prepared Formula Junior cars, he built the first Cosworth/Ford-engined F2 car in 1964 and he produced the original Lotus 49-Ford DFV F1 car in 1967. He died before his time at the end of 1982 of a heart attack on returning from a visit to France to discuss the latest controversial changes then being proposed for his beloved F1 programme.

*The original 'A-frame' Lotus-Cortina was launched in January 1963, went on sale later in that year, and would be built until 1965, when it was replaced by a more conventional 'leaf spring' model. James Allington's magnificent cutaway drawing shows that the Lotus-Ford engine was a snug fit in the engine bay, and that the battery had to be relocated into the right side of the boot.*

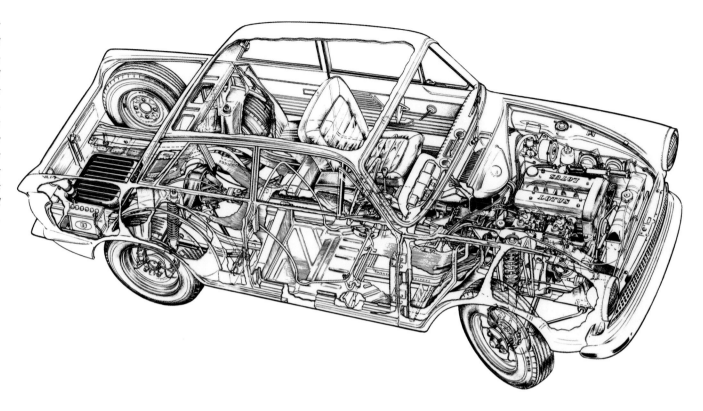

*The true architects of Ford's meteoric rise to success in production car motorsport were Ford's Walter Hayes (left), and Colin Chapman, the founder of Lotus. Here they pose behind an example of the Lotus-Ford twin-cam engine used in Lotus-Cortinas from 1963 to 1970.*

cation and used many light alloy body panels and castings. Meant for motor racing, the Lotus-Cortina soon became a sensation, though in road-going form it could be temperamental. To improve this, in 1965 the original coil-spring rear suspension, with what was known as its A-bracket location, was abandoned in favour of leaf springs and radius arms, which brought real reliability to a 110mph car, though only about three thousand were ever produced.

After selling a quarter of a million Cortinas in the first full year, 1963, – all of them except the Lotus-Cortinas being assembled at the Dagenham factory in Essex – Ford knew that its big gamble had started to pay off, though not even Terry Beckett could have seen that there would be Cortinas on sale for the next 20 years. A market leader when new, later versions of the Cortina would still be market leaders in the 1970s, and would still be respected cars in the early 1980s, before the Sierra project took over.

But Ford had no intention of sitting back complacently and introduced a series of improvements in the next few seasons. In late 1963 there was a new and more stylish fascia, while from late 1964 there was an external front-end facelift as well as the introduction of yet another design of fascia and instrument panel, and the incorporation of face-level ventilation – which was an innovation for British family cars.

Ford never seemed to lose the thread of what the Cortina was all about, which was to offer value-for-money car ownership to the motoring masses. By 1966, when the Mk I cars were approaching full maturity, the range encompassed 12 models, selling for between £648 and £1010. In addition, the Cortina had given rise to the pointed-nose Corsair, a larger and more expensive car, which used a stretched version of the Cortina's platform and running gear, topped by its own unique body style. By any standards, the original Cortina was a huge commercial and financial success, but after four years Ford was ready to replace it with a new and even better version. During the summer of 1966 the last of the 1,013,391 Mk Is was assembled – and a Mk II was on the way.

Then, as later, Ford was above all a pragmatic organisation, so when the time came to replace the original Cortina it moved cautiously, producing a thoroughly upgraded and visually different version of the original type. First with an entirely new body style and improved engines, and soon with new-generation engines too, the Mk II covered the same ground as the Mk I had always done, but with better fittings, more equipment, and an up-to-date look.

Announced in October 1966, the Cortina Mk II looked fresh, yet hidden away where fashion was not important but function was everything, Ford had saved much money by retaining the original pressed-steel platform, suspensions and running gear. Where the style of the original car had been craggy, that of the Cortina II was smooth – almost anonymous, in fact. Although each car rode on the same 98-inch (2489mm) wheelbase and was 168 inches (4267mm) long, the new car looked altogether larger and somehow more 'expensive'. The bodyshell was, 2.4 inches (61mm) wider, as were the wheel tracks, this having been done to provide a bit more elbow space in the cabin, but it was still a compact machine. No wonder, therefore, that the advertisements claimed 'New Cortina is more Cortina'.

The marketing thrust of the new car was like that of the old:

## LOTUS-FORD TWIN CAM

Picture it. The date was 1959 and Ford needed more powerful engines for use in racing and rallying. But the company didn't know how to do that. Suddenly over the horizon two possibilities appeared: one was that Keith Duckworth's tiny Cosworth company had started tuning the new ultra-short-stroke Anglia 105E engine, and the other was that Lotus was planning to make a small, light, road-going sports car, the Elan. The long-term result was the birth of the Lotus-Ford twin-cam engine and of a dynasty of truly fast Lotus and Ford cars.

Colin Chapman of Lotus and engine designer Harry Mundy were always close, for Mundy had designed the Coventry-Climax FPF F1 engine of the 1950s which Lotus and Cooper used so successfully. Later, while Mundy was *Autocar*'s Technical Editor, Chapman learned about the rock-solid little Ford engine, learned that it would eventually stretch to 1.5 litres, and persuaded Mundy to spend some spare time scheming up a twin-overhead-camshaft conversion on the basis of the engine's sturdy cylinder block. In later years Harry would insist that this had only ever been a cheap-and-cheerful project (typical of Chapman at the time) which was constrained by having to retain the existing mass-produced Ford crankshaft and connecting rods, and even to retain the existing camshaft as a jackshaft to drive the distributor and oil pump.

What happened in the next two years was complicated. Consultant engineer Richard Ansdale (who had previously worked with Lotus on other projects) completed the detail design. The very first prototype engine was a 1340cc unit using the three-bearing crankshaft bottom end of the Ford Classic, and it only produced 85bhp. There were breakages and problems, an enlarged 1477cc engine was built, Weslake was invited to look at the airflow characteristics, but it was not until the five-bearing 1498cc bottom end of the Cortina 1500 became available and Cosworth was invited to carry out a root-and-branch rework of the porting that 100bhp was achieved. Lotus awarded the JAP concern the contract to build road-car engines, the definitive 1558cc capacity was achieved by a modest over-bore, and the well-known rating of 105bhp was finally delivered.

The first Twin-Cam powered race car was the little Lotus 23 sports car which appeared in May 1962 and which Jim Clark drove at the Nurburgring, fitted with a 1.5-litre engine producing a mere 104bhp. It was not until Cosworth was asked to race-tune the engines (their internal code for this project was TA = Twin-Cam Series A) that real power was achieved. In almost every case the engines were fuelled by two dual-choke Weber carburettors, though fuel injection (Tecalemit Jackson, or occasionally Lucas) was tried on final developments at the end of the 1960s, when it was also found to be possible to enlarge some units to 1.8-litres.

Although the Twin-Cam's race-engine potential was limited by its eight-valve layout, it continued to be an extremely successful road-car power unit until 1975, when the last of the Lotus Europa Specials was built. Maybe it will not be remembered as the most powerful of all special 'Ford' engines but without the Twin-Cam engine there would have been no Lotus-Cortina, no Escort Twin-Cam, and probably no more fast Fords at all.

Harry Mundy, incidentally, once told the author that Colin Chapman offered him either £1000 for the twin-cam design work he had done, or £1 per engine built. Harry chose the lump sum, and soon regretted it – for 34,000 of all types were eventually manufactured. As he admitted, "It was the biggest financial mistake I ever made".

*Listening to the 'Gospel According to Colin Chapman', who was definitely making a strong point at Boreham. In this study, Ford Competitions Manager Alan Platt (back to camera), Walter Hayes (to Chapman's left) and Ford PR person Harry Calton (far right of shot) listen very carefully...*

two-door and four-door saloons plus an estate car, different trim levels, three different overhead-valve engines and (eventually) the super-sport twin-cam Lotus-Cortina model too. For the first model year the engines were merely improved versions of those already seen in earlier Cortinas, the big difference being that the smallest was now to be a 54bhp 1298cc unit.

The latest car was somehow less blatantly mid-Atlantic than before (Ford-UK, after all, had an American parent, so this had been understandable). The original bench-type front seat and steering-column gear change had been virtually eliminated, while the latest trim seemed more 'domestic', with carpets where the original version had used rubber mats, and with less bare painted metal in the cabin. For the first time, overseas manufacture also began in 1967, at Ford's Amsterdam plant.

As before, changes and improvements were introduced regularly. Early in 1967 the Cortina GT (and, later, other Ford models) benefited from a more suitable close-ratio gearbox (much appreciated by the motorsport fraternity), while the second-generation Lotus-Cortina arrived in March 1967, this time to be assembled by Ford at Dagenham, not by Lotus). Then, in October 1967, Ford phased in the new range of over-

head-valve Kent engines, which had crossflow cylinder heads with bowl-in-piston combustion chambers, and which were more powerful than before. At the same time the mid-size Cortina engine moved up from 1.5 litres to 1.6 litres, with 71bhp or in the GT 88bhp.

The big marketing surprise was the launch of the Cortina 1600E, where E stood for Executive. Here was a car that had cost mere petty cash to develop, but which was definitely a class above other Mk II Cortinas, and which because of its selling price (£982 at first) made Ford a great deal of money. In the next three years 55,833 four-door types and 2749 two-doors (these for export only) would be built.

Under the skin, the 1600E was pure Cortina GT, complete with a 88bhp 1599cc engine, but the suspension was lowered and given Lotus-Cortina (stiffer and shorter) spring and damper settings. Inside, the car was wall-to-wall luxury – plushy leather-look seat covers, thicker carpets, wooden fascia and door cappings, and an aluminium-spoked steering wheel – while outside there were unique Rostyle road wheels and special paint jobs to complete the makeover.

The customers (and the dealers, who found the 1600E easy

to sell) loved it, for here was a new model with all the pizzazz of a Lotus-Cortina (and a set of wheels that no other Ford would ever use) but with an unmodified GT engine that was still easy to service and maintain. It was a very appealing package, for there is no doubt that the 1600E handled better than its workaday relatives; when Cortinas eventually became seen as classics, it was the 1600E that qualified first, a reputation which has persisted to this day. In the next three years, however, there was more to come for all Cortinas: the GT-type remote gear change was brought in on less special versions, radial-ply tyres were gradually adopted, and reclining front seats also became available on all models.

Even though Ford had settled down to building its now customary quarter of a million Cortinas every year (and carried on disputing outright sales leadership in the United Kingdom with the Austin-Morris 1100/1300 range, which needed several different brand badges to achieve that), the product planners thought there was scope for yet more improvement. Accordingly, from October 1968, a mid-term facelift was introduced, which saw the cars looking good for another two seasons. Although the planners considered it worthwhile, one nevertheless had to look closely to see the differences. A new radiator grille appeared, while there was yet another version of the fascia layout. The bonnet release was now triggered

from inside the car (making it easier to protect the car against theft), the much criticised umbrella-handle handbrake of the original cars gave way to a proper pull-up lever, and there were new-style front seats.

Mechanically, the big changes were a new type of gearbox and gear change mechanism, and a fully fused electrical system. Although it was not fundamentally changed, at this time the Lotus-Cortina was officially renamed the Cortina Twin-Cam and got boot lid badges to prove it, though enthusiasts took absolutely no notice of this!

This was an impressive line-up, a range of 14 different models, with four different engines, a choice of manual or automatic transmission, and three body styles. Prices for 1969 started at £792 for a 1300 two-door De Luxe and peaked at £1163 for the Twin-Cam. (By this time the Race Proved company, led by former racing driver Jeff Uren, had developed a private-venture version of the Cortina, the Savage, in which there was a 128bhp 3-litre V6 Ford Zodiac engine; this gained approval from Ford, who supported it with a partial warranty, and it sold well.) For the next two years the Mk II cars led Ford's sales efforts, but for the 1970s an entirely new type of Cortina was on the way. Between 1966 and 1970 a total of 1,024,869 Mk IIs (4032 of them Lotus-Cortinas) had been produced.

*Competitions Co-ordinator Bill Barnett (left), driver Peter Procter (centre) and engineer Jack Welch discuss tactics before the start of an event.*

# CHAPTER 3:
# CORTINA AND GT MK I AND II IN RALLYING AND RECORD RUNS

You could say – and you would be right –that the author is emotionally attached to the rallying Cortinas, so this will be rather a personal chapter. In 1963 I was one of the very first co-drivers to sample a Cortina GT in British rallies, and in 1965 I was greatly privileged to sit alongside Roger Clark when he won the Welsh rally in a works Lotus-Cortina – the first time that this model had achieved a major British rallying success. But those were the days when cars still didn't really need twin-cam engines to be competitive, as the works pushrod-engined Cortina GT was a successful car for several seasons.

Even so, Roger's Welsh victory in his Lotus really brought the Cortina GT's career to a close. Before that victory, rallying's cynics had suggested that a Lotus-Cortina would never be strong enough to face up to the British forests and rugged European and African events. Afterwards they underwent an immediate change of heart.

From 1963 to 1965 I observed the Cortina GT rally cars from two distinct aspects. On the one hand I co-drove Ford

*Picture of a happy man: Bill Barnett at the end of the 1964 RAC rally and therefore the end of the rally season.*

main dealer Phil Simister's car to several victories in British events, while on the other I was managing the efforts of a rival team, Triumph, trying to get the larger, heavier and very solid Triumph 2000s on to terms with the Cortinas.

Incidentally, although the Cortina arrived more than 50 years ago, that doesn't mean that advanced technology, as we now know it, had not been created and harnessed. Fuel injection, roll cages, and ten-minute gearbox changes? Maybe not at the time, but in those days extensive test and practice sessions, driver-to-co-driver intercom headsets, close-ratio gearboxes, alternative final drive ratios, and much-tuned engines were already available. Safety belts? Of course, though not yet of the sophisticated full harness type. Special seats? Sometimes. And rallymanship? All the time...

Well in advance of the launch of the Cortina, in June 1962 works team co-ordinator Bill Barnett was already talking about the future of the car immediately before the French Alpine rally, even though it was still on Ford's secret list. In a tarmac event bound to be dominated by sports cars (the first four finishers were two Austin-Healey 3000s, a Porsche 356 Carrera and a Triumph TR4), his Zodiacs were beaten by front-wheel-drive Citroens, and his Anglias by the Mini-Coopers. "Next year it'll be OK," Bill said, rather slyly, "we'll have the Cortina then..." He would say no more at that time, and when the media first saw the original 49bhp Mk I Cortina 1200 they were not a bit impressed – not until the 78bhp Cortina GT arrived in April 1963 and the homologation process began.

The first major competitive appearance of a Cortina came in November 1962, when a previous Ford competitions manager, Jeff Uren, drove a highly-modified 1200 (TOO 528) on the RAC rally. Although this car had a 93bhp 1.2-litre Cosworth-modified engine, it had to make do with drum brakes, and that effort failed due to a multitude of problems, which included the entire exhaust system coming adrift.

Team captain Henry Taylor then took the same car on the 1963 Monte Carlo rally, though on that occasion it was in slower, FIA Group 2 trim, and managed second in the 1.3-litre class (to a rear-engined Skoda, which relished the blizzard-like conditions) though this was neither startling nor

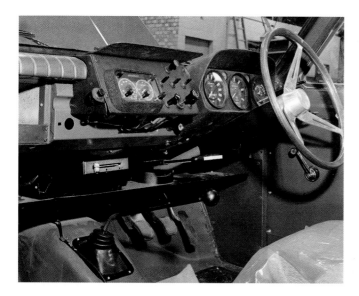

The original fleet of works Cortina GTs used an intriguing mixture of equipment – the latest instrument cowl ahead of the steering wheel, but a direct action rather than remote gear change. This image dates from late 1963.

Stuart Turner (left) was BMC's Competitions Manager from 1961 to 1967, while Alan Platt (right) was Ford's Competition Manager from 1963 to 1965. Turner became Director of Motorsport at Ford at the end of the 1960s, soon after the Lotus-Cortina programme was discontinued.

Henry Taylor had been on the fringes of an F1 career before joining Ford to go rallying. From 1962 he was effectively the team leader. From 1963 to 1965 he was certainly the most consistently effective driver in the team, after which he became Competitions Manager until 1969.

## BOREHAM IN 1963

As the early sections of this story make clear, the original works Cortinas – the well-known fleet of white GTs, and the Supers sent to contest the East African Safari – were originally prepared at the Lincoln Cars premises on the Great West Road, in Brentford, in south-west London. Newly-appointed PR chief Walter Hayes thought this unsatisfactory and arranged for a new Competitions Department building to be erected at Boreham Airfield, close to Chelmsford and the A12 trunk road, where Ford already had a truck proving ground and other facilities. The new building would take time to erect, and in the meantime staffing arrangements would have to be set in motion. As legendary mechanic Mick Jones (who was earlier working in another Ford department, at Rainham) once told the author, "Both Bill Meade and I were interested in motorsport. One day a notice appeared on the board, looking for mechanics in the new works rally department." That was in 1962, and the cars were still being built at Lincoln Cars, so, "I got that job in 1962, but didn't move house. For the first year or so, four of us – Bill Meade, Peter Ashcroft, Johnnie Rule and me – we used to meet up in a pub car park, the Six Bells near Boreham every morning, and commute round the North Circular Road twice a day! The first rally I ever did overseas for Ford was the 1963 Midnight Sun."

The new workshop was finally ready for occupation in October 1963, just in time to tackle the RAC rally, but then had to get on with the enormous job of building a new set of Cortina GTs for European events, new cars for the 1964 Safari, new practice cars, and Anglias too – 22 in all. As Mick Jones then added, "Alan Platt was the manager, he took over from Syd Henson. The rally engineer was Jack Welch. Then there was me, Bill Meade, Peter Ashcroft, Johnnie Rule, Norman Masters, 'Jolly Jack' Welsh – we were the original crew from Lincoln Cars. We then pulled in a few more people from other parts of Ford, including John May and Eric Bristow." And that was the way it all began, with the 'Band of Brothers' developing the workshops to their best advantage, which in those days included an engine build shop and test beds. There would be much change in the years which followed.

*For 1964, Boreham managed to get dual twin-choke Weber carburettors homologated into Group 1, which in theory meant that 5000 such cars existed. Very enterprising!*

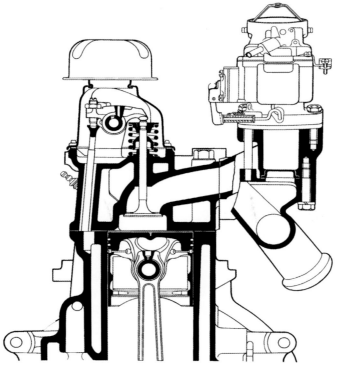

*Cross-section of the pre-crossflow engine as used in the Cortina Mk I of the 1963-66 and in the 1967 Mk II. As companies like Cosworth had already discovered, it was a remarkably robust and tuneable unit.*

very encouraging. But if this was all that could be expected, why had the famous Pat Moss, up to then a star of the rival BMC team, been persuaded to join Ford for 1963?

The answer became more obvious when the new Cortina GT was launched, immediately after a team of non-GT models appeared on the East African Safari without success. The GT was then first seen on the Tulip – but it was not until Henry Taylor and Pat Moss took fourth and sixth places overall in the Greek Acropolis that things suddenly looked up.

In the meantime, British eyes had already been well-and-truly opened. Teaming up with Ford main dealer Phil Simister for the 1963 rally season, the author had started the year in a much-modified Anglia (homologated as an Allardette, which allowed it to use front disc brakes), first with a 1340cc engine, then with a 1500cc engine, then with Cosworth tuning, and always with a bodyshell that didn't feel as it could ever be damaged. Along with rivals like Reg McBride in a similar car, these cars were winning *Motoring News* Championship events all round the country, and didn't seem to need to be quicker – until Phil Simister got his Cortina GT ready.

First time out, in the Kent rally, which ran all over the middle of Wales, he won the event, and two weeks later he won a smaller club event. Phil agreed that the new car might be bigger than his old 105E, but it was no heavier and seemed to handle better. We both loved it, for there was also more space in the co-driver's 'office'.

At which point Phil made a momentous discovery. The bodyshell had started to distort! There was already a crease across the roof between the door pillars, and other creases above the rear wheel-arches. The whole shell had started to bend. Boreham's engineers, it soon transpired, had already discovered the same problems, and they soon eliminated them on the works cars. Firstly they used the rather special heavy-duty export-market bodyshells, which had a much more robust floorpan and sundry reinforcements, and secondly they began to seam-weld and reinforce everything in a way that was still new to the world of rallying.

Amazingly, the new Cortina GT, which was really a sizeable thin-skinned body/chassis box compared with the small, over-engineered and virtually unbreakable Anglia 105E, was soon turned into a creditable rally car. Not just stronger than before, but a lot faster too.

Those, one should confirm, were still the days of 'fag-packet' engineering, where nothing was designed before it was made ("OK, let's try this..."), where things that broke were beefed up to make sure they did not break again, and where the accent was on easy-to-repair cars rather than 'don't-need-repairing' tanks.

Rally engineer Jack Welch and resourceful mechanics like Mick Jones and Bill Meade all had a hand in this. Oh yes, and Bill Barnett too. Bill was no engineer but he had a mind and a filing system like a computer, for nothing he learned or experienced at Lincoln Cars, and later at Boreham, was ever forgotten. That the Escorts which followed were so robust tells us a lot about the experience gained on the Cortinas during the 1960s.

The Cortina GT's problem, though – and for months it *was* seen as a problem – was that Ford only ever considered it as a stop-gap rally car, to be used until the Lotus-Cortina came along. Everyone was dazzled by Colin Chapman's engineering and by the way he had transformed the Cortina, and hopes were high – until, that is, the rear suspension and back axle failures for which the Lotus-Cortina became notorious started to appear.

Ford, who had signed up Pat Moss, David Seigle-Morris and Peter Riley for 1963 (all of them defecting from the BMC team, where they had starred) with the promise of the Lotus-Cortina being ready for rallying within a year, were embarrassed. They'd wanted to sign Saab's formidable Erik Carlsson too, but instead he turned down that deal, soon taking his new wife (Pat Moss!) back to Saab with him.

As described earlier, team boss Syd Henson had resigned in mid-1963, to be replaced by Alan Platt. Alan was a long-serving Ford insider who might have known little about rallying at first, but he listened and learned rapidly, and soon shook the team into place, running it more efficiently.

*Bill Meade started his 'comps' career as a mechanic at Lincoln Cars, but eventually became senior rally engineer at Boreham, including the period in the 1960s when the Cortina GT was being developed. Here he is seen seam-welding the brand-new bodyshell of a rally car.*

*Vic Elford joined the works team from Triumph for 1964 and soon proved to be the fastest driver in the line-up.*

Alan, along with team driver Henry Taylor, soon finalised the strategy which would serve Ford well for the next two years. First, the Cortina's structure would have to be made bomb-proof, the options and homologation list would have to be built up rapidly, the overhead-valve engine would be super-tuned just as far as possible – and the Lotus-Cortina would be ignored as a rally car until someone sorted out the rear suspension problems.

But, on rough rallies, who needed the Lotus-Cortinas? By the end of 1963 the fully-prepared works 1.5-litre Cortina GTs had 110bhp engines with twin-choke Weber carburettors, even in Group 1 trim, which made them easily as fast as a road-going Lotus, and they were a lot more reliable too.

Within months, private owners could drive up to Boreham, cheques in hand, to take delivery of all manner of other options – ultra-wide wheels, close-ratio gearboxes, limited-slip differentials, body brace stiffeners, auxiliary fuel tanks and rally seats among them – and there were many of them.

Cosworth, who were becoming ever closer to Ford's motorsport departments, helped with the engine tuning. It wasn't long before the 1.5-litre engines were fitted with twin horizontal dual-choke Weber carburettors, running the Spa-Sofia-Liège event as non-homologated machines, but how on earth did Ford then get them homologated into FIA Group 1 'showroom' trim when theoretically 5000 sets would have had to be sold? No-one ever counted the kits being sold, but

*It was typical of Walter Hayes's approach to PR exposure that at the end of 1964 (self-styled as the 'Year of the Cortina') he organised a massive party in the Italian Dolomites for all the team's race and rally drivers to enjoy themselves. How many of the famous faces in this group can be recognised?*

some of the company's rivals were mightily impressed by that administrative coup.

Even in mid-1963, when everyone was still learning, the results soon started to flow in. Taylor's fourth on the Acropolis was followed by Bo Ljungfeldt's third place in the Swedish 'Midnight Sun' (when only a Porsche and Erik Carlsson's Saab beat him). Henry Taylor's car then took second in the French Alpine touring car category (third overall, really, because it was beaten by a single Mini-Cooper S and a sports-racing Alfa Romeo). It wasn't just that the Cortinas were doing well, but that a special calibre of limited-production car was already needed to beat them.

Henry Taylor/Brian Melia even got a Lotus-twin-cam engined Cortina GT (*not* a Lotus-Cortina, you understand) into fourth place in the Spa-Sofia-Liège Marathon (behind a Mercedes-Benz 230SL, Erik Carlsson's Saab and a works Citroen DS19), an event where only 20 cars actually finished at all.

Now it was all looking a lot better, though Pat Moss could only finish seventh in the RAC rally, and that was not enough to persuade her to stay with Ford (she moved to Saab to join her new husband Erik Carlsson). At the end of the year Anne Hall and Peter Riley were both released from their contracts, but not even the signing of Vic Elford for 1964 could bring luck in the Monte Carlo rally, where Vic crashed into a non-competing car and Henry Taylor's car suffered a total

*No sooner had the works team moved in at Boreham than a concentrated barrage of new-car building took place. This image, dating from November 1963, shows the original white Cortina GTs alongside the new-for-1964 red cars, which would eventually take over the earlier registration plates.*

*Two shots of the workshop floor at Boreham immediately after it opened for business at the end of 1963. The shot on the left shows five brand-new GTs – the famous re-shelled 888 DOO – 893 DOO set which would be used extensively in 1964 and 1965, with one of the original white 1963 cars (which was about to be pensioned off) alongside...*

*...and this proves that there was space for no more than six cars to be worked on at the same time.*

*Boreham's works preparation block, modest then and no more flamboyant in later years, was built in 1963. This shot shows the side of the building which included the administrative offices and the small reception area. Principal access to the workshop floor was by roller shutter doors, which are just off to the right of this image.*

fuel blockage.

By the time the works team's operation had finally moved into the newly-constructed Boreham HQ, just to the north of Chelmsford (as confirmed by 'Mr Computer' Bill Barnett, that move was completed in October 1963, which may explain why there was not very much overt motorsport activity in September and October 1963 – effectively between the Spa-Sofia-Liège and RAC rallies). Almost immediately, the team's expertise, evolution, and output, all under the direction of the new manager, Alan Platt, began to improve very significantly.

Mick Jones, who in later years became something of a 'star

mechanic' in the Boreham family, once told the author that he personally unlocked the doors leading into the Boreham workshops on that first day in the autumn of 1963, and that the team 'never stopped running' after that. The rallying world soon realised why there had not been many works entries in events immediately after the Spa-Sofia-Liège. In its preview of the 1964 Monte Carlo rally, published in mid-January 1964, *Autocar* summed this up perfectly: "Ford's fine new Competition Department at Boreham has been working overtime since the RAC rally in mid-November, preparing a total of 22 rally cars. These comprise eight reconnaissance cars, three for the Monte Carlo Rally and five for the East African Safari Rally, five and six competing cars respectively for each of these events, and three cars for the Canadian Shell 4000 Rally. All are Cortinas except the Canadian cars, which are Anglias."

What was not spelt out in that survey was that all of the new European 'fleet' were to be painted red, and that these were to replace the original hard-working 1963 examples, but retaining their increasingly well-recognised registration plates. Equally significant was that the twin-choke Weber carburettor installation, and the fitment of an extra fuel tank across the back of the boot area (it was actually 'lifted' from a Cortina estate car) was now to be normal, while significant contracts had been signed with Dunlop (for tyres), and Ci-bié (for headlamps and auxiliary lamps). There was also the link-up with Total fuels, which allied neatly with Ford-USA's modern 'Total Performance' slogans!

What happened on the 1964 East African Safari at Easter, however, made up for everything. All six brand new Cortina

## BOREHAM IN 1964

First of all, the priority was to take possession of the building, which was still incomplete when the team first moved in in October 1963. Next the 'stock', or 'fleet' of new Cortinas had to be enhanced, for this was a time when motorsport programmes for the other now obsolete Ford models – specifically the Anglia 105Es and the Zodiacs – were rapidly being run down. As already noted (in Boreham in 1963), no fewer than 22 new competition cars were prepared in the winter of 1963/64, the last being sent off to compete in (and win!) the East African Safari at Easter time.

Because a massive team of rally cars, practice cars, service cars and personnel all went to East Africa for the Safari, there was something of a lull at Boreham in this period, which explains why there were no official team entries in the Tulip and Acropolis events, both held in May. Later in the summer, however, the team continued to persevere with the original A-frame Lotus-Cortinas, thinking that they could tame the eccentricities of that rear suspension (they were wrong). They built two brand-new cars of this type to compete in the Tour de France, while two new Lotus-engined Corsairs (now affectionately and unofficially known as Lotus-Corsairs) were also built to contest the Spa-Sofia-Liège marathon.

By this time Boreham had a working engine build/engine test facility, which would be of great importance until links were set up with Brian Hart Ltd in the 1970s. There was also a separate little operation where private owners could buy parts for their own competition cars. This, incidentally, was the year in which Vic Elford joined the team (from Triumph), and immediately set out to prove that he was the fastest of the drivers on the strength.

At this point it is important to emphasise the ever-expanding scope of Ford in motorsport. The Falcons which so nearly won the Monte Carlo rally and the Mustangs which won the Tour de France had been prepared by Alan Mann Racing at Byfleet, near the Brooklands circuit. The ETCC Lotus-Cortinas (also AMR) were also based at Byfleet, the Team Lotus BTCC Lotus-Cortinas were based at Cheshunt in North London, and the Jeff Uren/Willment cars were based in South West London.

*Walter Hayes commissioned the building of the Motorsport workshops at Boreham in 1962, and it opened for business in October 1963. This atmospheric study shows the first red 1964 works GTs being assembled, and one of the worn-out white 1963 cars is in the background. At most there was space for about six cars to be worked on at any one time.*

*At the end of a victorious 1964 season, PR chief Walter Hayes took all his contracted drivers and a handful of newly-facelifted Cortina GTs to Cortina d'Ampezzo in the Italian Dolomites for a celebratory weekend. Somehow or other he was persuaded to send a Cortina down the bobsleigh run, with predictable results...*

GTs proved to be highly competitive, and after five days of dust, mud, high speed and errant animals being dodged had been surmounted, the works cars finished first, third and tenth, with the Manufacturers' Team Prize also won. Local heroes Peter Hughes (the Ford importer to Kenya) and Bill Young drove the winning car. As with other Safari outings, this is covered in detail later in this book (see Interlude).

So the Cortina GT was now one of the fastest and the toughest of the current crop of rallying saloons, right? It certainly began to look like that, Boreham's problem being that they might be expected to repeat the trick every time they ventured out. But not always. No matter how hard he tried, Henry Taylor's much-modified (Group 3) Cortina GT couldn't quite overcome a performance handicap rating on the Dutch Tulip rally, though he took third in the entire Grand Touring category, behind a works Austin-Healey 3000 and a Porsche 356 Carrera Abarth. Neither did a Cortina GT always have to be a works car to be competitive, as proved by a young Roger Clark, who used his very own self-prepared Cortina GT to win the Scottish rally.

It was in June, in the classic French Alpine rally —all speed hill-climbs and high-speed sections in the mountains north of Cannes and Monte Carlo – where the Cortina GTs showed just how good they had become. Watching from the sidelines,

*Ford was so proud of its Cortina GT achievements worldwide in 1964 that it mounted this studio shot of all the trophies that had been amassed. The car was one of Boreham's practice/test cars, probably 553 UOO.*

one could appreciate the sheer pace of the latest red works machines, whose engines made all the right sort of noises and which certainly handled very well indeed. Almost throughout that long event, David Seigle-Morris's car led Vic Elford's sister car in the Touring Category, only for his engine's head gasket to fail just 25 miles from the finish, so handing victory to Vic Elford instead.

But this sort of success rate couldn't last for ever. In the last, fastest, greatest and toughest Spa-Sofia-Liege of all (a marathon which was nothing less than a four-day road race over Europe's worst roads, mainly in the Balkans), all the works cars crashed. Then, in the RAC rally which ended the season, Vic Elford's car should certainly have won outright, for it set many fastest stage times, but he also crashed the car twice (once taking a maximum stage penalty), and as a consequence could only take third place overall. That was the bad news. The good news was that Vic, Henry Taylor and David Seigle-Morris all held on, to win the Manufacturers' Team Prize. Ford was getting to like doing that.

However, that was virtually the end of the road for the works Cortina GTs. Although five cars started the 1965 Monte, only Henry Taylor's car (ninth) overcame the awful blizzards, and (unlike 1964) a team of locally-driven cars which started the Safari never led the event, though Vic 'Junior' Preston took third place. Weeks later Henry Taylor travelled to Canada, to take third place overall in the Shell 4000 rally in a privately-built car, an event whose route went all the way westwards across that continent from Montreal to Vancouver.

Here at home it was Roger Clark who made the GT head-lines, in the same hardworking and self-prepared car (registered 2 ANR, a personal identity). In a matter of months he took third place on the Circuit of Ireland, won the Scottish International, then won the four-day Gulf London rally as well!

But by this time it was nearly over, as commonsense had finally prevailed concerning the engineering of the Lotus-Cortina, which from mid-1965 was being manufactured with conventional leaf spring rear suspension. This was more robust than the coil spring/A-bracket layout used on earlier models. Just as hoped, this made the Lotus into a great race car *and* rally car. With 130 to 140 torquey horsepower now available, instead of a rather peaky 110bhp from the GT engine, it was immediately much faster than the Cortina GT, and soon began to prove it.

So whatever happened to all those famous works Cortina GTs? And why don't we see any of them around in today's classic events? The truth is, I believe, that not a single one of the well-known cars has survived. From early 1963 to mid-1965 the same identities – mainly 888 DOO to 893 DOO, six near-identical two-door cars, along with RWC 202 making seven – were often used on the Boreham cars used in Europe. The 'old' cars even survived the mid-term facelift, and therefore were not rallied as wide-grille 'Aeroflow' models. (Cars entered in the East African Safari, incidentally, carried local registration plates and were not re-exported from Kenya after the event.)

There were, in fact, rather more individual cars than this, for in those days (as later!) Ford was adept in throwing away the empties, and adopting old identities for the brand new cars which followed. The first set of cars had been painted white, but for 1964 (even before the end of 1963 if a white car had been severely crashed) they suddenly became red – but in essence these were brand-new cars with the existing registration numbers. When *Motoring News* visited Boreham soon after it opened, they took pictures showing the existence of rumpled old white cars, and pristine new red cars being worked on at the same time. Effectively we should consider white GTs as 'Lincoln Cars' machines, whereas the red cars were certainly all completed at Boreham.

The red DOOs had a very hard time, for almost all of them were rolled, crashed or written off at least once, and at the end of their careers they were well patched up, and more than one was looking very doggy indeed. And anyway, after the life they had had in 1964 and 1965, would you have paid good money to buy one? The historian's understanding (recently confirmed by that doyen of all things Ford in rallying, David Sutton) is that Ford's Boreham team either broke them up in mid-1965, or used them as practice cars and 'mules' until the time came to fill up another skip. There are well authenticated cases of old works cars being cut up at Boreham when they came to the end of their useful lives. This policy, however, was reversed when it came to the fate of the works leaf-spring Lotus-Cortinas, as is detailed in Chapter 5.

| REGISTRATION NUMBER | ENGINE SIZE | MODEL TYPE |
|---|---|---|
| **TOO 528** | **1198CC 4-CYL OHV** | **CORTINA 1200** |

Jeff Uren, one-time Ford works team manager, must have been bemused by the attention his 1962 RAC rally entry got, for he turned up in the very first works Cortina to be prepared (at Lincoln Cars, by the way, this being almost a year before the new Boreham competitions centre was completed).

Perhaps *The Autocar*'s pre-rally guide got it right with this comment: "Great interest was aroused by Jeff Uren's Ford Cortina (a two-door 1200),which was running in Group 3. Crowds collected round it, awaiting the moment [at scrutineering] when its bonnet was opened revealing, perhaps, the much-talked-of twin-cam Ford-Lotus engine. It was not this unit, but, almost as interesting, a Cosworth-tuned engine with two double-choke Weber carburettors, developing 93bhp – only about seven less than the road version of the twin-cam engine. Oddly enough, this very potent car has drum brakes all round, whereas the works Super Anglias had discs in front".(The other works Fords on this event were a team of three Anglia Supers, which were neither as striking, nor as newsworthy, as the new Cortina, though in the end Henry Taylor's car took sixth overall).

The new Cortina was only a 1.2-litre machine, and its engine did not have the right sort of torque delivery for forestry special stages, but Jeff Uren did his best to keep it going. Detail

development dramas held up the car at times – there was one occasion in Scotland, caught by *The Autocar*'s cameraman, when the entire exhaust system came adrift, so that in the end Uren was content to limp to the finish in Bournemouth.

For the 1963 Monte Carlo, the same car was re-prepared in

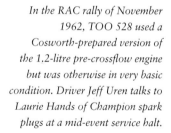

*In the RAC rally of November 1962, TOO 528 used a Cosworth-prepared version of the 1.2-litre pre-crossflow engine but was otherwise in very basic condition. Driver Jeff Uren talks to Laurie Hands of Champion spark plugs at a mid-event service halt.*

*The very first works Cortina to go rallying was TOO 528, which Jeff Uren (looking at the documents at scrutineering) drove in the 1962 RAC rally. This car had a highly tuned 1.2-litre engine.*

*TOO 528 at speed on the 1962 RAC rally, but early success eluded it.*

## Competition Record

| | | |
|---|---|---|
| 1962 RAC | Jeff Uren | Completed, well down. |
| 1963 Monte | Henry Taylor | 2nd in Class |
| 1963 'Autobog', Brands Hatch | Henry Taylor | DNF |
| 1963 Targa Rusticana rally, UK | David Seigle-Morris | DNF |

*As something of a suck-it-and-see exercise, Henry Taylor drove TOO 528, in strictly Group 2 form, in the 1963 Monte Carlo rally. It looked smart but was not a success.*

*Henry Taylor (right) and Brian Melia stand by TOO 528 after it had completed the 1963 Monte Carlo rally. That was its last appearance as a works car.*

something of a hurry (another car was to have been built but ...), this time in FIA Group 2 trim, in a factory team which also included three Zodiac Mk IIIs and two Anglia 105Es. Because very little tuning was allowed in Group 2 tune, this car had lost all its Cosworth kit, and cannot have had much more than 60bhp, which meant that it was distinctly underpowered by almost all its competitors' standards, so Henry

Taylor and Brian Melia could do no better than keep pushing on to the end.

This Monte was hard-hit by snow, which meant that traction was at a premium. It was no surprise, therefore, to see that the first seven finishers all had front-wheel-drive cars, and that even in its class the Cortina could not keep up with E.Gjolberg's rear-engined Skoda either. Starting from Monte Carlo itself, before spending the next three days circulating around France before the special stages began at Chambéry, Taylor and Melia kept going through blizzard-like conditions, even though they had to face blockages which decimated their group, and had to change a dynamo (without mechanics' assistance, for there were none positioned at Rennes where this occurred), which they did in just 15 minutes. They finished 36th overall, hampered by both a lack of traction and a lack of performance.

The Taylor/Cortina combination then appeared in what became known as the 'Autobog' held at a snowy Brands Hatch two weeks later (for the benefit of TV viewers of BBC Grandstand). If it hadn't been for the huge amount of snow on the ground one might even have called it the very first rallycross to be mounted in this country. This event was almost the end of its works career, though David Seigle-Morris shortly took it on a snowy British rally, the Targa Rusticana 'just for fun', but it did not finish.

Almost immediately the first of the Cortina GTs was homologated, in April, and would soon take over all the attention at Ford.

| REGISTRATION NUMBER | ENGINE SIZE | MODEL TYPE |
| --- | --- | --- |
| **MWC 448** | **1498CC 4-CYL OHV** | **CORTINA SUPER** |

To give the image of the newly-launched version of the Cortina Super a publicity boost, Eric Jackson and Ken Chambers were sent out to break the London-Cape Town overland record, in a two-door car. Few authentic records of the car's preparation survive, except that it is known to have been built at the Lincoln Cars depot in West London alongside the works team cars.

Starting from the RAC HQ at Pall Mall in London on 6 January 1963, the car finally arrived in Cape Town at 22.58 on 19 January. According to the official stats published by Ford, the journey took 13 days, 8 hours and 48 minutes to cover 11,621 miles, which equated to a running average of 36.2mph. There were no scheduled stops for rest at hotels along the way. Except for having the car flown across the English Channel (Lydd to Le Touquet), and by air from Marseilles to Tunis in North Africa, the trip was scheduled entirely by surface transport. Much detail, and the flavour, of this epic trip were captured by the author in an interview with Eric Jackson in later years, and the edited version is now included.

After competing in the 1962 Safari rally in a new Zodiac Mk 3, with *Autosport*'s Gregor Grant as his co-driver (starting from the back of the field, moving up to seventh place, then getting thoroughly bogged down in bottomless mud), Jackson got back home and made a fateful call to Walter Hayes. "I told Walter I'd met someone who held the unofficial London-Cape Town record, the new Cortina was coming along, and why didn't we have a go at that? He jumped at the idea, and that's how we got started on the long-distance lark."

By the end of 1962 Lincoln Cars in Brentford (who, at that time, were responsible for preparing the works rally cars) had built a new 1.5-litre Cortina Super, weighing it down with half a ton of extra fuel tanks, storage, parts, a fully reclining passenger seat and other gear, and the assault started.

"I took Ken Chambers with me – we'd never shared a car before, but we always got on well. He was as brave as a lion, such a good guy. We only ever had one row, in Africa in 1967, when he thought we were on the wrong road and I didn't – I was reading the compass!"

"He was another motor trader, with a Rover dealership in Barnet, North London, and later got a Ford dealership.

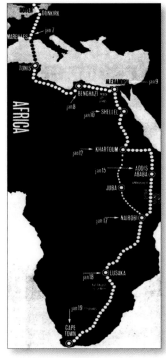

*In January 1963 Walter Hayes sent Eric Jackson and Ken Chambers to break the London-Cape Town record, which they duly did, before being fined by the RAC for 'racing on public roads'. This was the route, and the time schedule that they achieved.*

*MWC 448, the London-Cape Town record Cortina, prepares to leave the start outside the Pall Mall offices of the RAC in January 1963.*

*Eric Jackson and Ken Chambers (in dark glasses) pause to meet local dignitaries 'somewhere in Africa' on their race from London to Cape Town. The car was carrying temporary number plates at that moment.*

*Time for a pause, a mid-event service and (maybe) a bath for the crew. This was when Eric Jackson and Ken Chambers called in at Hughes Ltd., the Kenyan Ford importer, halfway from London to Cape Town.*

Anyway, we set off. In hindsight, it looks incredibly naive, but there had been no practice and no route surveys.

"We just set off on 6 January 1963, as green as grass, with maps and stuff. We had nothing pre-prepared. The biggest problem of all was to decide which way to go, and we didn't fancy the Sahara desert. So we went along the North African coast to Cairo, where we had service booked at the so-called Ford dealer, but our next service was to be at Hughes of Nairobi".

Having driven over icy roads to Marseilles, flown the car to Tunis, then pointed off eastwards, everything looked good. "There were TV crews, cameras, everything, and a motorcycle escort in a cavalcade. But five miles out of Tunis the tarmac ended, and so did the cavalcade. After that we were on our own in the desert. There were all kinds of adventures – we got pulled in at one point by Egyptian secret police who thought we were Israeli spies – but we made it to Cairo where the service crew was one mechanic and half-a-dozen young boys.

"In those days Ken and I were pretty good mechanics ourselves, but we didn't have spare gearboxes, axles, or anything like that, but we had things like valves, springs, dampers – and a belief we were going to make it."

Keeping up an insane speed, south along the Nile valley, in the middle of the night they crashed through a white mountain in the middle of the road, which turned out to be a harvest of cotton ("It was spread around a bit when we had passed through"), were refused permission to drive on from the Aswan dam to Wadi Halfa and had to take a 250-mile cruise on a very slow ferry.

Many hours later, at Khartoum, they discovered that the Nile had flooded, which caused a huge diversion into Ethiopia, and on to Addis Ababa ("We found a transport café at one point, hundreds of miles from anywhere.")

*MWC 448 at speed on the dash from London to Cape Town.*

"All this," Eric told me, "was without getting proper sleep, for we just had to keep going. We never slept in beds, not in hotels. We hadn't done this sort of thing at all. We had our own schedules – one drove while the other slept – and since Ken was a lousy navigator I had to write everything down for him. We always planned two hours on, two hours off – and we *really* slept in between – but we had a rule that we would wake up the other if we started nodding off. There was one occasion where Ken lasted only 14 minutes before nudging me again."

Needing new tyres in Addis Ababa, the duo bought six new tyres, six extra tyres and another 12 inner tubes. "At one point we did 192 miles, and it took us twenty-two hours, we were always changing wheels, mending punctures, or finding ways to ford rivers. When we finally reached Nairobi, we hadn't any spares left."

The big fright, so big that even in later years Eric didn't enjoy talking about it, came soon afterwards when they encountered a roadblock with stones across the dirt road, where they feared an ambush by bandits. Forewarned *and* armed, they had rehearsed the problem, and knew that to stop could literally be fatal, so Ken (who was driving) did a wall-of-death act into the ditch off the edge of the road to get by. "Then he stalled the engine! Before he could get started again they were all round us, thirty of them, waving guns and spears. They were Somalis, and they were enormous."

With bandits trying to drag them from the car there was

chaos for a time, but Ken eventually got the car started. "Then, only a few minutes up the road, we got a puncture and had to stop. Never has a wheel been changed so quietly and so quickly in the dark of an African night. That wasn't all, because we also got shot at on the Ethiopia/Kenya border because we were going fast and wiped off the border chain. In Africa, though, we developed an effective technique for getting through borders – we carried loads and loads of cig-

ARRIVED IN CAPETOWN
ON 20 JANUARY 1962
at 0058 HOURS.

Registration MWC 448
Vehicle No. 274B19897x

*The London-Cape Town record was only achieved with minutes to spare, and this document is what was signed to formalise their arrival in Cape Town.*

arettes, and we also carried a Polaroid camera. Ken was the heaviest smoker I ever knew, so he liked that too. The trick was to take a reluctant guard's picture, then present him immediately with a print and some cigarettes. It worked most of the time, but if we found someone who was *really* difficult it was time to reach for the fistful of US dollars. They never refused US dollars."

Back in Britain, meantime, Ford had little idea where they were or what was happening, for it was only in Khartoum, then in Nairobi, 11 days into the trip, that there was time to get messages back. Once past Nairobi, conditions eased a lot, on good tarmac roads, but after the huge delays the task looked hopeless at first. To break the record, the crew now had to average 61mph for 4000 miles all the way to Cape Town and, after more delays in Tanganyika, that rose to 71mph for the last 2000 miles.

"We were ready for packing it in, we didn't think we could do it, but Peter persuaded us to go on. Half way there we threw everything out of the car to lighten it – most of the tools, parts, everything – and then a miracle happened. Half way through South Africa the dynamo dropped off. We found a spare fan belt taped into the back of the car, we found a pair of Mole grips, but we still needed a bolt to replace the one we'd lost. We searched that car from end to end in the dark, and eventually found one in a door hinge,which did the trick."

Even then the drama wasn't over for, when arriving in Cape Town, only about an hour in hand and in the middle of the night, they didn't know how to find the RAC headquarters to 'clock in'. Commandeering a taxi driver didn't help ("He took us to the AA instead"), they finally stumbled across Edgy Fabris at the RAC, a mere 18 minutes in hand.

Ford was cock-a-hoop about this, but soon afterwards the RAC had what appears to be a complete change of mind, summoned Walter Hayes to their presence like a naughty school-boy, told him that they did not approve of record attempts on public roads, and fined Ford a considerable sum of money.

---

### Competition Record

| | | |
|---|---|---|
| 1963 London-Cape Town Record Run | Eric Jackson/Ken Chambers | Set new record, yet was later fined by the RAC for 'racing on public roads' |

---

| REGISTRATION NUMBER | ENGINE SIZE | MODEL TYPE |
|---|---|---|
| 785 BOO | 1498CC 4-CYL OHV | CORTINA GT MK1 |

One of the first Cortina GTs to be completed at Boreham in 1963 was given the identity of 785 BOO, but it was only used as a practice and test car at first, often with non-standard parts which might, or might not, be homologated in due course. It was not until January 1965 that it seems to have started an International rally, this being the Monte Carlo rally with Tour de France winner Peter Procter (he had been driving a Mustang on that event) taking part.

By this time, as the images confirm, it was a current-specification Group 2 car, and started the Monte from Paris alongside all the rest of the Boreham fleet. All went well until the special stages began south of Chambéry, and it was on the Col du Granier section that Peter caught up with team-mate David Seigle-Morris, tried to pass him on a wide stretch, failed, and ended up in a deep snow bank with the car on its side. As it was not possible for the crew to retrieve the car without

*785 BOO looks very smart as it starts from Monte Carlo in the 1965 Monte Carlo rally, where it was driven by Peter Procter and David Mabbs. When it crashed into a snow bank on the Col du Granier stage it could not be retrieved and had to retire.*

outside assistance, it was dark at the time, and in any case there were no spectators available, this meant that although the car was virtually undamaged, it had to retire.

Ford then found no more public work for this car until the Scottish, held in June 1965, where Boreham, almost in a bid to 'get rid of the empties' immediately before the leaf-spring Lotus-Cortinas were homologated, entered three regular drivers in three modified GTs, some in the Group 3 category with non-standard parts.

Henry Taylor himself ran the much-used 785 BOO with some glass-fibre body panels, and some Lotus-Cortina running gear in the transmission. It was the transmission internals which failed at an early stage of the event, in mid-special stage, which resulted in Taylor personally running to the end of the stage, organising a tow out of the stage from a Ford private owner, and having a complete new rear axle fitted! This axle also failed at another stage (this time in the ultra-fast Culbin forest, near Nairn), but another tow and another change somehow kept him going, and he eventually finished the event, actually winning a much depleted 1.6-litre Grand Touring class. Need one say that that car was never used again!

*Henry Taylor and Brian Melia drove 785 BOO in the 1965 Scottish rally and after a mechanically troubled week actually won its capacity class. The car was not used again after this.*

| Competition Record | | |
|---|---|---|
| 1965 Monte Carlo | Peter Procter | DNF |
| 1965 Scottish | Henry Taylor | 1st in Class |

| REGISTRATION NUMBER | ENGINE SIZE | MODEL TYPE |
|---|---|---|
| **128 CWC** | **1498CC 4-CYL OHV** | **CORTINA GT MK1** |

As *Autocar* magazine reported in its pre-Monte Carlo rally team survey of January 1964, Boreham had prepared no fewer than 22 cars since opening its doors in October 1963, including five Cortina GT team cars for the Monte, and three reconnaissance cars too. That was a luxury which could still be afforded at a time when the cars were still relatively simply engineered. The three modern recce cars at that time were 128 CWC, 129 CWC, and 553 UOO. The master plan did not involve any of these cars being entered for events but, like all the best such plans, it soon needed alteration.

For the 1964 Monte Carlo rally, Boreham planned to enter four cars (888 DOO, 890 DOO, 891 DOO, and RWC 202), but at a late stage their publicity machine (i.e. Walter Hayes) directed them to lend a car to Peter Dimmock of BBC Sportsview. The only car which was immediately available in the new red livery was 128 CWC, which was pressed into service as a Group 1 car, complete with the latest twin-choke Weber

engine kit, and all the other latest toys including a second fuel tank mounted behind the rear seat squab. There is no immediate record of Dimmock's performance on this event – he started from Monte Carlo itself (as did team professionals Henry Taylor and Vic Elford) but retired well before the end.

For the 1964 French Alpine Boreham allocated the car to the Finnish pairing of Esko Keinanen and Anssi Jarvi, which meant that the Boreham contingent on this event was made up of five cars. Keinanen had surprised the rallying establishment in January by pedalling a Plymouth Valiant very quickly until it expired, and this outing was Ford's way of finding out if they had spotted a future superstar. However, although the right-hand-drive 128 CWC was in the same state of tune as other team Cortina GTs, it did not seem to suit Keinanen, who must therefore have been relieved when its engine let go on the first night of the event. The same car fared no better on the Liège, which followed in August, when the Kenyan pair of

39

Peter Hughes (who had won the Safari of that year) and Mike Armstrong failed to finish.

Almost a year later, 128 CWC was dragged back into the limelight, to be driven by Vic Elford in the 1965 Scottish rally (where it joined 129 CWC and 585 BOO, also ex-practice/test cars), and where it ran with a non-standard engine. Not that this helped, for although Vic set several fastest times in the opening hours of the event, he finally up-ended the car and had to retire. This was the end of a rather inglorious career.

*This time it is the scenery, not necessarily the car itself – 128 CWC, driven by Eska Keinanen – which takes most of one's attention in this study of a 1964 French Alpine rally section.*

*The Kenyan pair Mike Armstrong (at the wheel of 128 CWC) and Safari-winner Peter Hughes contested the 1964 Spa-Sofia-Liège but failed to finish.*

### Competition Record

| | | |
|---|---|---|
| 1964 Monte Carlo | Peter Dimmock | DNF |
| 1964 French Alpine | Esko Keinanen | DNF |
| 1964 Spa-Sofia-Liège | Peter Hughes | DNF |
| 1965 Scottish | Vic Elford | DNF |

| REGISTRATION NUMBER | ENGINE SIZE | MODEL TYPE |
|---|---|---|
| **129 CWC** | **1498cc 4-cyl OHV** | **CORTINA GT Mk1** |

*129 CWC was rarely seen on rallies in 1963-65 as it spent much of its time as a practice and test car, but it was allocated to David Seigle-Morris for the 1965 Scottish rally. Unhappily for David he rolled it in an early forest special stage and had to retire.*

As noted above, 129 CWC was originally a practice/test car, but like 128 CWC it was suddenly pressed into service in mid-1964 as Geoff Mabbs' mount on the French Alpine rally, though that outing did not last long as the inlet manifold cracked during the first leg of the event, ruining the fuel-air mixture and making further progress impossible.

The car was then relegated to its original duties until June 1965, when it was one of the machines brought out to compete in the Scottish rally, but it had no luck on that event, for on the first day David Seigle-Morris went off the track in a forestry stage, overturned the car, and had to retire.

### Competition Record

| | | |
|---|---|---|
| 1964 Alpine | Geoff Mabbs | DNF |
| 1965 Scottish | David Seigle-Morris | DNF |

| REGISTRATION NUMBER | ENGINE SIZE | MODEL TYPE |
|---|---|---|
| **553 UOO** | **1498CC 4-CYL OHV** | **CORTINA GT MK1** |

Although this car figured strongly in publicity material put out by Ford in 1963/64, particularly when it came to displaying all the kit which could be fitted to a GT to make it more rally-worthy, and the many trophies which the team won in the early 1960s, it does not appear to have started in an event of any consequence. It was, of course, contemporary with the 888 DOO - 893 DOO sequence of more active works Cortinas, all of which were originally built in 1963.

### Competition Record
Not apparently used by the works team in International competition.

*This was the works layout of extra driving lamps and rubber bonnet straps which applied to all the Cortinas used by the factory in the 1960s. 553 UOO was a genuine Lincoln Cars-built machine dating from 1963, but seems only to have been used as a practice, test or (in this case) demonstration car.*

*This was a typical works instrument panel as used in a Cortina of the 1964-onwards period.*

*Soon after the Cortina GT was homologated, this extra fuel tank, 'lifted' from a current-model estate car, was made available. It fitted neatly behind the rear seats in the boot area. This explains the location of the twin fuel filler caps seen on the works rally cars.*

| REGISTRATION NUMBER | ENGINE SIZE | MODEL TYPE |
|---|---|---|
| **RWC 202** | **1498CC 4-CYL OHV** | **CORTINA GT MK1** |

If the registration number can be relied upon, when it was new this white two-door car must have been one of the very earliest Cortina GT cars to be registered, early in 1963. It was used by the works team as soon as the model was homologated, and was always allocated to Pat Moss during 1963.

When originally prepared, RWC 202 had an extremely basic specification, for all the modifications, improvements, and homologated extras for this model were still being developed.

For the Tulip rally of 1963 (which was based in Holland, but with all the competitive sections being in the French mountains), Pat collected it the day before the start and found it slow, so the mechanics who, like everyone else in rallying, had already fallen in love with this girl, worked all night to improve its performance.

This setback, and the need to get used to having a new co-driver (Jennifer Nadin) made it a difficult event, but Pat

*Pat Moss was a member of the Ford works team in 1963 and drove RWC 202 on several occasions. She never got her hands on a competitive or reliable Lotus-Cortina, which may have influenced her to leave Boreham and join the Saab team for 1964, alongside her husband Erik Carlsson.*

*Pat Moss in RWC 202. This was the newly-shelled 'second-generation' of that car, brand new for the 1963 RAC rally, in which Pat finished in a highly creditable seventh place and won her capacity class.*

plugged away, well out of the limelight, ending up second in her capacity class to Peter Harper's works' Sunbeam Rapier, and 12th overall in the Touring Car category. Creditable? Well, yes, because the class winner – a factory Sunbeam Rapier, a type of car which had already been in rallying for several years, and which was acknowledged as Ford's first target on their way to gaining supremacy – was a good yardstick.

Pat took part in the Acropolis rally in May, where she soon showed the men in the team that she was just as good as they were. At the end of rugged rally Ford team-leader Henry Taylor won the capacity class and finished fourth overall, while Pat was always close to him, taking second in class and a rousing sixth overall.

According to the existing Bill Barnett-inspired master plan, Pat was then scheduled to take part in the French Alpine event in RWC 202, immediately after competing in the Midnight Sun event in a Lotus-Cortina (see Chapter 5). However, she fell ill with pleurisy in Sweden, had to be rushed to hospital in London, and would not go rallying again for two months. RWC 202, therefore, might have been rally-ready for the French Alpine, but would not be used until September.

Pat then got married, joyfully, to Erik Carlsson, but it was not to be an entirely successful year for her, especially in RWC 202 on the Spa-Sofia-Liège rally. As related by Stuart Turner in her biography, *Harnessing Horsepower*, "In Yugoslavia, on one of the rare motorway sections, Pat handed over to Jenny and went to sleep. The next thing she knew, the car was going sideways down the road, scrubbing off speed from about 80mph for around 100 yards. The car had hit a Yugoslavian milestone, and this had thrown it sideways and ripped out the propeller shaft."

*Autosport's* rally story reported that the car was written off, which in normal circumstances it might have been, except that it re-appeared before the end of 1963, miraculously reborn, and was the very first works Cortina GT to get a bright red bodyshell. Running in FIA Group 3 specification, in the RAC rally, it was demonstrably faster than the other new GTs in the Boreham works team, and was beaten only narrowly to the finish, by Henry Taylor in a new and still unproven Lotus-Cortina.

Pat then left the team to join husband Erik Carlsson at Saab in 1964, which meant that RWC 202 lost its 'special-to-Pat' individuality, and became one of several team 'spares' to the re-shelled 'DOO' fleet. Immediately after this decision, however, it was allocated to Geoff Mabbs for the 1964 Monte, where he adapted well to what to him was a strange car, for he had never before driven a works Ford and his signing for this event was and still is rather mysterious. The ever-cheerful Mabbs finished in 22nd place, actually being the highest-placed of the works GTs to survive the event. Geoff then took the same car to compete in the BBC TV sprint spectacular at Prescott Hillclimb, where he finished third, close behind team-mate Henry Taylor and Terry Hunter's Mini.

At this point in 1964 the car and the rest of the 'European' fleet of Boreham-built Cortina GTs went back into hibernation as the team prepared for its massive (and, as it transpired, successful) assault on the East African Safari at Easter, so it was not seen again in public for some time.

Once again restored to front-line duty, and now with left-hand drive, but still with the original-style nose (*after the facelift/Aeroflow changes had been made to the production car range*), it was allocated to Esko Keinanen to drive in the 1965 Monte Carlo rally, where he retained the faithful support of Ford-of-Finland. Starting from Monte Carlo, he had to grapple with the worst of the blizzards which submerged the event that year, and dropped out even before the cars began their assault on the special stages.

## Competition Record

| | | |
|---|---|---|
| 1963 Tulip | Pat Moss | 2nd in Class, won Ladies' Prize |
| 1963 Acropolis | Pat Moss | 6th Overall, and Ladies' Prize |
| 1963 French Alpine | Pat Moss | Did not start (driver illness) |
| 1963 Spa-Sofia-Liège | Pat Moss | DNF |

**The car was then re-shelled and painted bright red**

| | | |
|---|---|---|
| 1963 RAC | Pat Moss | 7th, Class win |
| 1964 Monte Carlo | Geoff Mabbs | 22nd |
| 1964 TV Sprint, Prescott | Geoff Mabbs | 3rd |
| 1965 Monte Carlo | Esko Keinanen | DNF |

| REGISTRATION NUMBER | ENGINE SIZE | MODEL TYPE |
|---|---|---|
| **888 DOO** | **1498CC 4-CYL OHV** | **CORTINA GT MK1** |

Early in 1963 Syd Henson's team at Lincoln Cars had built up not one but up to 10 (the numbers are still not totally clear) new Cortina GT rally cars. RWC 202, and a complete run of 888 DOO to 893 DOO, were the planned principal fleet. As noted, RWC 202 started the Tulip rally in early May 1963, while three more of the 'DOOs' – 888 DOO, 890 DOO and 891 DOO – started the rough-and-tumble of the Greek Acropolis at the end of the same month.

As unofficial team leader, Henry Taylor took over 888 DOO, and would keep it 'as his own' for the next two years. As noted in the results panel it eventually became the hardest-working of all these cars. Right away Henry proved that it could be competitive, and several important homologated extras would follow in future months to make it even more so. In an Acropolis where established rallying 'tanks' like the Mercedes-Benz 330SEb and Volvo Amazon set all the standards, Taylor put up a remarkable performance by finishing fourth overall.

Next up was the French Alpine rally, where set averages on the sometimes serpentine, sometimes high, and always hot public road stages were extremely demanding. In an event where it was an achievement even to finish the event, it was a real achievement to make it back to the Riviera. On this occasion, only six Touring cars – two of them works Cortina GTs – completed the course without road penalties. Rauno Aaltonen's Mini-Cooper 1071S, and Rolland's Alfa Romeo Giulia SZ headed the list, but Henry Taylor and Brian Melia set a storming performance in 888 DOO to take second place overall in the Touring Car category. It is still not generally known that, when it was newly prepared, Taylor arranged to have his car delivered to Alan Mann's workshops in Sussex

*Henry Taylor's regular Boreham team car 888 DOO lined up for the Snetterton speed trial of the 1964 RAC rally, with 889 DOO right behind it and the Volvo of Tom Trana (which won the event) ahead.*

before it left for France, where significant preparation changes were made to the engine – so much so that team-mate Pat Moss was later heard to complain that her GT was much slower than his.

This for the time being was definitely Ford's star Cortina GT, for it was next re-engined with a Lotus-Ford twin-cam and entered on the 'anything-goes' Spa-Sofia-Liège rally, details of which are noted in Chapter 5.

Back at Boreham, it then had a rest (Taylor tackled the RAC rally in an A-bracket Lotus-Cortina – see Chapter 5 also) before gaining a new red bodyshell and an engine fitted with twin dual-choke Weber carburettors in time to contest the 1964 Monte Carlo rally. On the early special stages Taylor was going well, but on the one between Chorges and Savines (east of Gap) the car suffered a fuel pump blockage, stranding it for several minutes, and at a stroke his chances were ruined. His final finishing position, 77th, did not do justice to his or the car's potential. Even so, the car was still made fit and healthy at the close of the event, where Henry set second fastest time overall in the informal Manoeuvrability Test laid out on the Promenade in Monaco, being beaten by Gunther Klass's Porsche Carrera 2-litre by 1.10 seconds.

Then it was back home for a quick wash, and for the tyres to be kicked, before Taylor (along with David Seigle-Morris and Geoff Mabbs in their own Monte cars) performed for BBC TV cameras on an improved 'Rallysprint' course at Prescott hillclimb, near Cheltenham, which included parts of the hill and parts of the return roads.

Next, soon after Henry Taylor had returned from taking part in the East African Safari (see KHS 597 below), he was the only works driver to tackle the Tulip rally, using 888 DOO running in the Group 3 GT Cars category. This was done after the team had studied the pre-event regulations carefully, for as ever the Tulip was being run according to a very complex 'class-improvement' formula which seemed to favour the GT running with non-standard parts against privately-owned Porsche 356s.

There is no longer any record of what those non-standard pieces were – and on-event pictures of 888 DOO in action on this Tulip are rare – but they certainly included the use of lightweight Lotus-Cortina panels and other hardware. The result was gratifying, for Taylor and Brian Melia enjoyed a copybook run over the 48-hour/1750-mile route, did not put a foot or wheel wrong throughout, and finished a splendid third overall among the GT cars, behind the Morley Twins' works Austin-Healey 3000 and Berndt Jansson's Porsche 356 Carrera.

*By the end of 1964, 888 DOO was a very scruffy old works GT, here seen at Snetterton on the RAC rally in company with the two other GTs, 889 DOO and 893 DOO, which went on to win the Manufacturers' Team Prize...*

*...and in this shot, taken only moments later, Vic Elford in 893 DOO had taken over from the two sister cars.*

Taylor was not so fortunate on the French Alpine which followed. He started well but during the last frantic 24-hour hour run up and over most of the high passes inland of the Riviera he went off the crumbly tarmac, damaging the car, after which a following competitor in a Renault R8 completed the job.

Finally (and there is no question that this identity had had a hard life in the two years since it became Taylor's preferred Cortina GT), 888 DOO then started the 1964 RAC rally, which encompassed a massive 2500-mile London-to-London loop of the UK, with a night halt at Perth in Scotland and no fewer than 55 special stages.

Things started badly when Taylor put the car on its side in the very first stage (it needed manual assistance from team-

*Henry Taylor drove 888 DOO intensively in 1963 and 1964. Here he was pushing the old car along in the RAC rally of October 1964, its last-ever appearance.*

mate David Seigle-Morris to get it back on four wheels again), but there was little damage and only injured pride. Another off-road excursion in the Lake District didn't help, nor did a trip into the trees in Kielder, but the crew kept plugging on. The reward for all this was that, along with Vic Elford and David Seigle-Morris, three Cortina GT crews won the Manufacturers' team prize.

That was the end of 888 DOO's front-line career, for after all its 1964 adventures the red bodyshell was in a definitely secondhand condition. Taylor therefore changed his allegiance to 890 DOO for the 1965 Monte Carlo rally and 888 was not seen again, as after this the twin-cam engined Lotus-Cortinas were on the way.

As far as is known, the car was never sold on from Boreham but was scrapped. In later years, however, some confusion was caused when a freely-admitted replica appeared on classic events carrying '800 DOO' plates, but it was not the same vehicle. This is one important reason why the author has not attempted to trace a post-Boreham career for any of these cars!

## Competition Record

| | | |
|---|---|---|
| 1963 Acropolis | Henry Taylor | 4th, and Class Win |
| 1963 French Alpine | Henry Taylor | 2nd in Touring Category |
| 1963 Spa-Sofia-Liège | Henry Taylor. | The car was entered as a 'Lotus-Cortina prototype' (see Chapter 5), then along with other contemporary team GT cars was re-shelled and painted red in January 1964. |
| 1964 Monte Carlo | Henry Taylor | 77th |
| 1964 TV Sprint, Prescott hillclimb | Henry Taylor | 1st |
| 1964 Tulip | Henry Taylor | 3rd GT Category |
| 1964 French Alpine | Henry Taylor | DNF |
| 1964 RAC | Henry Taylor | 3rd in Class |

| REGISTRATION NUMBER | ENGINE SIZE | MODEL TYPE |
|---|---|---|
| **889 DOO** | **1498CC 4-CYL OHV** | **CORTINA GT MK1** |

This car had a rather short, undistinguished and disjointed career, for although it was originally commissioned with other examples of the 'DOO' fleet of 1963/64, it does not appear to have been used very often. It is not certain, indeed, that it was ever used Internationally in 1963 (as a 'white' car).

However, to gain more experience of rallying the Cortina (which was still quite scarce with this fleet in 1963), 889 DOO was entered in the British Rally of the Vales for David Seigle-Morris to drive. This was an important club event relying as much on the co-drivers' expertise as on the car being used, but the project came to nothing when David put the car off the road and damaged it significantly.

A rejuvenated 889 DOO was finally allocated to David Seigle-Morris for the 1964 RAC rally, and although he had his share of adventures – which included a multi-rally car accident in the Dovey Forest special stage – he kept going, to reach the finish in a plucky ninth place, the third of the red Cortinas to make it back to the end of this marathon event. The car was not seen again in a major event.

889 DOO was rarely seen on a rally in public in 1964 but here it is on the 1964 RAC rally with David Seigle-Morris at the wheel.

## Competition Record

| | | |
|---|---|---|
| 1963 Rally of the Vales | David Seigle-Morris | DNF |
| 1964 RAC | David Seigle-Morris | 9th |

| REGISTRATION NUMBER | ENGINE SIZE | MODEL TYPE |
|---|---|---|
| **890 DOO** | **1498CC 4-CYL OHV** | **CORTINA GT MK1** |

*Peter Riley bustling through a special stage of the 1963 RAC rally in 890 DOO, on his way to taking second in class.*

Peter Riley, newly signed from BMC, finished 11th overall in the 1963 Acropolis in this new GT, but must have been disappointed because he could not match the pace of Henry Taylor and Pat Moss. It was the start of a disappointing season for him at Ford, and his contract would not be extended for 1964.

Things got no better on the French Alpine, where his Cortina GT engine threw a fan blade, which punctured the water radiator, but even though Ford service at Chamonix rectified the problem in a matter of minutes, the engine had already overheated and retirement was inevitable. There was a better result on the rough Spa-Sofia-Liège Marathon, where Riley's GT was one of only two pushrod-engined Cortinas to keep going and ended up ninth overall, but a massive 48 minutes behind the flying Taylor/Melia twin-cam-engined sister car.

Riley's last drive in this machine was in FIA Group 3 tune in the 1963 RAC rally, where he finished in a creditable 15th place and second in the 2.5-litre class behind Pat Moss's leading team car.

Riley's contract with Ford was not extended, and Vic Elford was attracted to the team, having spent a fruitless season with the under-financed Triumph operation. Vic took over 890 DOO (now with a new red bodyshell) for the 1964 Monte Carlo rally. Unhappily, soon after the start of the event, his car hit a military truck on the open road near Epernay, and although every effort was made to restore the rally car to a good condition when it was being serviced before the Rheims control, this was never going to be possible in the time available and it had to be retired.

Vic Elford then took over the sister car 893 DOO for the French Alpine, and although Henry Taylor used 890 on the Spa-Sofia-Liège (while 888 DOO was being made good after its French Alpine misfortunes), 890 DOO does not seem to have been used again in major motorsport for the rest of 1964. However, when the 1965 Monte Carlo rally came around (and Henry Taylor's faithful old 888 DOO had finally

*Vic Elford (right) and his co-driver David Stone joined the Ford works team in January 1964.*

*Vic Elford made his debut for Ford in the 1964 Monte Carlo rally, driving 890 DOO.*

*Vic Elford in the 1964 Monte Carlo rally in 890 DOO soon after the start, on a mountainous section behind the principality...*

*...and here trying rather hard on a slippery tarmac section close to Nice.*

been given a decent burial after the 1964 RAC), 890 was allocated to Taylor, who finished a very creditable ninth overall in what was a blizzard-affected event, with five of the eight cars ahead of him being of the engine-over-driving-wheels type.

At Easter, Brian Melia got another chance to prove that he was not only an excellent co-driver for Henry Taylor but a fast driver too, when he took the car on the Circuit of Ireland (along with team-mates David Seigle-Morris and Vic Elford in sister cars). At the end of an event which Vic Elford so nearly won (in 893 DOO), Melia kept going steadily and unspectacularly, finally taking fourth place behind Paddy Hopkirk's Mini-Cooper S and the Cortina GTs of Vic Elford and Roger Clark.

It was at this time that Roger Clark, one of the most stellar of all personalities to get his hands on a rallying Cortina, enters the works story. As Roger later wrote in his autobiography *Sideways to Victory*, he was still not sure what Ford thought about his achievements in his own cars until, "Probably that Rover drive in the 1965 Monte did the trick," (Roger had won the GT Category in a Group 1 2000) "because soon afterwards Alan Platt (Ford's competitions manager at Boreham) started to make encouraging noises. When Fords duly offered me a ride in the Tulip rally that April I was delighted."

The story is that Platt was already planning for the future, for he knew that he would soon be promoted out of his job, and he had decided that Henry Taylor would take over from

*After staying faithful to 888 DOO for two full seasons, Henry Taylor then drove 890 DOO in the 1965 Monte Carlo rally, finishing ninth in very wintry conditions.*

him. For the Tulip, therefore, it made sense to 'borrow' Taylor's current team car (890 DOO) and his co-driver Brian Melia, for Roger Clark, and to send them out to tackle the Dutch-based event.

Not that this was a fairy-tale beginning, as there was heavy snow at one point in the Geneva-St Claude region which caused all manner of delays, after which the engine's electrics failed and retirement was inevitable. Roger therefore went back to his own car (2 ANR, see page 55), but would return to the team, permanently, at the end of 1965.

Finally, for the 1965 Gulf London, 890 DOO was loaned out to Brian Melia who, with the very minimum of service support, put up a stirring performance, kept going while cars fell about him in this marathon event, and finally finished third overall, beaten only by Roger Clark (in his own Cortina GT), and Jerry Larsson's front-wheel drive Saab 96. A marathon? Certainly, as only 17 of the original 92 starters made it to the finish.

*Occasionally, just occasionally, a rally driver has to do his own repairs. Above Henry Taylor is faced with making a wheel change on 890 DOO in the 1965 Monte Carlo rally.*

*890 DOO at speed in the 1965 Circuit of Ireland, where Brian Melia took fourth place overall.*

*This wonderful atmospheric shot shows the Boreham mechanics preparing the complex lighting system on an early example of the works GT fleet of 1963-65.*

## Competition Record

| | | |
|---|---|---|
| 1963 Acropolis | Peter Riley | 11th, 3rd in Class |
| 1963 French Alpine | Peter Riley | DNF |
| 1963 Spa-Sofia-Liège | Peter Riley | 9th, Class win |
| Then re-shelled, in red, for future use: | | |
| 1963 RAC | Peter Riley | 2nd in Class |
| 1964 Monte Carlo | Vic Elford | DNF |
| 1964 Spa-Sofia-Liège | Henry Taylor | DNF |
| 1965 Monte Carlo | Henry Taylor | 9th |
| 1965 Circuit of Ireland | Brian Melia | 4th |
| 1965 Tulip | Roger Clark | DNF |
| 1965 Gulf London | Brian Melia | 3rd |

| REGISTRATION NUMBER | ENGINE SIZE | MODEL TYPE |
|---|---|---|
| **891 DOO** | **1498cc 4-cyl OHV** | **CORTINA GT Mk1** |

Like Peter Riley in 890 DOO on the 1963 Acropolis rally, David Seigle-Morris must have been disappointed with his finish in 891 DOO on that event, for he only took 17th place. In France, however, things went much better for this combination, where they finished third overall in the Touring Category, close behind the team car of Henry Taylor. Unhappily, their luck turned sour on the gruelling Spa-Sofia-Liège marathon which followed, for after they had somehow twice struggled through the length and breadth of rock-strewn Yugoslavia, the car reached Gorizia in the Italian Dolomites where it blew a cylinder head gasket.

Nor was there any luck for Seigle-Morris on the 1963 RAC rally, where he started No. 22, along with four other team cars (driven by Pat Moss, Henry Taylor, Peter Riley and Anne Hall) in the car which had been prepared to Group 3 specification (which meant that it was running with several items of

*David Seigle-Morris has a problem here, and is explaining it to team co-ordinator Bill Barnett.*

*891 DOO was one the least often seen works GTs built at Boreham. This was David Seigle-Morris driving the car in the 1964 Monte Carlo rally, where it finished a lowly 24th overall.*

49

non-homologated equipment). The car was eliminated during the run through the special stages, the details of its demise not being reported in the specialist press.

For 1964 this car, like its companions in the contemporary Boreham fleet, gained a new red bodyshell, and for the Monte Carlo rally in January was equipped with the recently-homologated dual twin-choke Webers. Fortunately the works service plan was detailed and efficient, for on the way from Paris to The Hague, the Webers had partially swallowed a set of rubber O-rings, which were promptly replaced without the crew losing any time. In an event where the time penalties were massaged on handicap grounds (this explains why Bo Ljungfeldt's 4.2-litre Falcon beat Paddy Hopkirk's 1071cc Mini-Cooper S on the stages, but lost out in the final results),

David plugged on and finished 24th overall. Not only that, but soon after he returned home, with a still-healthy car, he took part in the TV spectacular 'Rally Sprint' which was held at Prescott, and which was won by team-mate Henry Taylor.

Preparation of a brand new team of GTs for the East African Safari meant that use of 891 DOO (and its sister cars in the same fleet) had to be deferred for a time. Used, it seems, as a practice car for the 1964 Spa-Sofia-Liège it was then allocated to Bo Lungfeldt (who had so nearly won the Monte Carlo rally in massive Ford Falcons) for the RAC rally, and for the 1965 Tulip rally, but had no further success.

After the arrival of a fleet of newly-homologated leaf-spring Lotus-Cortinas (see Chapter 5), the car became surplus to requirements and drops out of this story.

### Competition Record

| | | |
|---|---|---|
| 1963 Acropolis | David Seigle-Morris | 17th |
| 1963 French Alpine | David Seigle-Morris | 3rd Touring Category |
| 1963 Spa-Sofia-Liège | David Seigle-Morris | DNF |
| 1963 RAC | David Seigle-Morris | DNF |
| 1964 Monte Carlo | David Seigle-Morris | 24th |
| 1964 TV Sprint, Prescott hillclimb | David Seigle-Morris | 8th |
| 1964 RAC | Bo Ljungfeldt | DNF |
| 1965 Tulip | Bo Ljungfeldt | DNF |

| REGISTRATION NUMBER | ENGINE SIZE | MODEL TYPE |
|---|---|---|
| **892 DOO** | **1498CC 4-CYL OHV** | **CORTINA GT MK1** |

*It's off to work we go – four team members in the 1964 French Alpine rally – left to right Tony Nash, David Seigle-Morris, Vic Elford and David Stone.*

This car – or, to be more accurate, this vehicle identity – was allocated to Ford's established driver Anne Hall, but although the Cortina GT was homologated in good time to take part in the Acropolis rally of 1963, Ford preferred to send Anne to Greece in a Ford Anglia. Consequently, 892 DOO did not make its public debut until the French Alpine rally which followed a few weeks later.,

On that French Alpine, which was run in blisteringly hot weather to very demanding time schedules, Anne did not cover herself with glory as she crashed the car not once but three times, which ensured that she had to retire well before half distance. Nor was there any better luck in the Spa-Sofia-Liège, where the engine blew a head gasket. In her last drive in this white car, however, Anne took 16th place in the RAC rally, close behind her team mate Peter Riley (15th), but a long way behind Pat Moss, who took seventh overall. At that juncture Anne left the works team and, for the moment, it looked as if 892 DOO would take a rest before being re-created with a red bodyshell for use in 1964.

*David Seigle-Morris, driving 892 DOO, came so very close to winning the French Alpine rally in 1964. 892 DOO was one of the hardest-worked works GTs of the period.*

Some time later, the re-shelled car re-appeared, still ostensibly 892 DOO, but actually newly-built at Boreham with a few old bits included. Because of Boreham's heavy involvement in the 1964 Safari, with a different fleet of cars, it was not used until mid-1964, when it was allocated to David Seigle-Morris for use in the French Alpine rally. (For interest, there was a formidable five-car works effort in that event – 128 CWC, 129 CWC, 888 DOO and 893 DOO being the other four).

For David, who had had an unlucky stay at Boreham so far, things were definitely looking up on the Alpine. Right from the start he not only fought it out, car for car, against the other front-line drivers in the team (Henry Taylor and Vic Elford), but against every other machine in the outright Touring Car category. Fast from the start, he reached the overnight in Chamonix in the lead (Vic Elford in 893 DOO was close behind him), and up to the very last moment he held securely on to that position. Then, suddenly, only about 25 kilometres from the end of the event in Monte Carlo, his engine failed, which stopped him in his tracks and allowed Vic Elford to sweep past to take an outright win.

This was a shattering blow, and it was only a splendid run in the Tour de France in September (see the entry in Chapter 5) in an A-Frame Lotus-Cortina, ETW 362B, which brought him any solace. 892 DOO was not used again in 1964, as Seigle-Morris was allocated 889 DOO for the RAC rally.

Refreshed yet again for 1965, however, 892 DOO remained with him, but that season did not start happily as his run in the Monte Carlo rally ended abruptly on the third special stage, near Gap in the French Alps, when the gearbox suddenly broke and pitched him and his car off the road. Although David was devastated by this, the car was little damaged.

Recovered and rebuilt in time for Easter, the same car was used in the Circuit of Ireland, without success, thus ending its Boreham career.

## Competition Record

| | | |
|---|---|---|
| 1963 French Alpine | Anne Hall | DNF |
| 1963 Spa-Sofia-Liège | Anne Hall | DNF |
| 1963 RAC | Anne Hall | 16th |
| This was Anne's final drive in a works Cortina. 892 DOO was given a new red bodyshell for 1964 and 1965. | | |
| 1964 French Alpine | David Seigle-Morris | DNF |
| 1965 Monte Carlo | David Seigle-Morris | DNF |
| 1965 Circuit of Ireland | David Seigle-Morris | DNF |

| REGISTRATION NUMBER | ENGINE SIZE | MODEL TYPE |
|---|---|---|
| 893 DOO | 1498cc 4-cyl OHV | CORTINA GT MK1 |

*Vic Elford and David Stone with 893 DOO prepare to start the French Alpine rally of 1964, which they won outright.*

*Who said the French Alpine was always held on tarmac-surfaced public roads in France and Italy? This was Vic Elford on his way to winning in 1964.*

*Occasionally, just occasionally, Vic Elford would let co-driver David Stone take the wheel, as on this liaison section of the 1964 French Alpine rally.*

Although this identity was established in 1963 when other cars in the 'DOO' fleet were built, it does not appear to have been completed, or used on an event, until mid-1964 as it was 888, 889, 891 and 892 which did most of the regular work in the first series of works Cortina entries. In fact no white 'Lincoln Cars' Cortina GT carrying the identity 893 DOO seems to have appeared in public at all in 1963.

In mid-1964, however, all this changed, when a red-shelled 893 DOO took part in the first of several exciting outings for Vic Elford. With team orders certainly not applying, he fought stage after stage in the French Alpine Rally against his team-mate David Seigle-Morris in 892 DOO. Towards the end of the event, when Seigle-Morris looked sure to be on his way to winning the event, his engine suddenly failed, and Elford went on to win the Touring Car Category outright, against formidable opposition.

Unhappily, the same car/driver combination then failed to finish on the Spa-Sofia-Liège marathon, for Vic put the car off the road, hitting a wall near Perast on the Yugoslavian coast.

After his magnificent run on the Tour de France (with David Seigle-Morris in the A-Frame Lotus-Cortina, see Chapter 5), Vic returned to a rejuvenated 893 DOO for the RAC rally, and although he later admitted to the author that he did not enjoy driving 'blind' on British special stages (this is rally-speak for 'no pace notes'), he was always competitive. In spite of spinning the car several times, and going off the road

*No high-tech re-fuelling equipment in those days! The renowned senior mechanic Mick Jones adds fuel to Vic Elford's GT before the Snetterton test on the 1964 RAC rally.*

*Early in the 1964 RAC, in which he finished third, Elford was faced with thick fog on a road section.*

in the Lake District, he kept gamely on, pulling back from 11th place in mid-Wales to third overall behind the fighting duo of Tom Trana (Volvo PV544) and Timo Makinen (Austin-Healey 3000), all this after enduring a fuel pump failure on a Scottish stage. Evidence of how hard the car had been treated on that event is visible in pictures taken as the car was being prepared for the final circuit test at Snetterton!

There was less luck for this determined driver/crew/car

combination on the Monte Carlo rally of January 1965, an event beset by truly blizzard-like conditions towards the end of the route. Starting from Monte Carlo, the Weber-equipped red GT fought its way around in a loop to meet up with other competitors at St Claude and Chambéry before starting the special stages which led back to the Principality. On the very first of those stages, the Col du Granier, Elford's Monte came to an abrupt end when he rounded one corner to find specta-

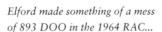

*Elford made something of a mess of 893 DOO in the 1964 RAC...*

*... so the mechanics had to work hard to get it to the finish.*

tors across the snow-covered road and had to decide whether to plough through them or go off the road. Choosing the humane option, the car plunged through a snowdrift and shortly stopped with a loud bang against an upside-down rally car which had just gone off ahead of him. The Cortina could not be retrieved.

Fortunately the damage to the car was relatively slight and it was soon made ready to compete in the Circuit of Ireland, which was due to take place on mainly tarmac roads at Easter.

Three works Cortina GTs started the event, plus Roger Clark in his own car (2 ANR), and a real battle developed between all of them as well as Paddy Hopkirk's Mini-Cooper 1275S. After one day it was the Mini which led, after two days it was Elford, after days three and four the Mini was back on top, then on the very last special stage (a forestry section) the Cortina GT picked up not one but two punctures and dropped finally into second place overall. That was the last works appearance for this hard-working car.

### Competition Record

| | | |
|---|---|---|
| 1964 French Alpine | Vic Elford | 1st overall, Touring Category |
| 1964 Spa-Sofa-Liège | Vic Elford | DNF |
| 1964 RAC | Vic Elford | 3rd |
| 1965 Monte Carlo | Vic Elford | DNF |
| 1965 Circuit of Ireland | Vic Elford | 2nd |

| REGISTRATION NUMBER | ENGINE SIZE | MODEL TYPE |
|---|---|---|
| **AVW 199B** | **1498CC 4-CYL OHV** | **CORTINA GT MK1** |

This car was owned by Boreham in 1964 but was not used competitively in International motorsport. Instead it was loaned out to team-driver David Seigle-Morris for him to use in selected British club rallies. It achieved no particular success in that period, and was eventually replaced by ETW 543B, one of two prototype 'Lotus-Corsairs'.

Its one claim to fame, however, came in December 1964, when it posed as an exhibit at the famous Hayes-inspired 'Cortina-in-Cortina' extravaganza in the Italian ski resort in the Dolomites, where many successful works, or supported, drivers got together to celebrate a very successful motorsport season. AVW 199B was used to front-up a group picture of the great and the good, and apparently was one of the cars to suffer from a typical Hayes stunt.

As team captain Henry Taylor once noted, "Walter couldn't decide what to do with the journalists on one particular day. So, as I had been in England's bobsleigh team, he asked me to see if a Cortina would go down the bobsleigh run! There wasn't much snow, so I said I would have a look. Jim Clark was sitting next to me when we drove down the run. It was very narrow but maybe just wide enough. We actually pranged three cars trying this out. The first one was my fault. Jim then had a go, got too high on a corner, turned it over, and slid down the track on the roof. With the third car I drove it all the way down, but damaged both front corners just keeping it between the walls." One of those cars (which one is not recorded) was AVW 199B.

*When Walter Hayes organised a Cortina Car of the Year event at Cortina in the Italian Dolomites in December 1964, the team took along AVW 199B (a Boreham-based practice/test car) to see if it could be driven down the bobsleigh run. It could, but not without damaging the front corners.*

| REGISTRATION NUMBER | ENGINE SIZE | MODEL TYPE |
|---|---|---|
| 2 ANR | 1498CC 4-CYL OHV | CORTINA GT MK1 |

I had to wrestle with all my carefully-crafted definitions before deciding that 2 ANR, the Cortina GT made famous by Roger Clark in 1964 and 1965, might indeed have started as a private entry prepared with Boreham-supplied pieces, but ended up in 1965 as a factory car in all but name. Prepared by Roger himself at the family-owned Ford dealership at Narborough, a suburb of Leicester, it started life as a clubman's machine, tackling British International and *Motoring News* Championship events, but after Roger and his long-time co-driver Jim Porter had won the rough-and-dusty Scottish rally of 1964, Boreham rapidly started to take an interest in it. By the time it ended its career in mid-1965, it had a Boreham-supplied bodyshell and some running gear, and finished off with back-to-back outright victories in the 1965 Scottish and Gulf London events. Thereafter Roger was swept into the Ford factory team, soon collecting a Boreham-built works Lotus-Cortina (KPU 383C) in which he immediately won the Welsh rally.

In his autobiography *Sideways to Victory*, Roger recalls originally preparing the white two-door car himself in 1964,

*Strictly speaking 2 ANR was not a works car, having started life being prepared by Roger Clark in his own Ford dealership near Leicester. Due to his success and after it had been re-shelled in bright red, it became a factory car in all but name. This was Roger on his way to outright victory in the Scottish rally of 1964...*

*...a feat which he repeated in 1965, this time with the re-shelled 2 ANR.*

*Roger Clark won the Scottish rally twice, in 1964 and 1965, in his own Cortina GT before being swept into the works team on a permanent basis. Thereafter he became Boreham's most famous driver until the end of the 1970s.*

became justifiably famous.

The next few months were not as upbeat, as this extract from the autobiography confirms: "I shunted the white car on the Gulf London – very aggravating because of a phenomenal £1000 waiting for somebody as first prize (big money for 1964!) – and it then fell to pieces on me in the first of the 1965 Welsh Internationals. I say 'fell to pieces' because the body started to fall apart. A rear spring actually punched its way into the bodywork with a piece of the spring hanger still attached, which made such a mess of the rear end that a new bodyshell was needed".

That was the Bad News. The Good News, though, was that: "Alan Platt, who was competitions manager at Boreham by then, offered me a new works body-shell. 'Works' meant a scarlet body with all the latest strengthening bits and an up-to-date fascia with lots of instruments, Aeroflow ventilation, the lot. It was still 2 ANR, and most of the old parts went into it, but it all looked brand new and sparkling."

The 'new' 2 ANR, effectively the second iteration of this identity, then had a short and stellar career in British events, all compressed into the April 1965 to July 1965 period. First of all, Roger took it out to compete in the Circuit of Ireland, where the presence of a team of Boreham-built cars made it tactically desirable to run with a few non-standard pieces, and compete as a 'Grand Touring' car for the Easter weekend. This worked very well for Roger, as he eventually finished third overall, beaten only by Paddy Hopkirk's works Mini-Cooper 1275S, and Vic Elford's works Cortina GT (893 DOO).

Then came the true highlights of this car's career. In June Roger won the 1965 Scottish Rally outright, and followed it up, just three weeks later, by taking outright victory in the four-day/no-overnight-rest-halts Gulf London. As already noted in earlier entries, Boreham had supported (but not officially entered) a full team of four Cortina GTs (which were about to be replaced by newly-homologated leaf-spring Lotus-Cortinas), but as they all fell out of close contention (three accidents and one broken differential) it was left to Roger to battle on against Timo Makinen's formidable works Austin-Healey 3000. When the Healey also broke down, it was left to Roger to cruise to victory, though on at least one occasion he put the GT off the track *after* the end of a special stage.

with a standard bodyshell, a home-designed set of sump shields and petrol tank guards, an Alexander-modified engine, a close-ratio Lotus-Cortina gearbox borrowed from a second-hand car which just happened to be in stock at the time, and a 4.44:1 axle from another showroom model. Suspension was standard at first, though wide-rim Lotus-Cortina road wheels were used.

This was the car in which Roger started his Ford rallying career, first taking third place in a one-night navigational event in Wales, then having to retire from the Circuit of Ireland with a failed dynamo (and no available spare). Only weeks later, however, the same car and crew tackled the five-day Scottish rally, which had no fewer than 44 special stages in the Highlands of Scotland on a 1600 mile route. The result was that 2 ANR won convincingly, beating Adrian Boyd's works Sunbeam Rapier by several minutes, and demonstrating the newly-acquired 'sideways' style for which Clark

It was then a rush and a struggle to re-prepare the car for the Gulf London (and with 400 miles of special stages to be completed in a four-day event, the preparation job had to be done really carefully), but Roger and 2 ANR took the lead at an early stage and held it throughout. Only 15 cars reached the end of the 1,400-mile event, but Roger won by a huge margin from Jerry Larsson's works Saab Sport and Brian Melia's works Cortina GT (890 DOO). That was the end of an illustrious car, for the registration number was transferred to one of Clark's road cars and the battered old rally car was sold off.

## Competition Record

| | | |
|---|---|---|
| 1964 Express & Star rally | Roger Clark | 3rd |
| 1964 Circuit of Ireland | Roger Clark | DNF |
| 1964 Scottish | Roger Clark | 1st |
| 1964 Rally of the Vales | Roger Clark | 20th |
| 1964 Gulf London | Roger Clark | DNF |
| 1965 Welsh | Roger Clark | DNF |
| (January, the first of two such events held in that year) | | |
| 1965 Circuit if Ireland | Roger Clark | 3rd |
| 1965 Scottish | Roger Clark | 1st |
| 1965 Gulf London | Roger Clark | 1st |

| REGISTRATION NUMBER | ENGINE SIZE | MODEL TYPE |
| --- | --- | --- |
| **SOO 293D** | **1498CC 4-CYL OHV** | **CORTINA GT MkII** |

During the winter of 1966/67, Boreham began development of the Mk II-bodied GT and Lotus versions of the Cortina, with rallying, circuit racing and rallycross in mind. The first and as far as one can see only road-registered example of a test car was SOO 293D, a two-door Mk II GT registered in the late autumn of 1966 but which appeared only briefly in the spring of 1967. Not only was it used as a test car at Boreham but it was driven by Roger Clark in TV rallycross events in the first weeks of 1967.

### Competition Record

| | |
| --- | --- |
| 1967 testing and TV rallycross events | Roger Clark |

*Ford was always keen to sell competition parts to underline the honest homologation process which continued throughout the life of the GT, and this 1967 display of Mk II parts makes a strong point. Among the kit available were lightweight panels, special seating, long-range fuel tanks, engine tune-up pieces, high-ratio steering gear, competition brake materials, suspension components, and much much more.*

# CHAPTER 4:
# CORSAIR IN MOTORSPORT

Without PR chief Walter Hayes's instinctive eye for a stunt, the Corsair would surely not have gathered much publicity in its seven-year life. In those days at Ford, if wasn't the Lotus-Cortina which made headlines it was F1, and if it wasn't F1 it was the Escort Twin-Cam, and if it wasn't any of those it was the big Marathon rallies which got much more exposure for Ford at the time.

As we know, 331,095 Corsairs of all types were eventually built, most of them at Halewood, where Land Rover Evoques are now born in big numbers, but none of them were ever to be serious race or rally cars. Were they too big? Too heavy? Underpowered? Maybe so, but that didn't deter Hayes (especially as he had promotional money to spend), who knew how to get his old friends on the national newspapers to take an interest.

Hayes, who was well advised by Competitions Manager Alan Platt, wanted a big promotional push for the new Corsair, but speedily realised that this could never become a front-line race or rally car. Instead, he decided that a series of stunts, record attempts, or very occasional forays into mainstream motorsport, might do the job instead. Accordingly, it was even before the Corsair was introduced to the public that this process began.

The original Corsairs – 1500s or 1500GTs – were to be launched in October 1963, but by this time Hayes had already unleashed his two record-breaking heroes, Eric Jackson and Ken Chambers, on a Round-the-World driving stunt. They were already seasoned contenders, for they had recently set a new fastest time from London to Cape Town, by way of Egypt and Kenya, but when Hayes suggested that a 'Round the World in Forty Days' stunt had a nice ring to it, everything went quiet for a few minutes.

It couldn't (still can't, by the way) be done without thumbing a lift on the occasional long sea voyage or aircraft sector. By going west-about, how could one get from North America to Asia, for instance, or Australia to almost anywhere else, especially because this was a period when it was politically impossible for a Westerner to drive across either China or the USSR?

The job was done, but as it involved the use of aircraft, ships, unscheduled contact with bandits, breakdowns, and the unplanned assistance of Ford dealerships around the world, was it any wonder that car and crew were quite exhausted by the end, and that it took more than 43 days for them to make it back to London? With no less than 29,991 miles on the trip-meter the battered Corsair car was fit only for the scrap heap where, apparently, it went.

Less than a year later, in the spring of 1964, Hayes fell for another persuasive spiel, this time from the cheerfully anarchic members of the Cambridge University Automobile Club, who asked him, quite baldly: "Why don't we try to average more than 100mph for seven days at Monza?"

And so it came about, with a team of no fewer than six drivers (including Michael Bowler of *Motor* magazine). A crude form of experimental 'aerodynamic' nose was applied, front and rear bumpers were removed, and this eccentric enterprise was ready to go. Total provided the fuel to fill the 28-gallon petrol tank, Castrol provided the lubricants, and the rest was down to the crew, who were well schooled in this sort of activity.

History now tells us that after 114 hours or just under 5 days, with the average speed just below 99mph (and the team was aiming for the three-figure mark), there was an almighty bang: the engine had broken its crankshaft, which was of course irreparable. And what happened to the car? Does anyone know?

Later in the year there was a more serious one-off attempt to prove that the Corsair was a rugged performance machine. At Boreham, Ford Motorsport was still in its first year of operation. It had already won the Safari rally with a Cortina GT (as already noted in Chapter 6), but could still make little sense of the A-frame suspended Lotus-Cortina as a rally car. Then, suddenly, for the Spa-Sofia-Liège of August 1964, where homologation rules did not apply, Ford was inspired to build two brand-new cars which we might call Lotus-Corsairs – effectively two-door Corsair GTs, but powered by rally-prepared Lotus-Cortina twin-cam engines. In the end, though, this was a wasted effort, as both cars dropped out at an early stage.

It was an intriguing prospect, as all the Cortina GT structural and chassis improvements were made to the slightly longer-than-Cortina platform (the Lotus-Corsairs retained leaf-spring rear suspension), allied to a Lotus-Cortina engine. A good idea, for sure, the two cars being allocated to David Seigle-Morris (ETW 542B) and Esko Keinanen (ETW 543B). There was no happy ending though, as Keinanen disappeared at an early stage, and Seigle-Morris's car ended up on its roof on the way into Bulgaria.

The last major Corsair stunt, of course, is that well-known Jackson + Chambers escapade, where Walter Hayes accepted a wager from the Union Castle shipping line, and set a Corsair 2000E to 'race' the *Windsor Castle* liner from Cape Town to Southampton in May 1967. The car left the quayside as the liner cast off. In the next 12 days the liner would make only its usual scheduled call at Las Palmas in the Canary Islands, whereas the Corsair was faced with crossing 14 borders, traversing the Sahara desert, and having a two-man crew who would get very little sleep.

Exhaustion set in, the car suffered a spate of punctures and it was refused entry into Cameroon in Central Africa but the Corsair kept going. Apart from getting stuck more than once in deep sand, and suffering some front end damage on occasion, it arrived in the UK the evening before the *Windsor Castle* was due.

In a typically staged close finish, Jackson and Chambers arranged to reach the quayside as the liner edged in to its dock. All parties agreed that it had been a 'Good Draw', and the headline writers had their story.

The 'sporting Corsair' story really ends there, though we also ought to salute the crew of the privately entered 2000E which contested the London-Sydney Marathon of November/December 1968. Messrs Wilson, Mackelden, Dwyer and Maxwell started at No. 23 from Crystal Palace, and must have had a cramped time. However, on the first truly tight section in Turkey, from Sivas to Erzincan, they lost no less than 101 minutes, passed through Teheran without further penalty, but only hours later the unfortunate Corsair went off the road, rolled, was badly damaged, and had to retire.

And that was really the end of the Corsair's sporting endeavours. From 1968 the Escort, in particular the Twin-Cam, had come on to the scene, even the Lotus-Cortinas then retreated into the background, and the Corsair was left to complete its seven-year road-car career in 1970.

## Corsair Round the World, 1963

For Eric Jackson, born in a gypsy caravan near Doncaster, fame as a round-the-world record breaker was vastly different from his origins. His father soon moved to Barnsley, started working for the local Ford dealer, and established a Jackson-Barnsley connection which has never been broken. Eric eventually started selling cars too: "Getting a Ford retail dealership, selling cars from two Nissen huts in the town." Years later he became the Ford main dealer in Barnsley, at Service Garage, eventually moving up to buy other outlets in Bradford and York, and setting up the Polar Group.

Like many motor traders of the day, rallying was an obvious way of letting off steam at weekends, and Eric eventually moved up into the works team, after which Ford's Public Affairs supremo Walter Hayes agreed that he and fellow motor trader Ken Chambers should attack the 'unofficial' London-Cape Town record, which they duly did, successfully, in a Cortina.

Only months later, with Eric back in his Barnsley dealership in mid-1963, Walter Hayes called again, this time to ask for more suggestions. "'I had heard that the Round-the-World record was over 80 days'", Hayes once told me, so I said "Why not have a go at 'Round the World in 40 Days' in a Corsair GT?". Readily convinced – both, after all, were motor traders, and both knew how important successful stunts like this could be – Jackson and Chambers blocked out their diaries and started to plan the itinerary. Just as a previous R-t-W trip had found (Austin, with an A40 Sports in the 1950s),

*Very smart, kitted out at Lincoln Cars, and ready to tackle the Corsair's Round-the-World dash.*

*The fascia/instrument layout of the Round-the-World Corsair of 1963 was remarkably simple, with only three extra auxiliary instruments and a pocket at the side of the tunnel for maps and documents.*

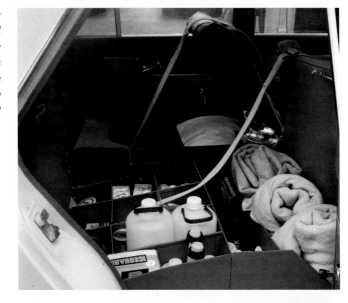

*The rear seat of the Corsair had been removed and replaced by stowage bins for spares. Full-harness seat belts were fitted, there were blankets and pillows and – very important, this – a teapot!*

*The Round-the-World Corsair of 1963 actually started the run before the new model was officially announced. As is clear from this, the boot was filled with a massive fuel tank, two spare wheels and sundry spares.*

several long air or shipboard sectors would be involved, and since it was still politically impossible to traverse the USSR or China, their route had to make a big jump from Western Australia (Fremantle, close to Perth) and transit to Sri Lanka (which was still known as Ceylon in those days). Was a 40-day trip possible? Maybe, just maybe.

This time the record car – a four-door pilot-build Corsair from Halewood, registered 590 UOO – was prepared by Bert Havard's team at Ford's R & D Centre in Essex, ahead of the new car's launch in September 1963. A roof rack was fitted, and because no-one, anywhere, had ever seen a Corsair before, there were no spares around the world, so up to 450lb of extra equipment was also carried – oil, gaskets, pushrods, bearings, distributors and points, for instance.

Inside the car was a passenger seat which could be let down to form a bed, four water bottles, a wander light, an ample supply of tinned food, a retractable can opener – and a teapot. An extra 16-gallon fuel tank helped produce a formidable range, very useful indeed for the Nullabor Plain in Australia, and for sections in the Middle East, but the duo hoped they would not need the sand channels and the winching gear which they also carried.

Goodyear and Castrol, both active supporters of the works rally team, provided tyres and precious fluids, while Mobil agreed to provide fuel. If they were lucky, the team thought, they might achieve more than 600 miles between refills, though it was only in Western Australia, or in the Afghanistan/Iran/Turkey wilderness, that they thought this might not be enough.

As before, there was no pre-event publicity (Hayes knew full well that if something went wrong private failure was preferable to public humiliation), so that even before the new model was officially launched the Chambers/Jackson duo left the UK on 2 September 1963 without fanfare. If all went well – and, as it happens, it did not go perfectly – they hoped to be back by the 11th or 12th of October. Round-the-World in Forty Days? Hmm.

"We started by putting the car on a Pan American 707 at Heathrow Airport, at dead of night, and flew it to New York. From there to San Francisco there was little to report, except that we got pulled up once for speeding. I was in the left-hand seat, and got a real bollocking from the speed cop – it took him time to realise that we were in a right-hand-drive car, and that Ken was actually driving!

"Then the problems started. Ford gave us a lovely welcome in San Francisco, and at nine-o-clock the following day we were due to go on a ship to Hawaii, and eventually to Sydney. But when we drove down to the docks, an hour early, we couldn't see a ship – it had already left and was out in the bay."

With the next ship not due to leave for days, there was pandemonium, only settled when calls were made to the local USAF base, space was found in a transport plane, and the

Corsair hitched a lift to Hawaii. "So we had two days off, in Hawaii, waiting for the ship to arrive. Days later, and after the *Oriana* got to Sydney, we started work again, driving all the way across Australia by the Nullabor Plain, and I'll never forget seeing a notice-board which said 'Caution, next water supply 880 miles'. We could hold whatever speed the car would do out there."

After that, and with the car still in excellent condition, things suddenly got difficult. Although they were nicely up on the record schedule, Eric accepted that there was still more than 12,000 miles to go, and that the motoring which lay ahead would be more demanding. Following a passenger ship journey from Fremantle (the port for Perth) to Ceylon, a sprint across Ceylon through jungle-flanked roads, with a police car escort ("Not that that helped, for at one point we hit an ox, though that did only minor damage to the car"), and a ferry trip across to the southern tip of India, they settled down to face the long grind back to Europe.

Here was where the Corsair just had to show its merits, for the dynamic duo intended to keep going, turn and turn about, every three hours, if possible. They had achieved this on the way to Cape Town in the Cortina, so why not do it again? "There were few problems at first," Eric told me, "except that we once stopped for a pee, got back into the car, switched on the lights, and found a tiger watching us with great interest from thirty yards away."

"Then, when Ken was driving in India, we hit a water buffalo, fair and square, which charged us, broke the windscreen,

*The Round-the-World Corsair in New York City soon after the start of its frantic dash to drive round the world in 40 days in the autumn of 1963. Ken Chambers was at the wheel at this moment.*

*Here we go again. Having reached Sydney by a combination of air, sea, and surface travel, the Corsair started the dash to Perth (in Western Australia) by leaving Sydney docks.*

smashed some of the lamps, and dented the bonnet. For the last few days, then, we had a hole in the screen on the passenger's side". It had to be patched up with Sellotape but was eventually replaced.

Border delays and customs officials were described in quite unrepeatable language. It was these, rather than mechanical incidents, which began to make the Forty Days target increasingly difficult. Things, however, got worse, much worse, when there was a bandit drama in Pakistan. Ford's own information service was positively restrained when it stated that "The crew found the road blocked by a chain slung across it. The Corsair charged this with the chain skating over the roof and in the process removing the roof rack holding the sand channels, fuel cans and an ice box," but because men with guns were then seen to be running towards the crippled car Chambers, who was driving, decided not to stop but rushed off up the road.

Even then the drama was not over, for in Iran, where temperatures were extremely high, the engine thermostat jammed closed, the car boiled, and a head gasket blew...then another... and finally the last one. "We were stuck in Iran," Eric told me, "'I had to go find help in the next village (Ken was bigger than me, and stayed to guard the car). The importer in Teheran came out with more gaskets, but this held us up for at least a day."

Then there was the moment, also in Iran and on the way to the Turkish border, when the car was forced off the road by two large trucks approaching them side by side, which forced them to leave the road to avoid a head-on collision. This ruined the rear axle, hitch-hiking back to the nearest telephone in Tabriz was essential, and the Ford importer in Teheran had to be found. The result was that a complete Cortina axle (which was very similar to the Corsair component) was trucked out to the Corsair, which was beginning to look like a 'breakers' yard special', and the repair was made. This all added a day's delay, and the schedule was now unachievable.

After such a struggle, so far and so fast, this was not their finest hour, but the two kept going, on roads which they now knew so well from previous exploits, holidays and long distance rallies. After what they had been through, a final three-day dash up through Greece, Yugoslavia (which has now sundered into several different countries), Austria and Germany was a positive cake-walk.

Three-hours on/three-hours off continued, they once achieved 1200 miles in 24 hours, and in the end were delighted to find that Ford had arranged for the now worn-out Corsair (and its crew) to be flown by a regular car-ferry from Rotterdam airport to Southend airport. To the intrepid pair, who had slept peacefully across the English Channel, the last hour of the journey down the A127 to the Dagenham factory was something of an anti-climax – but they had done their job, just. Somehow, though, 43 days for this amazing trip didn't sound quite as dramatic as 40 would have done.

## Corsair - 100mph at Monza

By launching the Lotus-Cortina Ford made a rod for its own back. If that car was so outstanding, how on earth was Ford going to get a lot of publicity for slower but still sporting cars like the other Cortinas, and the new Corsair? Not easy – but Walter Hayes squeezed every ounce out of the cars by sending them off on record runs, endurance escapades and simply mad outings.

Now think of this one. The Corsair, newly launched in October 1963, might have looked smart enough, but it wasn't as quick as the Cortina GT and it was left trailing by the Lotus-Cortina. First of all, as already noted, Hayes had already sent the Jackson/Chambers duo round the world in one, but then he got a phone call from ex-Cambridge University AC stalwart Gerry Boxall, who had recently run a successful Anglia 105E stunt at Montlhéry. "Walter, I've had an idea. The standard Corsair GT has a 95mph top speed, right? It wouldn't take much to make it do 100-plus. Then, if we kept it going round a banked track like Montlhéry, we could set up another record run. How about it?"

Hayes, who knew little about engineering but everything about publicity, was soon convinced and gave the go-ahead. At the time, though, he really did not know how much of a gamble he was about to take. At 95mph a Corsair GT engine was already running at 5460rpm. At 100mph it would be turning at 5750rpm, which was perilously close to a major vibration 'period' in this engine which tuning guru Keith Duckworth of Cosworth had already discovered when preparing engines for motorsport. Larger wheels and tyres, or a different axle ratio, were considered, with 6.00-section tyres eventually chosen.

No matter, Hayes gave some money, Total and Castrol, both of whom were already supporting the works rally team, chipped in, and the project got started. Ford's press garage (not the works team at Boreham, which was up to its neck in building Cortina GTs to take part in the East African Safari), run at that time by the redoubtable Alf Belson, would develop and build the car, while Boxall would assemble drivers and book the location.

The objective was to run at more than 100mph for seven days – no rest halts, no overnight close-downs - and to take a series of International class records in the process. As he had already done with the Anglia, Boxall wanted to run at Montlhéry, but eventually settled on the banked track at Monza instead. Not only was Monza wider and flatter (though rough and crumbly, maybe) but it was not as busy.

Even so, this was a real gamble. Monza's banked oval (it's still there, but no longer in use) had been built in the 1950s, and could certainly guarantee hands-off, braking-free conditions for the Corsair, but within five years of its construction few races were being scheduled as the concrete surface was rough (and accidents, if they happened, were at horrendous speeds). Previous record runs by the CUAC brigade, in

*The only sign of this Corsair being a long-distance record attempt car, to be driven at Monza for seven days, was the twin fuel filler caps and the oversized tyres.*

*Apart from the specially shaped nose cone, the Corsair Monza record car was mechanically close to standard, but it could reach and exceed 100mph for hours on end.*

*By any standards that is a massive fuel tank, very necessary on the Monza Corsair record attempt car and allowing it to go flat out for three hours at time.*

Austin-Healeys and Triumph TRs, had all achieved their objectives on this site, but mechanical carnage had been high.

So, how to prepare the car? Ford chose a two-door Corsair GT, the fastest and lightest type in the range, and craftily re-arranged the paint scheme so that the registration number, BOO 782B, was partly obscured and only the '007' section was still on show.

Belson sent the 1498cc pre-crossflow engine off to tuner Don Moore to be fettled. A gas-flowed head, a different camshaft profile, and re-jetted compound Weber carburettor all helped, though the actual peak power was never quoted. Larger-section Lotus-Cortina tyres and wheels were fitted at the rear, and the top speed turned out to be 104mph. Interestingly enough, standard Corsair GTs used a remote gear-change, but the record car was finally given the simpler, direct-action lever of other Corsair/Cortina models.

Springs, dampers and steering were all left alone, but Alf Belson's men produced an absolutely enormous fuel tank

which virtually filled the boot, and a new-type nose panel was crafted which not only had a smaller air intake than standard but looked as if it might be more wind-cheating. Wind-tunnel tested? Certainly not. No time for that.

At the same time, front and rear bumpers were discarded, a full-length undertray was added, and after testing some air ducts were added to keep the standard rear axle cool. Testing showed that the car would achieve 5200rpm in top without the undertray, and 5400rpm with it fitted – worth it, therefore, if it didn't cook anything in the process.

After high-speed testing at Monza, experience showed that there was the occasional bump in the concrete to be avoided, and that with the throttle buried to the floor, lap speeds of 102-104mph (depending on the prevailing wind) could be achieved – no steering, no braking, and no gear-changing at all. For the drivers this would be extremely boring, and for the car a real test of endurance. Although the technology was available at that time, 'ship-to-shore' radio contact with the

*This was the driving compartment of the Corsair prepared for the Monza record attempt. No special seats and no roll cage either – just a few extra instruments well out of the normal sweep of the driver's eye.*

*'007', as it became known, and its intrepid crew, ready for the start at Monza.*

*At the end of yet another three-hour stint the Corsair rolls into the pits for a routine refuelling session and driver change.*

pits was not fitted to the car.

Once the attempt began, it was the tedium and the routine, not the speeds, which dominated the proceedings. Flat out within a couple of minutes of the start line, the driver would then keep the Corsair at 5400rpm, keep it on the 'neutral'/hands-off line around the bankings – about half-way up the slope as it transpired – and try not to fall asleep.

Thanks to Boxall's planning, each of the six active drivers would have three hours on duty, followed by 15 hours off. What did they do in those 15 hours? Not a lot really, except sleep, read a good book, and try not to die of boredom. Each lap took almost exactly 92 seconds, and after every three hours the car swept into the pits for refuelling, a driver change and an anxious look at the tyres (which needed to be changed every 18 hours or so). Fuel economy? Let's assume that at least 25 of the 28 gallons were used in 300 miles, which equated to about 12mpg. If the car was to achieve its target, it would complete 16,800 miles and drink 1400 gallons of Total's best. Oh yes, and ten sets of tyres too.

Once unleashed, the car soon settled down to its routine, lapping at more than 102mph, refuelling and changing drivers every three hours or so – and keeping going day and night in this dry and warm Italian spring week of 1964. Although the drivers were convinced that the Corsair could have found its own way around the banking, it needed to be steered on to and off the straights, so no-one tried any show-business heroics.

So what else happened? The starter motor broke at an early stage (battering from the rough track saw to that) so push-starts were needed eight times a day thereafter. After 84 hours a front wheel bearing collapsed and ruined the stub axle by the time the car limped back to the pits. Because FIA Endurance Record rules stated that all spares had to be carried on

*Belting up, and ready for a three-hour driving shift around Monza's banked track.*

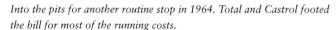

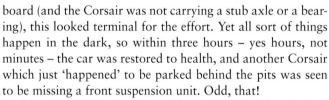

*Into the pits for another routine stop in 1964. Total and Castrol footed the bill for most of the running costs.*

*Anything to keep the driver interested and awake. The thumbs-up was to say that another speed mark had just been achieved.*

board (and the Corsair was not carrying a stub axle or a bearing), this looked terminal for the effort. Yet all sort of things happen in the dark, so within three hours – yes hours, not minutes – the car was restored to health, and another Corsair which just 'happened' to be parked behind the pits was seen to be missing a front suspension unit. Odd, that!

The running average, therefore, was cut back from 101.7mph to 98.8mph, but the crew was determined to claw back that deficit in the next three days. As it happened, the gallant car kept going for a further 30 hours before there was a big bang, all drive was lost, and after the Corsair coasted back to the pits, it was found to have a broken crankshaft. Keith Duckworth could have been excused for saying 'I told you so', but did not.

In spite of the disaster the intrepid crew realised that records were still available even though the car was now broken, so Alf Belson and his associate Lionel Sangster mended the broken starter motor in no great hurry, and just before the five days ticked up they motored the car across the line on starter motor power.

100mph for seven days? Well, no, as the car expired after four days and 18 hours, but what a remarkable attempt. Ford did not worship its memories, returned the car to standard, and it eventually disappeared.

| Records set at Monza in 1964 | |
| --- | --- |
| Distance/time | Speed set (mph) |
| 1 day | 101.6 |
| 2000 miles | 101.1 |
| 4000 kilometres | 101.6 |
| 3000 miles | 101.7 |
| 5000 kilometres | 101.3 |
| 4000 miles | 101.3 |
| 5000 miles | 101.3 |
| 2 days | 101.75 |
| 10,000 kilometres | 101.1 |
| 3 days | 101.7 |
| 15,000 kilometres | 98.8 |
| 10,000 miles | 99.1 |
| 4 days | 99.0 |
| 5 days | 95.4 |
| 6 days | 79.5 |

## Drivers

| | |
| --- | --- |
| Gerry Boxall | ex-Cambridge University AC |
| Michael Brookes | ex-Ford |
| Tony Brookes | ex-Ford |
| John Clarke | ex-Ford |
| Ben Porter | ex-Ford |
| Arthur Taylor | ex-Ford |
| Michael Bowler | *Motor* magazine |

*Timekeeping for the record run, with stopwatches, reams of paper, observers – and with the broken Corsair parked outside the window after its crankshaft had broken!*

### Lotus-Corsair on the Liège

Once, just once, Ford Motorsport indulged itself by entering special Corsairs for a major rally, but this an occasion with a difference. The Corsair was still a relatively new model – it was less than a year since production had begun – and PR chief Walter Hayes was keen to see it given as much publicity as possible. Accordingly, as soon as preparations for the Spa-Sofia-Liège rally of 1964 were published, Boreham began to prepare its usual Cortina GTs to take part, but also to send along two very special Corsairs.

As almost every rally enthusiast is aware, 'the Liège', as it was always affectionately known, was a major International rally which had become dauntingly famous in the 1960s for combining high-target average speeds with an immense mileage, a four-day event on public roads with a complete absence of night halts, and some of the roughest terrain in the Balkan states north and east of the Adriatic sea. And did I also say that the route was 3,500 miles long?

On the other hand, the Belgian organisers took a refreshingly relaxed view of homologation, allowing entrants to use any car with almost any modifications, just so long as the result was still roadworthy. Homologation, therefore, was not a factor, and any amount of special kit, fixtures and fittings was acceptable. All this, and the fact that the event usually took place at the end of August/early September, meant that major teams usually flocked to take part.

In 1964 therefore, Boreham decided to take advantage of these regulations (or rather the lack of them), by blending the best of the still-evolving Cortina and Lotus-Cortina range with the structure of the Corsair. This was made more straightforward because the main chassis structure of the Corsair was a longer-wheelbase version of the Cortina's, the Corsair having a 101in wheelbase, the Cortina 98in. Since the Corsair also shared its suspension and steering layout with the Cortina (both the GT types had the same rugged leaf spring/radius arm rear suspension), the only basic difference was the use of a longer propeller shaft on the Corsair.

Boreham set out to build two heavy-duty Corsairs and to power them with mildly tuned versions of the still-new Lotus-Cortina twin-cam engine (the power output of these engines was never revealed). These became the only official 'Lotus-Corsairs' ever to be seen in public (other engineering prototypes were built, but never shown), and they only appeared on this one International event, both of them without success. This was not an experiment which was ever repeated.

| REGISTRATION NUMBER | ENGINE SIZE | MODEL TYPE |
|---|---|---|
| **ETW 542B** | **1558CC 4-CYL DOHC** | **CORSAIR PROTOTYPE** |

Two new works Lotus-Corsairs were prepared at Boreham specifically to take part in the four-day Spa-Sofia-Liège Marathon rally of August 1964. Although these cars started life as two-door 1500GTs when built at Halewood, they were rapidly turned into works rally cars combining every still-developing feature of the team's Cortina GTs (those which had recently won the Safari rally were used as development templates), but were fitted with 1.6-litre Lotus-Cortina-type twin-overhead camshaft engines and gearboxes.

The engines were by no means highly tuned, not only to ensure that they would keep going for more than 3500 miles, but also because the quality of petrol available in Yugoslavia and Bulgaria was still awful, to say the least. To save weight perhaps, Lotus-Cortina front quarter bumpers replaced the normal full-width bumper of the Corsair road cars, while

*In the summer of 1964 Boreham built two Lotus twin-cam engined Corsairs to tackle the Spa-Sofia-Liège rally, one to be driven by David Seigle-Morris (seen here), the other by Esko Keinanen. Neither car finished, though the second car (ETW 543B) was used in British rallies several times by David Seigle-Morris.*

a much simplified front grille was fitted to allow as much cooling air as possible to enter the engine bay.

ETW 542B, a right-hand-drive car, was allocated to David Seigle-Morris and Tony Nash. They started well but suddenly disappeared just as they entered Bulgaria, approaching Sofia where there would be a brief pause for a meal (but no night halt!). The official reason for retirement was that the car had a burst tyre and subsequently overturned, with the result that it was badly damaged and could not continue in the event. Although it was eventually retrieved and later returned to the UK, it was never used again by the factory team.

*David Seigle-Morris at the start of the 1964 Spa-Sofia-Liège rally in the first of the Lotus-Corsairs, ETW 542B.*

### Competition Record

| | | |
|---|---|---|
| 1964 Spa-Sofia-Liège | David Seigle-Morris | DNF (accident) |

| REGISTRATION NUMBER | ENGINE SIZE | MODEL TYPE |
|---|---|---|
| **ETW543B** | **1558CC 4-CYL DOHC** | **CORSAIR PROTOTYPE** |

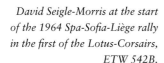

The second of the works Lotus-Corsairs was an almost identically-specified clone of ETW 542B and was allocated to the Finnish pair of Esko Keinanen and Anssi Jarvi, who had been recommended to the Boreham management by the even more famous Ford-driving Finn, Bo Ljungfeldt. This was one of the rare occasions on which Keinanen was a member of the Boreham team.

The car was eliminated from the 1964 Liège at an early stage during the passage through Yugoslavia, with a mechanical problem (not specified in detail) and was not seen again as a works car in International motorsport.

In 1965, however, it was refurbished and loaned to team driver David Seigle-Morris for him to tackle whichever British club and national events took his fancy. There were no particular successes in this programme.

*This Boreham preparation shot shows how neatly the Lotus-Cortina twin-cam engine fitted into the Corsair engine bay for the Spa-Sofia-Liège entry.*

### Competition Record

| | | |
|---|---|---|
| 1964 Spa-Sofia-Liège | Esko Keinanen | DNF |
| 1965 British rallies | David Seigle-Morris | No major successes/incidents. |

### Corsair 2000E versus ocean liner, May 1967

These days it takes only 12 non-stop hours to fly from Cape Town to London – any self-respecting Boeing 747 would see to that – and there isn't an alternative. In the 1960s it could take 12 *days* by sea if, you took one of the elegant Union Castle liners. Nearly 50 years ago a Corsair raced a liner and the match was officially drawn. You can credit Walter Hayes for this wheeze. He thought that a fast Ford could drive overland,

*The hardworking V4 engines fitted to Corsairs and 2000Es after 1965 rarely get more than a passing mention, so here is a smart studio shot of this compact 60-degree vee unit. It wasn't meant to be elegant or powerful – just to do a job.*

*In a staged 'race start', the Corsair 2000E rushed off from the quayside in Cape Town to race the* Windsor Castle *liner back to Southampton. Ken Chambers is at the wheel at this moment, with Eric Jackson in the passenger seat.*

through Equatorial Africa, and across the Sahara desert, and beat the Union Castle's best. Worth a try, anyway?

Hayes's call to Ford long-distance expert Eric Jackson was short and sweet: "Eric, it's time for another marathon drive. Call Ken Chambers, reserve two weeks in May – you're going to race the *Windsor Castle* back from Cape Town." Jackson, a long-time member of the Ford rally team, didn't even blink. He and fellow Yorkshireman Ken Chambers had tackled stunts like this before. So what if it was through Africa, the Congo and the Sahara? He'd been there in 1963 in a Cortina.

For Hayes, it all started with a bet. Union Castle representatives had attended a Ford dealer convention in Nairobi at Easter. The shipping line thought they could always provide faster, more reliable and more comfortable travel from South Africa to the Old Country. Hayes, and Ford, disagreed. Hayes, in fact, wanted to publicise the newly-launched Corsair 2000E, complete with its 97bhp 2000cc V4 engine, even though the dice were loaded against the car – the ship would steam 6939 miles, against an estimated 9800 miles for the car. The ship would be on a normal scheduled voyage from Cape Town to Southampton, would carry freight and hundreds of passengers, but the Corsair would have to find its own way.

Were there any rules? Only that the Corsair should be driven almost the whole way, except for taking an aircraft across the Mediterranean from Algiers to Marseilles, and a short ferry trip across the English Channel. The ship's scheduled stop would be at Las Palmas in the Canary Islands, and it would averaging 24mph for the entire trip. Jackson and Chambers needed to cross 14 borders and average 35mph – and they were rarely planning to stop off in hotels for a rest.

According to the pre-race map which Ford sent out to the media in advance, the Corsair's schedule included a programmed halt in Nairobi (in Kenya) and another in Kano (Nigeria), but little else. While the *Windsor Castle*'s passengers were enjoying the sun, the Crossing-the-Line ceremony as the Equator was passed, and the seven-course meals, Chambers and Jackson would be flogging on, and on, and on.

Service and support would be difficult. Although Ford had dealers in most of the countries involved (a good proportion of the African map was of ex-British colonial nations) they could only survey part of the recommended routes in advance and talk to a few of the border officials. There were good tarmac roads in the south – most of the way from Cape Town to the Congo (later renamed Zaire) – but the rest of the battle to Algeria would be on dirt and gravel and across thousands of miles of sand.

Those were the days when there was more strife in Africa than there is today. This explains why the Corsair's original chosen route went due north to Kenya, avoiding Namibia, Angola and Uganda, then struck west through the Congo and the Central African Republic to Kano, before attacking due north on the 'main highway' across the desert, through Tamanrasset towards Algiers. After that, in the Jackson/Chambers language, Marseilles to the UK would be kids' stuff.

Surprisingly, the works motorsport department at Boreham was never involved in this escapade. 'Edgy' Fabris, one-time competitions manager, but still running the Ford press fleet, got the job of preparing the Corsair 2000E (UVW 999E) at Lincoln Cars in Brentford, which kept its standard engine but gained an oil cooler and a special fan. The chassis was given Safari-type heavy-duty suspension and sump shielding. Firestone crossply tyres were chosen (they were thought to be more puncture resistant than radials), there were extra fuel tanks, and spare fuel cans were strapped on to a roof rack.

Jackson and Chambers were old hands at this sort of challenge: they insisted on having a matt black anti-glare bonnet panel, asbestos padding on the floor, and also took along all their (British manufactured) food in cans, their water in a special tank, and took every possible precaution against mosquito bites. Other home comforts included a dual-purpose kettle, a tinned food heater, retractable trays with cup holders, and a reclining passenger seat. The loaded-up roof rack, the 'roo' bar and all the rally-type equipment made this a seriously overloaded Corsair.

Working out the way was one thing, but getting permission to cross every country was always going to be difficult. According to the maps, it was going to take 9752 miles, and it relied on every country greeting the Corsair at its borders and waving it through.

Even at the planning stage there was one major snag. For no obvious reason Cameroon refused passage, even though Ford only wanted to use 50 miles across its northern tip so that the Corsair could get from Chad to Nigeria. A diversion would add thousands of miles, for there were no car-worthy routes from Chad to Nigeria. Eventually, Ford and the Union Castle line agreed to the Corsair taking a short air ferry trip over Lake Chad, from Fort Lamy to Maiduguri.

The *Windsor Castle* was ready to leave Cape Town harbour at 4.00pm on 10 May, and so was the Corsair, but when Captain Alec Hart shook hands with the Corsair drivers, he can have had no idea of what was ahead of them. He was, we now know, confident that he would win.

Jackson and Chambers had made this trip once before, via Cairo, in 1963, in 14 days, so they recognised the hazards – real hazards – along the way. It wasn't just other traffic, particularly buses and trucks, but wild animals, awful track surfaces, and even hostile locals could all be expected. Eric and Ken planned four-hour turns behind the wheel, though they both knew that as tiredness – real dog-weary, bone-aching, exhaustion – set in, they would be swopping seats more frequently. Because they expected big problems in central Africa, they scheduled a 55mph average for the first three days, and a 50mph average to the Congo. After that, they thought, 40mph might be possible, though they wisely reckoned on only 30mph in the middle of the Sahara.

To ease the pain, Ford co-opted Castrol as sponsors for the

trip. Fabris and Castrol's Jimmy Simpson chartered a private plane, arranging to fly ahead, hoping to ease the border passages, and somehow to find and arrange a flight to airlift the Corsair around the northern edges of Cameroon.

After the formal send-off from Cape Town everything went well, and for two days the crew piled on the miles. Even so, in Tanzania the car suffered no fewer than 17 punctures in quick succession. Naturally this all happened at night, miles

*Already looking travelworn, and with a spotlight missing, the Corsair 2000E poses briefly for the camera in Kenya.*

*This snapshot, taken in Kenya, shows that the more usual means of transport was a Land Rover.*

*At this point in the trans-African dash the Corsair 2000E was well ahead of its planned schedule. Here is Eric Jackson on the outskirts of Nairobi, approaching a rendezvous with the Hughes mechanics in the Ford garage.*

*A quick pitstop and a chance for Ford to snatch a picture or two as the Corsair reaches Nairobi.*

from anywhere. After the crew had run out of spare wheels, tyres and inner tubes, Jackson had to walk several miles to the nearest village (would you have liked to do that, at night, in a still untamed country?) to find a garage, knock up the owners, and beg new supplies. So much time was lost that the Corsair was eight hours late arriving in Nairobi, where Ford importer (and rally star) Peter Hughes worked miracles in giving the car a quick check-over and threw in lots more spare parts (and inner tubes!) before the Dynamic Duo set out again.

Almost immediately the master plan fell apart, for officials in The Congo (which was still emerging from a bloody civ-

il war) were less helpful than expected. No sooner had Fabris's light plane arrived at Paulis (now known as Isiro) than it was impounded. Seeing the plane's South African registration number, the authorities arrested the entire crew – pilots, Fabris, Simpson and all – clapping them into jail as suspected spies. That, at a stroke, was the end of Ford-in-the-air support for this epic trip; they were released days later and never caught up again. Murphy's Law then kicked in, for there were no other Ford officials within hundreds of miles to confirm their story. Jimmy Simpson, in fact, feared for his life: "Spies were shot, without trial, and without discussion, in those days," and all were relieved to get away, though too late to see the Corsair again until it reached the Mediterranean.

Jackson and Chambers never found out what happened to their support crew, but carried on alone, just as they had had to do several times before. As Jackson later confirmed, the Corsair was in good shape so the crew kept going. It was only the sometimes-chaotic African countries and their border officials which threatened to stop them.

Getting out of the Congo into the Central African Republic, for instance, should have been easy, but it wasn't. The chosen border crossing at Bangui was actually a river ferry over the River Oubangu, there being no alternative for hundreds of miles. The Corsair and its dust-caked crew arrived on the eastern bank early one evening, still in daylight, just before the service was meant to close down for the night.

Because the ferry was on the Central African Republic side, the two hired a native with a canoe, paddled across, and tried to bribe the ferry captain to make one more return trip. He refused (was the bribe offered not quite high enough?), and Central African Republic customs men arrested them as illegal immigrants as their passports were still on the Congo side! Overnight house arrest in Bangui, and a 12-hour delay, ensued.

The biggest delay came at Fort Lamy, for the Corsair was not to be allowed to enter Cameroon. With 'Edgy' Fabris's crew still in jail, no plane had been hired, and none could be found which would fly them into Nigeria. Was this the end of a brave effort? Jackson thought not, and somehow managed to get messages back to Walter Hayes in the UK. Both Hayes and the Union Castle line saw a good newspaper story dissolving in central African chaos, and agreed that if only the Corsair could be flown anywhere northwards, preferably into Algeria, the race was still on.

Finding a plane to airlift the Corsair 1000 miles to Tamanrasset, and the use of brute force and sheer people power to get it on to and off the aircraft, made a story which Jackson often related in later years. When the job was eventually done, the car was ready to roll northwards, but to preserve fair play the drivers rested, and did not restart until their original projected 'schedule' time.

In the meantime the *Windsor Castle* ploughed serenely and majestically on, crossing the Equator on 15 May, and made

*Cleaned up (the crew, not the car, that is) and ready to go again, Eric Jackson (dark shirt) and Ken Chambers (moustache) chat to Ford officials in Kenya before leaving for central Africa.*

*Not looking as smart at the end of the trip as it had been 43 days earlier, this was the Corsair which Eric Jackson and Ken Chambers took round the world in the autumn of 1963.*

*According to the post-race press release, the contest between the Corsair 2000E and the liner Windsor Castle ended in a draw. This was the quayside in Southampton, where a simultaneous arrival was staged and the ship's master posed with Eric Jackson (left) and Ken Chambers.*

its planned call in the Canary Islands on 19 May. The Corsair drove out of Tamanrasset on 17 May, using what passed for the main road north. By this time the crew were refreshed, so navigating with a compass and oil drum markers seemed straightforward enough. Until, that is, a hard piste gave way to soft sand, the Corsair bucked, plunged, then nosedived. Yet apart from front panel damage, all was well, except that the front-suspension crossmember was knocked out of true (Boreham knew all about that one), and the impact caused the heavily-laden roof rack to bend the roof panel itself.

From Algiers, though, it really was downhill all the way. The trans-Mediterranean ferry was waiting, the French roads felt blissfully smooth, and the Corsair actually arrived on British soil, Gatwick Airport, on the evening of 21 May. It was nine hours before the *Windsor Castle* was due to dock at Southampton. Walter Hayes's Fleet Street-trained brain then worked its magic, for he decided to turn this contest into a staged draw, with the car rushing into the docks on Southampton Water before the ship arrived. Accordingly, the crew had a short night's sleep before driving off to Southampton and a dockside rendezvous with Captain Hart.

But it wasn't quite over. For all the obvious publicity reasons, the Corsair hadn't been washed for 12 days and was filthy (and so, rather artistically, was the crew!). Newsworthy perhaps, but not to the liking of a British police patrolman who insisted that the number plates be washed to make them road legal!

On the quayside the ship and Captain Hart looked just as pin-neat as they had done 12 days earlier. But not the car or its crew. The 'roo bar was distorted, the front number plate

was crumpled, the roof was bent under a bedraggled heap of stores on the roof rack, and some of the sponsor's stickers were missing. And except for the front number plate (which looked as if it had suffered from machine-gun practice), it carried the dirt of many African nations on its flanks. UVW 999E. Was it ever seen again?

# CHAPTER 5:
# LOTUS-CORTINA MK I AND MK II IN RALLYING

*This display exhibit shows the Lotus-Ford twin-cam engine and its related gearbox, as used in the Lotus-Cortina from 1963 onwards. It was a 1.6-litre unit producing about 105bhp in road car form but could be persuaded to give more than 150hp for rallying or up to 175bhp for circuit racing. The cylinder block and many bottom-end components were the same as those of the Cortina 1500 engine.*

Once it was made reliable for use in rugged long-distance events, the Lotus-Cortina became Ford's works rallying mainstay for three busy years, but it was all very discouraging at first. In 1963 and 1964 none of the works drivers really wanted to use an A-frame car in a rally, and even after five years of motorsport activity, engine failures were still likely to occur. However, the good news was that works Lotus-Cortinas eventually won major events like the RAC rally, the Swedish rally, the Shell 4000 rally (of Canada), the Scottish rally, the Gulf London rally – and would so nearly win several other big events in 1966, 1967 as well as the London-Sydney Marathon of 1968.

It was Pat Moss who first rallied a Lotus-Cortina, on the

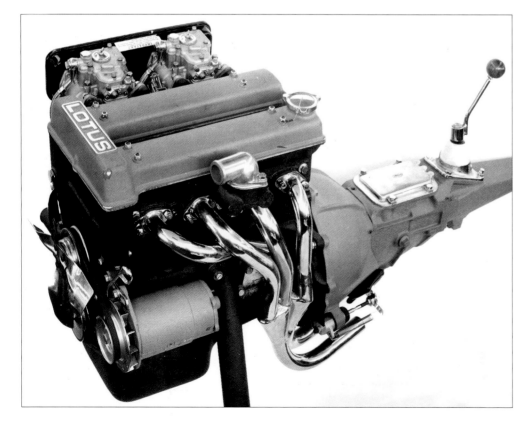

Swedish Midnight Sun event in mid-1963, where it shocked the Boreham mechanics with its fragility and she was apparently not impressed. Homologation into FIA Group 2 was delayed until 1 September 1963, but even before then the next works quasi-Lotus-Cortina to go rallying was driven by Henry Taylor in the rugged Spa-Sofia-Liège rally (again, an event where non-homologated cars could compete), though I must point out that that machine was really a hybrid, actually a regular (but re-engined with a Lotus-Cortina engine) works Cortina GT (888 DOO), complete with conventional leaf-spring rear suspension. It finished fourth, a great result.

Team captain Henry Taylor then took a deep breath and in a real act of faith used an original type works Lotus-Cortina on the 1963 RAC rally. Complete with A-bracket rear suspension, and with constant TLC from Boreham's mechanics, it somehow managed to finish sixth overall, but once again it was a very troublesome five-day event, a very traumatic rally for everyone.

But what about tarmac events, where works-sponsored cars from Alan Mann Racing had proved that they could survive six hard racing hours at a time? Boreham's rally team took a big 'Brave Pill', and found out a lot more in September 1964, when two newly-built cars were sent to tackle the 10-day 4000-mile Tour de France, which was half-race, half-rally. Although one car crashed, this proved to be a real triumph, for the Vic Elford/David Seigle-Morris car not only survived but won the prestigious Touring Car Handicap category outright.

Soon after this (as already noted in Chapter 2), Lotus-Cortina road cars were re-engineered to use conventional leaf-spring rear suspension like the existing Cortina GTs in place of the troublesome A-frame/coil spring layout. Production began in the late spring of 1965, Group 2 sporting homologation was achieved almost immediately (even though very few road cars had even been delivered – but who was counting?), and Boreham set out to build a fleet of new cars, originally using BRM-prepared twin-cam engines. At about the same time Alan Platt moved out of the manager's post in favour of Henry Taylor, who became Competitions Manager on 1 October 1965 and would remain in that position until mid-1969.

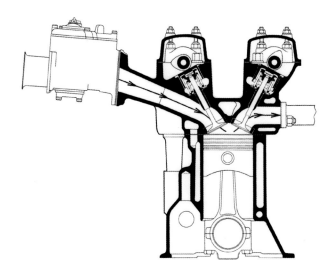

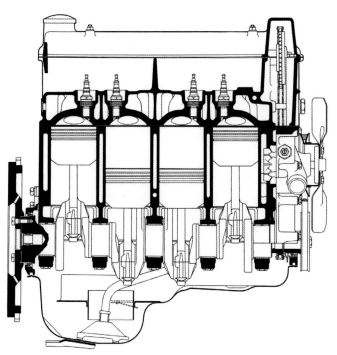

*The Lotus-Ford engine was simple but efficient, with the twin over-head camshafts driven by chain from the front of the engine.*

*As conceived by ex-Coventry Climax chief designer Harry Mundy, the Lotus-Ford twin-cam engine had classic part-spherical combustion chambers and opposed valves. The cylinder block was an unmodified Ford Cortina casting.*

*James Allington's excellent cut-away drawing shows that the Lotus-Cortina engine was definitely state-of-the-art for the period.*

Four new cars started the French Alpine (where the route and schedule were fast but gruelling, sometimes at high altitude, and usually in high-summer temperatures, but there wasn't quite a fairy-tale beginning. Vic Elford's car (KPU 395C) led this high-speed event for days, but with only hours remaining the engine's Lucas distributor broke and stranded the car. It was not until the end of the season that Roger Clark gave the Lotus-Cortina its first major success by winning the Welsh International in December 1965.

Somehow the Lotus-Cortina was then re-homologated into Group 1 for 1966. The regulations required 5000 cars to have been built in a year, and Ford and Lotus swore, with wide-eyed innocence, that this had been done, but the truth, uncovered years later, is that a mere 1112 examples had been built in 1965. In theory, and in comparison with the obvious rival products of the day, this meant that the latest cars, running in Group 1 or Group 2 depending on which categories favoured their entry, should have won event after event, especially as both Roger Clark and Bengt Soderstrom (of Sweden) had joined the team by that time. That year, though, there was often something, whether fate, unhelpful scrutineers or sheer damned hard luck, to frustrate them. During the season the record shows only one undisputed and emphatic victory, by Bengt Soderstrom in the RAC rally, and the cars' unreliability was a major reason for Vic Elford deciding to leave the team and defect to Porsche, who did not even have a rally team at the time.

For the Monte, which was confined to Group 1 cars, Boreham built new cars and immediately ran into a huge political scandal. On the event itself, the works Fords and BMC

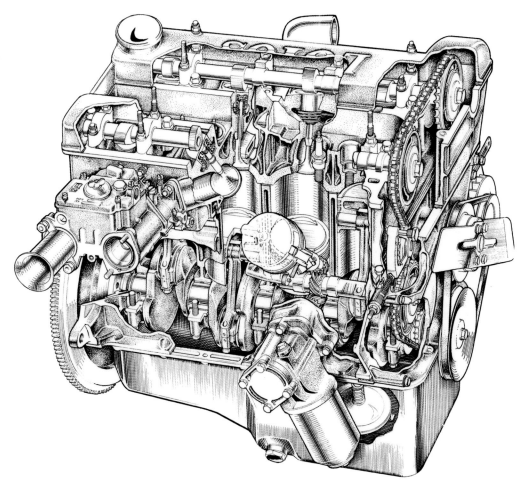

*This was the combustion chamber layout of the Lotus-Ford twin-cam engine used in the Lotus-Cortina, with two valves per cylinder and a single sparking plug. The four-valve BDA engine which would eventually displace it was still several years into the future.*

Mini-Cooper Ss were so much more effective than the front-wheel-drive Citroens that the chauvinistic Monegasque organisers suspected foul play. How could 'showroom' cars like that be so fast, they wondered (especially as they were not French)?

The real reason was simple: weeks of careful pre-event practice and the correct choice of tyres stage by stage. Roger Clark had set the third-fastest aggregate times, but was relegated to fourth (behind the three works Mini-Coopers) once the complex Monte Carlo handicap, which considered engine size, had been applied. Then came the scandal, about which millions of words have been written already. Roger lost fourth place when he was disqualified in the 'lighting fiasco', through no fault of his own or, for that matter, through any sharp practice by the works team.

Weeks later Vic Elford 'won' the Rally of the Flowers in Italy, but was immediately disqualified when the gearbox internals were found to differ from the homologation papers; the fact that there had been a mis-type in compiling homologation forms was not about to sway the Italian scrutineers. Elford then finished second in the Tulip, while Bengt Soderstrom was handed victory on the Acropolis when the winning Mini-Cooper S was disqualified for a service infringement.

More new cars were then built up during the summer, and a team of three tackled the French Alpine, using Minilite magnesium road wheels for the first time. These 'tarmac-spe-

cials' matched the pace of the factory-supported Alfa Romeo GTAs until Elford's car blew its engine. Roger Clark, less comfortable on tarmac, carried on to finish a strong second overall. The RAC rally then wound up the season, where four works Boreham cars started. Bengt Soderstrom won outright, which delighted his employers, but this event was also the unique occasion on which F1 Champion Jim Clark also tried his hand at loose-surface rallying, driving a Boreham machine.

Jim admitted that he knew little about rallying before the event, but after a day or two's brisk training at the military-owned Bagshot rough-road testing facility, where Roger Clark acted as his tutor and cheer-leader, he soon settled down and began to set a series of phenomenally fast special stage times. His car, however, went off the tracks at least twice before he finally found a high-speed blind brow on a Scottish stage, and, "Rally cars don't steer," Jim complained, "when the front wheels are off the ground." That was the end of his immensely popular appearance on that event, and in fact the last time he ever tackled a rally.

During the winter Boreham then built up a set of new-style GT Mk IIs (see Chapter 3) and an old-style Lotus-Cortina to contest the 1967 East African Safari, and also sent old-type Lotus-Cortinas out to Sweden for Bengt Soderstrom and Ove Andersson to drive. This was where Soderstrom triumphed in the snowy Swedish rally of February 1967 to provide a final victory for the Mk I car.

In the meantime, Boreham still saw the Safari as unfinished business, for their ambition was to repeat their 1964 victory. Held, as usual at Easter-time, no fewer than six Boreham-built cars appeared, two of them being old-shape Lotus-Cortinas. Apart from being slightly de-tuned from their usual European rally level, to 135bhp to take account of the dodgy local petrol supplies, the Lotus-Cortinas looked exactly like the European machines which we now knew so well. Ford mounted a colossal effort in this event, but it was the GTs which performed so well. Yet there were various mechanical dramas, and in the end it was Vic Preston's Lotus-Cortina which finished second overall.

## Mk II cars

Shortly after this Roger Clark, whose Lotus-Cortina had fallen to pieces around him during the Safari, made better headlines, first by winning the Canadian Shell 4000 rally (with a local co-driver) in a locally-prepared Mk I Lotus-Cortina, and then by dashing back to win the hot-and-dusty Scottish in a new Lotus-Cortina Mk II.

In the meantime, Bengt Soderstrom took a new car to third place in the Acropolis, where Paddy Hopkirk's Mini-Cooper S got its revenge for disqualification from the 1966 rally. After this Ove Andersson used the self-same car, a few weeks later, to win the incredibly long and tiring Gulf London 'forestry marathon' rally outright.

Two other brand-new cars were prepared for the London, for Clark and Soderstrom to drive, whose engines had Tecalemit-Jackson fuel injection. Neither car would finish the Gulf London. Late in the season, the team then came very close to winning the Three Cities (Munich, Vienna and Budapest) event, when Soderstrom's car led until the very last circuit test, where the clutch exploded, which demoted him to second place.

No fewer than six works cars were then prepared for the RAC rally. Two of them, for Clark and Soderstrom, were the ex-Gulf London cars, still fitted with fuel injection and designated as Group 6 'prototypes', while two others were allocated to F1 star Graham Hill and to a rising young British driver, Ford dealer Tony Chappell, from South Wales.

Unhappily, the event was cancelled at the last moment before the start. A nationwide outbreak of bovine foot-and-mouth disease had spread so rapidly that whole areas of Britain were progressively being closed off to the rally, in fact to all wheeled traffic. Even after pre-event scrutineering, on the evening before the scheduled start in London, Government officials arrived at the Headquarters hotel to 'invite' the RAC organisers to cancel the event. Less than 12 hours before the first cars were due to be flagged off, they did.

This meant that the regular Lotus-Cortina rally cars would eventually be pensioned off in 1968 as the Escort Twin-Cam was to be launched in January, but to make this story tidy I should now report on the two long-distance events which followed in that year – the 1968 East African Safari, and the London-Sydney Marathon of November-December 1968 – for which Lotus-Cortinas were considered most suitable.

A three-car team of Boreham cars was sent to Kenya to tackle the Safari (it might have been four, but Ove Andersson's entry was abandoned in favour of him concentrating on the new Escort Twin-Cam programme), but all of them faded before the end, though morale was partly maintained when local man Peter Huth's example (with works pieces, but self-prepared in East Africa) kept going, to finish second. This was a particularly demanding Safari, certainly the wettest so far held. Only seven of the 92 starters managed to complete the 3073-mile route. Vic Preston's Lotus-Cortina led at the half-way halt, only to be disqualified for a missing stamp in his Road Book; Bengt Soderstrom's car, lying second, then failed with a suspension breakage; and near the end Peter Huth lost the lead, his car becoming bogged down in yet more seas of mud following a cloudburst. To take second place, 22 minutes off the pace, was no consolation.

There was similar misfortune on the London-Sydney Marathon. As forecast by the pundits, Roger Clark's car duly led the entire event on the slog from London to Bombay (no night halts, please note), and after a lengthy transit from India to Australia by sea, it set out on the three-day dash across Australia from Perth to Sydney, with every hope of recording a comfortable victory. Other Ford works drivers had struck trouble – Peter Harper's fuel-injected car suffered a failed water pump, and Bengt Soderstrom's engine broke a cam follower (even after five years the Lotus-Ford twin-cam was still not bomb-proof), while Nick Brittan's car hit a horse in Turkey.

By the time the cars reached Bombay, only two works Lotus-Cortinas were still in the running. Roger Clark's car led, with only 11 minutes lost, while the Jackson/Chambers car was down in ninth, with a 31-minute penalty.

Unhappily, as so often with cars fitted with the twin-cam Lotus engine, in Australia it all went wrong again. Roger Clark's Lotus engine damaged its top end on the way to the Quorn control in southern Australia. Eric Jackson's sister car was then called in for the cylinder heads to be swapped over (which ruined Eric's chances of finishing as high as third, perhaps, and he was not best pleased by this decision). There was more misery to come for Clark: on the final night, in the hills west of Sydney, the Lotus-Cortina's axle failed. Could the Lotus-Cortina have been made even better if there had been more time, and if the Escort Twin-Cam had not arrived to take its place? For sure it could, although, as Roger Clark once told me, it wasn't perfect: "You know, you could do anything with a Lotus-Cortina in a forest, anything at all – but when you got it sideways it began to feel just a bit too big. But I loved 'em".

Below is the car-by-car, event-by-event, chronicle.

| Registration Number | Engine Size | Model Type |
|---|---|---|
| **779 BOO** | **1558cc 4-cyl 2OHC** | **Lotus Cortina Mk I** |

Once identified, wrongly as it transpired, as the Lotus-Cortina which Pat Moss drove in the 1963 Midnight Sun rally, 779 BOO (a very early A-frame car) was loaned during 1963 to David Seigle-Morris, along with Brian Melia, to compete in a series of British club rallies. There is no point in relating its event by event career, mainly in Wales, because it habitually broke down, with failures connected with the rear suspension, serving only to convince the factory team (first at Lincoln Cars, later at Boreham) that A-frame cars would never be successful on rough rallies. The fact that it crashed and burnt out, without injury to the occupants, during the Welsh rally at the end of the season was a merciful release.

| REGISTRATION NUMBER | ENGINE SIZE | MODEL TYPE |
|---|---|---|
| 786 BOO | 1558CC 4-CYL 2OHC | LOTUS CORTINA MK I |

*Henry Taylor and Brian Melia completed a gritty performance on the 1963 RAC rally by bringing this A-frame Lotus-Cortina (786 BOO) home on what had been a rough and demanding event.*

Although the Lotus-Cortina could not officially start rallying until it was homologated, Ford was anxious to 'blood' it as soon as possible. Accordingly, when they discovered that there was a class in the 1963 Swedish Midnight Sun rally (lots of high-speed gravel stages, in high summer) where non-homologated cars could run, they made haste to indulge their new star driver, Pat Moss, who rather fancied a trip to an event she had rarely tackled before.

786 BOO was a very early A-frame car which had been built soon after launch in January 1963 and prepared in haste for this occasion at Lincoln Cars in Brentford, and frankly it was virtually undeveloped. Indeed, as Pat's biographer Stuart Turner recounted, "The Lotus had just come out, and Ford had not had time to do much development, but Pat persuaded it to let her try one, just to see what fell off. The car gave her

no trouble, but it was in the class with the Porsche, which won outright, so they hadn't much chance of doing anything about it. They enjoyed the rally, though, regarding the Lotus-Cortina as a pleasant car, although not fast enough as standard in spite of its twin-cam engine".

That, one feels, is being kind to the car, for pictures obtained by mechanic Mick Jones seem to catch him under the car at service points, rather more than he might have hoped! Even so, apart from worrying about the behaviour of the A-frame rear suspension, the rest of the chassis seems to have behaved itself.

It was after this event that Pat developed pleurisy and had to take time off rallying, which explains partly why this car was not seen again for some time – and why poor Pat did not take part in the French Alpine rally of 1963 (see Chapter 3).

Five months later (Ford Motorsport having been very active in the meantime, getting its brand-new Boreham premises completed, equipping the buildings, and moving in during the autumn) the works team tried again, using 786 BOO and entering it for Henry Taylor/Brian Melia in the RAC rally. This was a more serious attempt, for in the meantime the body shell had received all the strengthening tweaks which were currently being developed for the works GTs, and this time it was hoped that the car would be truly competitive.

Within a five-day event linking Blackpool to Bournemouth, by way of 43 stages spread across Scotland, the Lake District and Wales, this was a considerable challenge for all concerned. Running against the cream of Europe's rally teams, including a full entry of four GTs from Boreham, Taylor soon settled down, though he was not able to beat his GT-powered team mates until much later in the event.

Much work by the dedicated mechanics was needed to keep the car motoring, not least of them connected with the troublesome A-bracket linkage, but Taylor at least showed the car's potential pace by being fastest of all on the Oulton Park and Porlock (both tarmac) sections. In the end, this gallant effort was rewarded by sixth place overall, with four of the drivers ahead of them being Scandinavian and thoroughly used to loose-surfaced special sections.

Unhappily, this convinced Taylor that the original-specification car was still not capable of beating his fast-developing GTs in such events, so no further use of this car took place in 1963/64, and although it carried out some development duties behind the scenes in 1964, it was not used again in motorsport.

**Competition Record**

| | | |
|---|---|---|
| 1963 Midnight Sun rally | Pat Moss | 3rd in Class. |
| 1963 RAC | Henry Taylor | 6th, plus winning Team Prize member. |

| REGISTRATION NUMBER | ENGINE SIZE | MODEL TYPE |
|---|---|---|
| **888 DOO** | **1558CC 4-CYL 2OHC** | **CORTINA GT/LOTUS MK I** |

The story of 888 DOO's rallying career overall has already been told in Chapter 3, but there was one diversion which should be included in this, the Lotus-Cortina Chapter. During the summer of 1963, with the real Lotus-Cortina not yet homologated, Ford was anxious to use the new-fangled twin-overhead camshaft engine whenever and wherever possible. Accordingly, for the Spa-Sofia-Liège marathon, where non-homologated cars were welcomed, it was decided to create a hybrid, so in one of their last preparation efforts at Lincoln Cars the mechanics added a Lotus-Cortina engine to Henry Taylor's regular Cortina GT, 888 DOO (which had already completed several events earlier in the season), and sent out their senior driver to see how it would fare in the rough, tumble, dust and awful roads of Yugoslavia.

By any standards the result was a triumph, for in a four-day marathon, with no night halt, the intrepid pairing of Henry Taylor and Brian Melia took a remarkable fourth place, beaten only by the formidable Bohringer (Mercedes-Benz 230SL), Carlsson (Saab) and Lucien Bianchi (Citroen DS19). This was an excellent performance, for in a 3430 mile event, in which only 20 cars finished, the car proved its rugged nature, and somehow the engine proved it could keep going too. As a long-term prospect this was extremely promising, and just to prove the ruggedness of the developing car, 888 DOO was speedily re-converted to Cortina GT-specification and given a brand-new red bodyshell for 1964.

**Competition Record**
1963 Spa-Sofia-Liège    Henry Taylor    4th

| REGISTRATION NUMBER | ENGINE SIZE | MODEL TYPE |
|---|---|---|
| **ETW 361B** | **1558CC 4-CYL 2OHC** | **LOTUS CORTINA MK I** |

During 1964 Ford had concluded that the A-Frame Lotus-Cortina was never going to be a successful rally car, though it already knew that, with a lot of attention at pit stops, the same type of car could not only be kept going through a series of long races, but could also win them outright. The decision to convert the A-frame production lines into building leaf-spring derivatives instead was yet to be taken, but there seemed to be hope for the future.

In the autumn of 1964, therefore, the works team (still relatively newly established at Boreham) decided to have another go at Europe's premier race/rally, the Tour de France. Here was a phenomenal event, heavily sponsored by Shell, which lasted for 10 days (yes, days) and covered 4000 miles. It was a fabulous combination of lengthy races, special stages, and sheer muscle-sapping road miles, an all-tarmac event which in 1964 was to include eight one-hour races, many speed hill-climbs in the French Alps and Pyrenees, and a good deal of high-speed rallying at night around twisty mountain roads in

*The two works A-frame Lotus-Cortinas circulating in close company in the 1964 Tour de France, with Vic Elford (ETW 362B) slightly ahead of Henry Taylor in ETW 361B.*

the Alpes Maritimes between Geneva and the Riviera.

No other event in the motor racing calendar combined flat-out races at Le Mans, Rheims, Rouen, Clermont Ferrand, Monza and the like with classic stages such as ascents of Mont Ventoux, the Col de Turini and the Col de Braus, and no other could witness the start of racing sports cars such as Ferrari's 250 GTO from control tables in the middle of otherwise peaceful French villages!

Although there were several overnight rest halts, and each circuit race occupied much of the day at a particular location, it was all extremely tiring and hard on the cars, not to mention the drivers, for there was one interesting quirk of the rules which demanded that the co-driver had to tackle at least two of the speed tests; this explains the unique pairing of Boreham personalities, though we must never forget that Brian Melia (though a navigator by profession) was already becoming an accomplished rally driver at British national level.

In 1964 the start was from Lille, in north-eastern France, and the finish in Nice, but the whole of the nation seemed to be covered in the next 10 days. Faced with competition from Alan Mann Racing Ford Mustangs (which eventually won the event) and several fast Alfa Romeo Giulia Ti Supers, the two Lotus-Cortinas started steadily, but soon settled into the top few positions in the Touring Category.

After three days, the two cars were lying second and third in the Handicap section (the 'Handicap' was calculated according to engine size), with Henry Taylor in ETW 361B just ahead of Elford. Unhappily, when the event reached the Pyrenees, to tackle what we all know as 'Tour de France cycle race' hillclimbs, ETW 361B crashed, rolled, and had to retire. It was not seen again in works motorsport.

## Competition Record

| | | |
|---|---|---|
| 1964 Tour de France | Henry Taylor/Brian Melia | DNF |

| REGISTRATION NUMBER | ENGINE SIZE | MODEL TYPE |
|---|---|---|
| **ETW 362B** | **1558cc 4-cyl 2OHC** | **LOTUS CORTINA MK I** |

*Vic Elford (left) and David Seigle-Morris congratulate each other on their Handicap success in ETW 362B in the Tour de France.*

This was the second of the two new A-frame Lotus-Cortina cars prepared at Boreham to compete in the Tour de France of 1964. This car, driven by Vic Elford and David Seigle-Morris, was always reliable, always competitive, survived the 10 days remarkably well, and astonished everyone (including, to be frank, the factory team themselves) by surviving to the end. A historical note is that Vic Elford had started his works career at BMC as David Seigle-Morris's co-driver, but had eventually become a driver in his own right. On this Tour de France it was Vic who tackled all the racing events, with David tackling the hillclimbs and special stages.

Well before the end, the running order in the Touring Category had settled, with Alan Mann Racing's Mustangs fighting for outright victory, Bernard Consten's Jaguar 3.8-litre still close behind them, and ETW 362B in fourth place, having outpaced all the Alfa Romeos and other Jaguars along the way. At the finish there was genuine joy when it became clear that the Elford/Seigle-Morris car had not only finished fourth overall in the Touring Category, but had won its engine capacity class *and* lifted the Handicap award too.

Once again, this car was then not seen again in works events. According to the Ford policy of the day it should have been cut up, rather than sold on, but after a considerable period of being parked at Boreham it was sold off to David Sutton and used in British events.

## Competition Record

| | | |
|---|---|---|
| 1964 Tour de France | Vic Elford/David Seigle-Morris | 4th Touring Car Category |
| | | 1st in Handicap Category |
| | | 1st in Class. |

| REGISTRATION NUMBER | ENGINE SIZE | MODEL TYPE |
|---|---|---|
| **KPU 380C** | **1558CC 4-CYL 2OHC** | **LOTUS CORTINA MK I** |

Soon after production of leaf-spring Lotus-Cortinas began (officially in the spring of 1965, though prototypes had run at Boreham well before then), Ford gained Group 2 homologation of this new derivative of the car. At the same time, a whole series of consecutive Essex (not Boreham) registration numbers were allocated to works race, works rally, practice/ test and press cars. The lowest of these numbers was KPU 380C, and apparently the highest of the batch, some of which were never used on competition cars, was KPU 398C.

KPU 380C, therefore, was one of an original group of Group 2 cars made ready to start the French Alpine rally of July 1965, and like its immediate GT predecessors it was painted in red. Except for the use of Lotus-type quarter front bumpers, and the usual 5.5in steel road wheels, it was only the Lotus badging (and, of course, the wider-mouth front grille and 'Aeroflow' ventilation outlets in the rear quarters) which allowed these new cars to be distinguished from their GT predecessors.

For its debut in what turned out to be a very demanding and high-speed event (held, of course, on public highways in the glorious summer close to the French Riviera coast), it was allocated to David Seigle Morris. Immaculate at the start in Marseilles, it was by no means so pristine at the end, for it suffered one serious accident which resulted in the mechanics having to patch up the front wing with a hastily re-shaped piece of metal advertising sign from a nearby service point. In addition, there had been a brake wheel cylinder failure on a tight section which caused David to lose his penalty-free run.

This was a great shame, for until then the car had been keeping abreast of the flying team cars of Vic Elford and Henry Taylor. David's own result was further ruined because when he came upon the stricken sister car of Vic Elford (KPU 395C, see below) close to the end of the event, he stopped, offered a tow to get it mobile again, and lugged the car over the hill to the next control. In the end both cars suffered huge road penalties.

The same car was then re-prepared for the 1965 RAC rally, a five day marathon which started and finished in London, with a single night halt in Perth, and which included no fewer than 57 special stages in the 2464 mile route. Starting at No. 40, and driven by David Seigle-Morris, this was one of four works leaf-spring cars in the event. Like the other team cars it ran in Group 2 condition, with a quoted 132bhp engine, and it was noticeable that the company had turned over to running Lucas instead of Cibié lighting, for contractual reasons.

This was one of those events where fortune never seemed

to be on Ford's side, for all four works Lotus-Cortinas retired. Although he went off the slippery, icy and sometimes snow-covered tracks on several occasions, Seigle-Morris kept going for as long as he could until he finally went off, irretrievably, in the Lake District some hours after the half-way halt.

This identity would not reappear until mid-1966, at which time it was given to a brand-new car, with a white/green spear bodyshell, and becomes one more in that confusing list which rally historians have had to deal with ever since. The 1966 car

*KPU 380C had been new for the 1965 French Alpine rally and continued its career in David Seigle-Morris's hands in the 1965 RAC rally.*

**BOREHAM IN 1965**

The two major changes at Boreham were that the works team changed over decisively to using leaf-spring Lotus-Cortinas, ending their intensive Cortina GT programme (except for the 1967 Safari) in June 1965. A completely new team of Lotus-Cortina cars was prepared, along with several others for use by contracted drivers like Vic Elford and Roger Clark in lesser events.

The major managerial change was that during the year Henry Taylor hung up his driving helmet to become Competitions Manager, while Alan Platt moved back to another post within the Ford mainstream management team.

*Reborn in mid-1966, this time with a white shell, KPU 380C led the French Alpine rally for hours before the engine failed. Vic Elford and David Stone were the unfortunate crew.*

might have been the same, theoretically, as the red machine of 1965, but there was really no physical connection.

The new/reborn car was one of three such machines, and was allocated to Vic Elford for use in the French Alpine rally. Like the other cars (NVW 239C and NVW 242C), it was state-of-the-Boreham-art Group 2, white with green spears along the flanks, black anti-dazzle bonnet panel, 'Ford' go-faster speed stripes down at sill level, a BRM-tuned engine, and recently homologated 6.5in magnesium alloy road wheels from Minilite.

For the first two days of this hot-and-high event (held in September, just at the end of a torrid Mediterranean summer) Elford was leading, matching Jean Rolland's Alfa Romeo GTA second for second on the hillclimbs and selective sections, but on the second leg, from Aix to Aix, tackling the forbidding Mont Ventoux hillclimb, his engine began to break

up, with a broken tappet bucket which eventually broke the precious engine.

Boreham, and Elford, made one final attempt to retrieve this ill-starred car's reputation by entering it in the 1966 RAC rally, where Vic started from London carrying No. 24. High hopes lasted only a matter of hours, for an oil pipe came adrift at an early stage and there were immediate fears for the life of the engine.

Days later, when the car was in the depths of the Kielder forest complex, the end came at last, as the author's own *Autocar* report made clear: "Days of misery for Vic Elford finally culminated in Wark forest when a damaged shield pushed up the sump and upset an oil pipe in the engine. Right from the start of the rally Elford's car had suffered from misfiring at high revs, which was only traced after some time to a faulty distributor condenser. Having at last got the car going well, setting four fastest times and nine second fastest, this cruel luck intervened."

Finally, and only two weeks later, this seemingly unlucky car, now refurbished, was used by Brian Melia to take fourth place on the Welsh rally. That was the end of its works career, and so it was for Vic Elford at Ford, who left to join Porsche, where he soon turned to circuit racing and the 200mph 917s, regularly surprising all the Old Hands with his bravery and expertise.

## Competition Record

| | | |
|---|---|---|
| 1965 French Alpine | David Seigle-Morris | 19th in Touring Category |
| 1965 RAC | David-Seigle-Morris | DNF |
| 1966 French Alpine | Vic Elford | DNF |
| 1966 RAC | Vic Elford | DNF |
| 1966 Welsh | Brian Melia | 4th |

*Photographed recently, KPU 380C had a strenuous life as a works rally car, complete with leaf-spring rear suspension. This was its second iteration, with the white/black-bonneted style adopted from mid-1966.*

*Those were the days when visual sponsorship of rally cars was still absent from rally cars. The only real clues to KPU 380C's purpose was the fitment of Minilite wheels, the rubber hold-down straps to the bonnet and boot panels, and the big reverse lamp.*

*'Speed stripes' were considered to be trendy for a time in the mid-to-late 1960s, though they did not figure on the standard road cars.*

*Magnesium Minilite wheels became available in the mid-1960s, and were speedily homologated by Ford for use on the Lotus-Cortinas. They were not, of course, a feature of the standard road cars.*

*When the leaf-spring Lotus-Cortina was homologated in 1965, Ford reserved a whole batch of KPU .... registration plates for the factory cars. KPU 380C was the lowest of the batch, which stretched all the way up to KPU 396C, that one actually being used on a works Team Lotus race car.*

*The rubber hold-down straps were a 'just in case' addition to the lift-up panels of 'works' rally cars of the period, just in case accident damage caused the panels to fly up. The black painted bonnets were a fashionable anti-glare feature.*

*Twin fuel tanks were homologated, that under the rear window being the extra one essential to stretch the range of works cars with thirsty race or rally-prepared 1.6-litre engines.*

*Modern features added to make this historic car useful on modern classic events are neatly blended in with the traditional layout of KPU 380C's cockpit features.*

*Although Boreham retained its own engine build shop, by 1966 BRM (of Bourne in Lincolnshire), where Mike Hall was a senior development engineer, had become a favoured supplier of engines for works rally and some of the contractors' race cars.*

| REGISTRATION NUMBER | ENGINE SIZE | MODEL TYPE |
|---|---|---|
| **KPU 381C** | **1558CC 4-CYL 2OHC** | **LOTUS CORTINA MK I** |

This identity dates from mid-1965, when Boreham's first batch of leaf-spring Lotus-Cortinas was prepared for rallying, but it does not seem to have appeared in public until 1966. In the same way as a more significant team car (KPU 383C) was allocated to Roger Clark for non-team use, this car, KPU 381C, was allocated to Vic Elford, who was about to start a turbulent third year with the works team which ended when he left the team to join Porsche.

Vic seems to have had very little chance to use this particular car in motorsport (he started no fewer than six events in Boreham-based team cars in the first five months of 1966), so the first and it seems the only time that KPU 381C started a major rally was the Gulf London of July 1966, an event where

*Allocated to Vic Elford for use in British events in 1966, KPU 381C was rarely seen in public. Here it was seen starting the Gulf London rally of that year, where Vic unfortunately crashed it in a Yorkshire stage.*

Boreham could not provide full support as the event itself was not within certain rules being policed by the industry's governing body, the SMM&T. In the meantime, it seems, it had often been used as a practicing/testing machine.

Along with Roger Clark and Brian Melia, Vic was one of the well-known Boreham drivers to start this event, for which he was a much fancied runner. It was all in vain, for after a long motorway drag north, from the start in London to the fast forestry stages of Yorkshire, Elford put the car off the road in Wykeham, took time retrieve it, and soon afterwards limped into the control after the Allerstone stage with a smashed exhaust system and a broken steering wheel. And that, it seems, was the last time this particular works car was seen on a major event.

| Competition Record | | |
| --- | --- | --- |
| 1966 Gulf London | Vic Elford | DNF |

| REGISTRATION NUMBER | ENGINE SIZE | MODEL TYPE |
| --- | --- | --- |
| KPU 382C | 1558CC 4-CYL 2OHC | LOTUS CORTINA MK I |

This identity was issued to Boreham in the spring of 1965 but was not applied to a car starting a rally until the 1966 Circuit of Ireland, when Roger Clark used it to begin its career. In the next five months it started three events, finished twice, and was not seen again after August.

One of three works cars to start the Circuit, it was well-fancied. Roger Clark had taken third place in his own Cortina GT in the previous year, and was known to enjoy the format and the atmosphere of the event. After the first night Clark was leading, with Vic Elford's sister car second, and he held this place when the cars reached the overnight halt in Killarney. Unhappily, on the very next morning his highly-tuned twin-cam engine suffered a stuck oil pressure release valve, the engine shortly failed, and that was that.

Six weeks later the re-built car appeared again, this time carrying Competition number 44, and starting the incredibly demanding Acropolis rally in Greece. In a rough, fast and dusty event where the battle for the final victory was always between Bengt Soderstrom's Lotus-Cortina (KPU 387C, see below) and Paddy Hopkirk's Mini-Cooper S, Roger Clark put in a fast and consistent performance. Finally, and without the drama accorded to his teammates (where protests, disqualifications, and changes of ranking were all involved), he and co-driver Brian Melia finished a serene second overall.

The car then made one final works appearance in the Polish rally held in August 1966. In a scantily-reported event, where Tony Fall's Mini-Cooper S won outright, Roger Clark took fourth place in the first of the cars which was not of the 'engine-over-driving-wheels' variety. Only 11 cars of the 49 starters actually completed the event.

| Competition Record | | |
| --- | --- | --- |
| 1966 Circuit of Ireland | Roger Clark | DNF |
| 1966 Acropolis rally | Roger Clark | 2nd |
| 1966 Polish rally | Roger Clark | 4th |

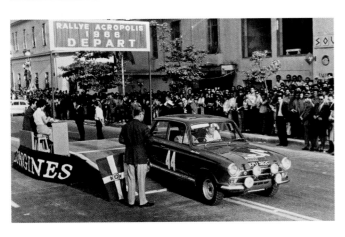

*Roger Clark took a fine second place overall in KPU 382C in the 1966 Acropolis rally, here seen taking the start of the event.*

*Roger celebrating the oversteering habits of KPU 382C on his way to second place in the 1966 Acropolis.*

| REGISTRATION NUMBER | ENGINE SIZE | MODEL TYPE |
|---|---|---|
| **KPU 383C** | **1558CC 4-CYL 2OHC** | **LOTUS CORTINA MK I** |

This particular leaf-spring car holds the distinction of being the first-ever works Lotus-Cortina to win an International rally outright. It was issued to Roger Clark towards the end of 1965, and Clark promptly drove it to win the Welsh International rally in December. To deflect any confusion, one should emphasise that this was the second Welsh International to be held in 1965, the first of the two being promoted in January of that year.

KPU 383C was one of a whole batch of new rally cars prepared at Boreham in the spring/summer of 1965. It was a right-hand-drive car and was apparently first used by Bo Ljungfeldt on the RAC rally with a 132bhp engine. He retired the car on the ninth special stage, in the Forest of Dean as the route entered Wales, by (as Eric Dymock's *Autosport* report told us) going "off the road a long way".

Suitably refurbished, it was then allocated to Clark so that he could carry out a programme of events in the UK in the coming months. Unhappily, and although it started so well, it became a one-hit wonder, as Roger drove it in several events during 1966 and retired every time.

By comparison with what was to follow, the debut Welsh was a straightforward weekend event, witnessed first-hand by the author, who was privileged to be Roger's co-driver. Not that it was an easy victory, as Roger had to fight tooth-and-nail against Simo Lampinen in a fast but heavy works Group 3 Triumph 2000, and there was one heart-stopping moment when the car clouted a rock and badly deranged its steering geometry.

First time out in 1966, the car was leading the Circuit of Ireland when (to use Roger's own words from *Sideways to Victory*) it "landed hard on its sump shield, which then punched the sump and the oil pump out of place," ensuring that the engine, though not the rest of the car, was ruined. Two months later, on the hot-and-dusty Scottish, the car was once again leading a strong field when the differential failed, and four weeks after that (once again to quote Roger), "Darn me if the same thing didn't happen again to Jim Porter and I in the same car on the Gulf London".

*KPU 383C, having already won the 1965 Welsh Rally in Roger Clark's hands, was then allocated to Roger for British events in 1966. Here, on the Scottish, it was battling for the lead before suffering a rear axle failure.*

### Competition Record

| | | |
|---|---|---|
| 1965 RAC | Bo Ljungfeldt | DNF |
| 1965 Welsh | Roger Clark | 1st |
| 1966 Circuit of Ireland | Roger Clark | DNF |
| 1966 Scottish | Roger Clark | DNF |
| 1966 Gulf London | Roger Clark | DNF |

| REGISTRATION NUMBER | ENGINE SIZE | MODEL TYPE |
|---|---|---|
| **KPU 385C** | **1558CC 4-CYL 2OHC** | **LOTUS CORTINA MK I** |

This early example of the works leaf-spring fleet of 1965 began its career on the French Alpine rally, driven by team captain Henry Taylor and prepared to the same specification as cars such as KPU 380C and KPU 395C. Having gone off the road at one point in the early hours of the event, bursting a tyre and bending the front suspension, Taylor and co-driver Brian Melia somehow managed to retain their unpenalised position on the road until the end of the first night halt at Grenoble, where they were in sixth place. In a gritty performance, facing the incredibly high target average speeds set, Taylor and Melia hung on, passing their team mates following Vic Elford's problems, and ended up third in the closely fought Touring Category, beaten only by Trautmann's winning Lancia Flavia Zagato and Timo Makinen's Mini-Cooper 1275S. As far as is known, this was the only appearance, in a rally as opposed to testing and reconnaissance, of this particular car.

*Boreham built a team of new leaf-spring Lotus-Cortinas in 1965, including KPU 385C, which started its short career in the French Alpine of that year, winning its capacity class and finishing third in the entire Touring Car category, with Henry Taylor at the wheel.*

**Competition Record**

| 1965 French Alpine | Henry Taylor | 1st in Class, 3rd in Touring Category |
|---|---|---|

| REGISTRATION NUMBER | ENGINE SIZE | MODEL TYPE |
|---|---|---|
| **KPU 387C** | **1558CC 4-CYL 2OHC** | **LOTUS CORTINA MK I** |

Bo Ljungfeldt drove the fourth of the brand-new team cars on the French Alpine rally of July 1965, and was going well until, on the first timed climb of the Col d'Allos, his engine expired and that was that.

Bengt Soderstrom then took it over for the RAC rally of November 1965, this being a long, arduous but snowy event where conventionally engineered cars (i.e., those with front-engine/rear-drive layouts) cars struggled to stay competitive. Well before the half-way rest halt in Perth, and soon after leaving the Oulton Park special stages, the engine expired and, like the entire Ford factory team on this event, the car had to retire.

Soderstrom then persevered with it almost throughout the 1966 season, starting four major events, winning one (the Acropolis) and taking second place once (Vltava), before it was retired from front-line duties. Backed by two of the ex-1966 Monte Group 1 cars, Bengt took this rebuilt RAC rally machine to Sweden in February 1966, struggled to stay on terms with the leaders, holding 10th place at half-distance, and then saw his car break its rear axle as the second leg got under way.

Three months later (and having used his still-fresh Monte Carlo car twice – on the Rally dei Fiore and the Tulip), he tackled the rough, hot, dusty and gruelling Acropolis rally in Greece where, to Ford's joy, he was acclaimed as the winner. Right from the start the battle was between the works Cortinas of Soderstrom, Elford and Roger Clark and the works BMC Mini-Cooper Ss, the Lancias, the Volvos and the Saabs.

Victory might have gone to team-mate Vic Elford (see the entry for MNO 761C) or to rival Paddy Hopkirk (Mini-Cooper S), for when the results were initially published Elford had been disqualified while Hopkirk was declared the winner with Soderstrom second. Shortly (and no firm evidence was ever given for this, though BMC always blamed Ford's Henry Taylor) a protest was raised against Hopkirk on the grounds of his taking 'illegal' service inside a control zone. This was up-

held, a penalty was applied which dropped him to third place, and Soderstrom became the unexpected and delighted winner.

Only a few weeks later, while some of his team mates were preparing to tackle the British Gulf London rally as 'private owners' (full-blooded works entries were forbidden in this event for trade and sponsorship reasons), the Acropolis-winning car was rebuilt, and sent out to Czechoslovakia for Soderstrom to contest the Vltava (sometimes called Moldau) rally. In a battle which went on throughout, Soderstrom scrapped closely with Aaltonen's works Mini-Cooper S, finally finishing second overall.

The final public appearance came on the Finnish 1000 Lakes in August 1966, a little-reported event in which Soderstrom eventually retired from the field.

*Bengt Soderstrom and Gunnar Palm on their way to outright victory in the 1966 Acropolis rally, driving KPU 387C.*

**Competition Record**

| | | |
|---|---|---|
| 1965 French Alpine | Bo Ljungfeldt | DNF |
| 1965 RAC | Bengt Soderstrom | DNF |
| 1966 Swedish | Bengt Soderstrom | DNF |
| 1966 Acropolis | Bengt Soderstrom | 1st |
| 1966 Vltava (Czech) | Bengt Soderstrom | 2nd |
| 1966 1000 Lakes | Bengt Soderstrom | DNF |

| REGISTRATION NUMBER | ENGINE SIZE | MODEL TYPE |
|---|---|---|
| **KPU 395C** | **1558CC 4-CYL 2OHC** | **LOTUS CORTINA MK I** |

*Vic Elford and David Stone looked set to win the 1965 French Alpine in this newly-shelled leaf-spring Lotus-Cortina but the engine faltered just hours from the finish.*

This car, one of the early batch of leaf-spring Lotus-Cortinas prepared at Boreham in the spring of 1965, looked ready to win its very first event, the French Alpine rally (held in July 1965), except that cruel luck held it back very near the finish. Vic Elford, who had struggled to get an A-frame car through the Tour de France in 1964, revelled in the newly-found reliability of the leaf spring car along with the BRM-tuned engine, and was well placed to win the entire event -- not just the Touring section but the entire rally.

By the time the depleted column was making its way towards Monte Carlo and the end of the event, Elford was still more than three minutes clear of the field and still unpenalised on the tight road sections, when (in Vic's own words), "The last special stage was typical; up one side of the mountain, down the other. It was so easy we did not even bother with a service point at the end since it was only about twenty kilometres to the finish in Monte Carlo. On the way up, the car suddenly stopped. We had no idea why and eventually David [Seigle-Morris] took pity on us, stopped and towed us to the summit, where we coasted down past the finish where we found Rootes Group service team. They hunted around and eventually found that the 'heel' on the Lucas distributor points had broken off. They managed to adjust it so it worked just enough to get us to the finish, but of course it was too late". That one tiny failure dropped the team from a commanding lead to a lowly 21st place, and handed victory to René Trautmann's Lancia Flavia Zagato.

Vic Elford then had the good fortune to be allocated Competition Number 3 for the 1965 RAC rally – in fact due to Tom Trana's Volvo withdrawal, the only car to start ahead of him was Timo Makinen's works Austin-Healey 3000 – but it actually brought him little luck. On Stage 5, at Brendon Hill in the West Country, Vic crashed the car (this was claimed to be due to a rear axle problem) and took a maximum penalty before he could be retrieved and the car could be patched up. For the next two days he experienced what the author later reported in *Autocar* as an 'on and off' performance, with some very fast stage times and with yet more excursions into ditches, before finally going off the road for good in the Lake District as the route began to return from Scotland. There was one piece of drama which almost caused a big crash: Elford was in mid-stage when the steering wheel began to disintegrate, so that the rim came adrift from the aluminium spokes!

Although this car was not used again as an actual competing rally car by the works team, it was used in practice, for testing, for the occasional flutter in rallycross, and – most significantly – as a test car by Jim Clark at the Bagshot rough-road track, where he learned something about driving rally cars (and took some 'tuition' from his namesake Roger Clark) before starting the 1966 RAC rally himself.

### Competition Record

| | | |
|---|---|---|
| 1965 French Alpine | Vic Elford | 21st |
| 1965 RAC | Vic Elford | DNF |

For 1966, when significantly different and more stringent FIA sporting homologation regulations came into force, the works Ford factory team prepared a fresh fleet of so-called 'standard' Group 1 and modified (Group 2) cars for the early part of the season. A batch of brand-new leaf-spring Lotus-Cortinas – the NVW 239C to NVW 243C series – were all prepared at Boreham. The table below lists original (not final) allocation of those cars. This was the original master plan, but as the 1966 season progressed further changes had to be made. What follows summarises their careers.

| | |
|---|---|
| NVW 239C | Not completed at first, then used by Bengt Soderstrom (LHD) when finally completed to Group 2 specification |
| NVW 240C | Bengt Soderstrom (LHD) |
| NVW 241C | Roger Clark and later Jim Clark (RHD), Group 2 |
| NVW 242C | Vic Elford (RHD), later converted to Group 2 |
| NVW 243C | Roger Clark (RHD), later converted to Group 2 |

| REGISTRATION NUMBER | ENGINE SIZE | MODEL TYPE |
|---|---|---|
| **NVW 239C** | **1558CC 4-CYL 2OHC** | **LOTUS CORTINA MK I** |

This (later famous) car was one of three brand-new white-with-green-spear cars made ready for the French Alpine rally of August 1966, an event which was set to be one of the fastest held on the demanding cols and private by-roads of the French Alps.

Unlike its sister cars on this particular event (KPU 380C and NVW 242C, both of which had started life as right-hand-drive red machines), this really was a brand-new left-hand-drive car and would only appear twice. The minor mystery, insoluble after all these years, is that although the registration number/identity was reserved before the end of 1965, the car itself was not even made ready to appear until September 1966.

The pace on this French Alpine was so hot that even the fastest works drivers had to go flat out on the *sélectif* sections, and it was on the Col de la Chaudière (north of Mont Ventoux) that Bengt Soderstrom misjudged his braking distance *after* the flying finish of the section, hit a wall hard enough to damage the oil cooler and the radiator so that all the vital fluids rapidly drained away, and had to retire on the spot.

After (by Boreham standards) quite a leisurely rebuild, the car was made ready for the RAC rally, where Bengt Soderstrom had the (for Boreham) unique arrangement of four low-mounted extra driving lamps, but otherwise ran in the same white/green livery with Minilite wheels as the cars of team mates Jim Clark, Roger Clark and Vic Elford.

Right from the start Soderstrom, managed cleverly and serenely by Gunnar Palm, settled down among the leaders, with stage times always up among them, but never actually out in front. Special stage times so usefully published in *Autosport* immediately afterwards show that Soderstrom did not actually set up a fastest time until Stage 17, which was the long and demanding Dovey Forest.

*Bengt Soderstrom's RAC victory in NVW 239C brought Boreham's troubled 1966 season to a successful close. Here he was cruising towards the win at the Silverstone time trial.*

**BOREHAM IN 1966**

Apart from a significant re-shuffle in the front-line driving strength, Boreham progressed logically from 1965 to 1966. Bo Ljungfeldt and David Seigle-Morris were released at the end of 1965, and Roger Clark and Bengt Soderstrom became regular team members in their places. The works team concentrated purely on the refinement and improvement of the existing Lotus-Cortina, though as the road car went out of production before the end of the year a new model would be required in 1967.

This was a year in which the team should have been dominant – when its cars were going well they were always pace-setters, but it was also a year in which the team was let down (sometimes in a self-inflicted manner) by technical or administrative failures. Caught up in the 'headlamps fiasco' of the Monte Carlo rally, the team was then robbed of victory in the Flowers rally because the Italian scrutineers uncovered mistakes in the homologation papers. In spite of much effort by Boreham and BRM (who built most of the power units) the engines were often unreliable, as were the rear axles. Vic Elford was so unhappy about the way these events built up that he decided to leave the team at the end of 1966, precipitating more driver changes for 1967.

There were no dramas, no histrionics and, above all, no set-backs. When the depleted field finally reached the mid-event rest halt at Aviemore in the Scottish Highlands, the Lotus-Cortina was in second place, though no less than six minutes behind Timo Makinen's works Mini-Cooper 1275S. In the next 24 hours, and even while attacking the much-feared complex of stages in Kielder (on the English/Scottish border), Soderstrom

was still rarely setting fastest times, but neither was he losing positions, and when Makinen's Mini-Cooper suddenly broke its transmission in Pundershaw, Bengt found himself in the lead by well over 10 minutes over any rival.

And so it remained, for there were few stages left to tackle, and no narrowing gap of timing to worry about. Much of the final day was spent on the road, and *Autosport* was finally able to report that "The only person without worries was Bengt Soderstrom, who toured round in his Lotus-Cortina knowing that he had no need to hurry".

It was a wonderful way for Ford to finish their 1966 season, especially as this victory also handed them the Manufacturers' Rally Championship.

## Competition Record

| | | |
|---|---|---|
| 1966 French Alpine | Bengt Soderstrom | DNF |
| 1966 RAC | Bengt Soderstrom | 1st |

| REGISTRATION NUMBER | ENGINE SIZE | MODEL TYPE |
|---|---|---|
| **NVW 240C** | **1558CC 4-CYL 2OHC** | **LOTUS CORTINA MK I** |

Group 1 cars should be used, NVW 240C, 242C and 243C were all as close to 'showroom standard' as necessary. Because Bengt Soderstrom, the brawny Swedish truck driver who had joined the team, was to drive NVW 240C, it had left-hand drive.

Although the engines were blueprinted by BRM (a horse-power figure was never revealed, the project being run by Mike Hall, who later joined Cosworth), they were little more powerful than standard. The transmission *was* standard, the back axle ratio was the optional 4.4:1, and the team had to use the standard tiny 8-gallon fuel tank. Rather cleverly detailed slip-over covers were used to make the standard seats more supportive, but otherwise there was little apart from Britax safety belts to hold the crews in place.

On the Monte Carlo rally, and before the rumpus over Ford's 'illegal' lighting blew up (for details of this, see the entry for NVW 243C), Bengt put in a stirring performance, and if any normal situation would have been eighth overall. Significantly, all but one faster car, Roger Clark's sister works car, had front-wheel drive.

Only four weeks later the same car/driver combination tackled the Rally of the Flowers, which was centred on San Remo, just on the Italian side of the border from Monte Carlo. Although this was the same car which had competed in Group 1 in the Monte, for the Flowers it appeared with four forward facing auxiliary lamps, which automatically upgraded it to Group 2. Unhappily, there was no happy ending, for it was only on the second special stage that Bengt's car picked up a puncture, ran off the road, and smashed its front suspension.

After a short lay-off, and restored to Group 1 specification, the car then started the Tulip rally. Team mate Vic Elford was in a Group 2 car, MNO 761C, for this event, and there-

*The first works appearance of a Group 1 Lotus-Cortina, the 1966 Monte Carlo rally. Bengt Soderstrom drove NVW 240C but it was disqualified for a spurious 'lighting infringement' after the end of the event.*

In the late autumn 1965 and early weeks of 1966 this was one of three cars built specifically to meet the revised FIA Homologation regulations for 1966, when Ford had some-how persuaded the sporting authorities that they had produced more than 5000 Lotus-Cortinas during 1965 to make them eligible for Group 1. For the Monte Carlo rally, there-fore, in which the regulations made it almost essential that

fore not competing for the same set of awards. Bengt battled throughout with Timo Makinen's Mini-Cooper S, and ended up second overall to Timo, but by a mere 7.7 seconds. Although it was still hale and hearty, this was where the works career of NVW 240C came to an end.

*NVW 240C started its second event within weeks in the Rallye dei Fiori (based on San Remo) in February 1966 but crashed out after picking up an unexpected puncture.*

### Competition Record
| | | |
|---|---|---|
| 1966 Monte Carlo | Bengt Soderstrom | 8th (then disqualified) |
| 1966 Rallye dei Fiore (Flowers) | Bengt Soderstrom | DNF |
| 1966 Tulip | Bengt Soderstrom | 2nd in Group 1 Category |

| REGISTRATION NUMBER | ENGINE SIZE | MODEL TYPE |
|---|---|---|
| **NVW 241C** | **1558cc 4-cyl 2OHC** | **LOTUS CORTINA MK I** |

Here was a car which only appeared twice, once without fanfare, and once with the spotlight of the specialist media on it at all times. The mystery, however, is not why it was used so little, but why it appeared so late in the life of the 'NVW' family.

As noted above, the 1966 works fleet of five new Lotus-Cortinas was commissioned before the end of 1965, and three of them then competed (in Group 1 tune) in the Monte Carlo rally of January 1966, but nothing was seen of NVW 241C until it was allocated to Roger Clark for the Finnish 1000 Lakes event.

Although it was already in full Group 2 tune, with a BRM-tuned twin-cam engine, and could have been competitive on this event, Roger clearly did not enjoy himself. For one thing he had never before rallied in Finland, and for another he seems to be have rather overawed by the sheer pace of the local Finnish pilots. All in all, it must have been a relief for him to have finished at all, which he did in 20th place.

Three months later, however, things could not have been more different, for this time it was entered for the RAC rally, where race driver Jim Clark, already a double F1 World Champion in 1963 and 1965, was determined to prove that he could also shine on loose surfaces, without previously having seen any of the forestry stages which made up the vast majority of this event's competitive mileage.

This was no 'just-for-show-business' appearance either, for before the event Jim Clark practiced assiduously, sometimes with his name-sake Roger as a 'tutor', sometimes with Brian Melia, who would be his rally co-driver, alongside him, and

always with one or other of the sizeable fleet of Boreham rally cars and practice/test cars to use at venues such as the Bagshot rough road tracks, near Camberley in Surrey.

Seeded at No. 8, Jim left the start surrounded by famous rallying names including Paddy Hopkirk, Bengt Soderstrom, Timo Makinen and Pauli Toivonen immediately behind him. From the beginning Jim was on the pace, setting third and fifth fastest times, his progress through the stages looking

*The two famous Clarks, Jim (left) and Roger, ready to start the 1966 RAC rally. The car they are sitting on, NVW 241C, was the one Jim Clark would use in the event.*

spectacular to say the least. He set fastest times in the Towy and Myherin stages (both of them Welsh 'classics'), and in spite of having more than one minor excursion which in his words "rounded off the corners of the car", four punctures, and a very brief panic when the earth lead jumped off the battery, he was in sixth place overall at the half-way halt at Aviemore.

It was in the second half of the event that the drama kicked in. Soon after the re-start, Clark put the car off the road on the Loch Achray stage, damaging the front suspension and steering against a bit of solid Scottish scenery and being delayed by up to 45 minutes before the car could struggle to a Ford

service vehicle and be patched up. Nothing daunted, he carried on until, in John Davenport's words in *Autosport*, "In the stage at Glengap, Jim Clark's rally came to an end when he got airborne over some humps and flipped twice into some trees." According to Philip Turner of *Motor*, "It took a large breakdown vehicle one-and-a-half hours to recover the car, in which all the glass was still intact, and the engine still working."

This was the sad end to a very spectacular outing, and the end for this car, which was later photographed back at Boreham before being finally dismantled. In later years, rumours spread that the wreckage had been spirited away, and might resurface, but these seemed to be without foundation.

**Competition Record**

| | | |
|---|---|---|
| 1966 1000 Lakes rally | Roger Clark | 20th |
| 1966 RAC rally | Jim Clark | DNF |

*Testing times compared at Bagshot in November 1966. Left to right are Roger Clark, Jim Clark, rally engineer Bill Meade and co-driver/co-ordinator Brian Melia.*

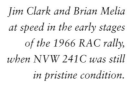

*Jim Clark and Brian Melia at speed in the early stages of the 1966 RAC rally, when NVW 241C was still in pristine condition.*

*Clark and Melia in the 1966 RAC, where Jim surprised everyone with his pace and his obvious enjoyment of the event. Just one tiny dent in the front wing at this stage shows how hard he was trying.*

*Oh dear – this is how Jim Clark left NVW 241C after the last of its accidents on the 1966 RAC rally. It is thought that it was stripped and quietly scrapped soon afterwards.*

| REGISTRATION NUMBER | ENGINE SIZE | MODEL TYPE |
|---|---|---|
| NVW 242C | 1558CC 4-CYL 2OHC | LOTUS CORTINA MK I |

Here was the second of the original Group 1 cars which Boreham built up to start the 1966 Monte Carlo rally, and it was one which Vic Elford came to dislike. As he once told the author, "For the Monte, my new co-driver, John Davenport, went off the road on the way to our start point in Warsaw, Poland, damaging the steering. My engineering apprenticeship was called in to action again and I took a complete steering assembly with me by plane, and spent an afternoon under the car replacing it."

"The first common mountain section developed into a battle between Timo [Makinen] and me, and we were only seconds apart when we tackled the last special section before arriving in Monaco – the Levens hillclimb. Half-way up the hill the engine suddenly shut down and we coasted to a stop. After checking around, we found that a brisk bash with a hammer was all that was needed to get the Lucas fuel pump to work again! But of course by then it was too late".

Hastily returned to Boreham, rebuilt, then readied for its next outing, it was then sent on to Sweden, still in Group 1 tune, and although practice was forbidden, Elford spent some time learning to drive quicker on snow and ice at other sites. Having started steadily from Orebro, well before half time everything came to a halt. Having gone off a stage into a snowdrift, Elford found that the engine would not restart for 20 minutes, and it wasn't until then that he discovered that the long air-cleaner trunking which directed air from the front of the car to the Weber carburettors had filled up with snow, which had frozen solid, as a result of the accident. Nevertheless he finally got going again and, because Group 1 was well depleted by then, ended up taking 10th place and winning his class.

Two starts and two disappointments, and it wasn't long before they made it three out of three, as Vic's short outing on the Circuit of Ireland, in full Group 2 form, soon ended in disaster. On the very first special stage after the start in Ballymena, in darkness – well, let Vic take up the story: "The first special stage was over a very long, narrow, switchback road with stone walls on either side. Being a public road, we had only been able to do a recce run slowly, in daylight. On the rally I was building up speed and accelerating over the first hump, over the second, over the third when, next time we were about three feet in the air, the road suddenly dropped away and bent slightly to the left. We came down astride the wall, bounced off and shot across the road into the other wall, destroying the car in the process".

Although Vic could never be persuaded to drive that car

again, the miracle is that it was eventually reborn for use in the French Alpine rally, where the existing identity was given to an all-new Group 2 car. It had a brand-new bodyshell, resplendent in white-with-green paintwork, 'go faster' stripes along the flanks, and the latest in Minilite magnesium wheels. On that occasion it was allocated to Roger Clark, while Vic took over KPU 380C, which had been David Seigle-Morris's red car in 1965. Make of that what you will.

What followed on the French Alpine was that Roger put up one of the finest performances of his career, even though in the end he had to settle for second place overall, (a mere 67 seconds behind Jean Rolland's Alfa Romeo Giulia GTA. In fact, Roger was one of only seven drivers who achieved a penalty-free run on the harum-scarum road section, and was not only the only works Ford driver to finish, but was one of the 19 survivors overall. Yet it cannot have helped his preparations when, on the day before the start, his car collided with a non-competitor near the team's hotel in La Ciotat,

*Vic Elford and John Davenport in the new Group 1 works car, NVW 242C, shortly before mechanical problems forced retirement from the 1966 Monte Carlo rally.*

damaging it, and causing Henry Taylor's mechanics to have to work overtime to get it looking presentable again. In spite of the car eventually suffering from a blowing exhaust system and (guess what!) a rear axle which threatened to disintegrate in what was now a familiar fashion, he made it to the finish.

Two months later the car was made ready to take part in the RAC rally, where Roger started from No. 31 (which was really quite an insult for such a successful British driver). With team mates Jim Clark, Bengt Soderstrom and Vic Elford all starting ahead of him, he set out from London quite determined to make amends, and he certainly made an early impression by being fastest on each of the first three forestry stages. Then, as Roger later wrote, "On the Puddletown Forest stage, near Dorchester, my car slid off the outside of a gentle downhill bend, the nose hit a tree head-on, and we split the radiator. I

wasn't quite used to the new type of limited-slip differential in the car, which is no excuse. The radiator was split, we lost all the water, and before we could even get to our next service car a few miles away, the head gasket had blown".

Things could only get better. Or could they? Suitably refreshed, the same car then tackled the Welsh International (which Roger had won in 1965). Roger was seeded No. 1 and "This time I had another freak accident. Jim and I were running first on the road in the Lotus-Cortina, it was a dark and dirty night, and we charged over a brow to land smack in the middle of a very large pool of water. The problem was that it only covered one side of the road, and it pulled the steering wheel clean out of my hands. We spun, hit the bank, and the wretched thing fell over." Which was no way for the career of such a good car to come to an end.

### Competition Record

| | | |
|---|---|---|
| 1966 Monte Carlo | Vic Elford | DNF |
| 1966 Swedish | Vic Elford | 10th, and Class win |
| 1966 Circuit of Ireland | Vic Elford | DNF |
| Then a new car was built, using the old identity, for | | |
| 1966 French Alpine | Roger Clark | 2nd |
| 1966 RAC | Roger Clark | DNF |
| 1966 Welsh | Roger Clark | DNF |

| REGISTRATION NUMBER | ENGINE SIZE | MODEL TYPE |
|---|---|---|
| **NVW 243C** | **1558CC 4-CYL 2OHC** | **LOTUS CORTINA MK I** |

Technically this right-hand-drive car was to the same Group 1 state of preparation as the other 'NVW' cars which started the 1966 Monte Carlo rally. Although it was not as powerful as other works cars which he was used to driving, it was clearly to Roger Clark's satisfaction, as he soon

*Roger Clark in the Group 1 car, NVW 243C, in the 1966 Monte Carlo rally, in which he finished fourth 'on the road' but was finally disqualified on a technicality.*

settled down to be one of the very fastest front-engine/rear-drive competitors in the event, matched only by Bo Ljungfeldt in one of the pair of Alan Mann Racing cars (NNO 822C).

When the final night of stages started from the Promenade in Monte Carlo, two works Minis led the event, with Clark and Ljungfeldt close behind them. During the night, Ljungfeldt disappeared, though Paddy Hopkirk's Mini Cooper 1275S squeezed past, which left Clark as the leading Ford driver, and the leading front-engine/rear-drive exponent.

All was well, it seemed, and Clark duly finished fourth overall – or so he (and Boreham) thought, until the post-event scrutineers did their best to penalise British ingenuity by declaring that the single-filament quartz-halogen bulbs (which mean that the headlamps had to 'dip' on to alternative lamps) was 'illegal'. Disqualification duly followed, and no amount of appealing to the smug, chauvinistic organisers could make them relent.

As Roger Clark later wrote in his autobiography, "We knew there was a lot of pro-French hysteria about when we heard it suggested that both BMC and ourselves were using non-standard cars, that homologation papers were fiddled, and that at times we were even swapping cars for race-tuned versions to tackle certain tests and hill-climbs... It all pointed to hysteria by a group of very nationalistic people. At the finish the organisers stripped the winning Minis almost to the last nut-and-bolt, but they left the Lotus-Cortina alone: they could find nothing at all wrong."

Outwardly not too disappointed, Roger then waited for the same car to be refurbished, and used it to start the Swedish rally just three weeks later. However, although he was soon setting competitive times and matching team-mate Vic Elford in another ex-Monte Group 1 car, the BRM-prepared engine let him down several times in the opening hours, so he was forced to retire.

For its next (and last, as it transpired) outing, this car was allocated to Brian Melia (normally a Boreham co-driver, but an accomplished driver too), to tackle the Circuit of Ireland at Easter weekend, when it appeared in full-blown Group 2 tune. Faced with stiff opposition, which included other Boreham-prepared cars for Roger Clark and Vic Elford, Melia soon settled in to one of the leading positions, and at the halfway halt in Killarney he was in a strong second place, behind Roger Clark.

Soon after this, when Clark's team car lost its engine (see KPU 382C), Melia found himself in the lead, but shortly he was passed by Tony Fall's works Mini-Cooper S, which led him to the end. Fortunately the car lasted, in spite of what sounded like impending trouble from the back axle, which was a perennial complaint from high-powered Cortinas at the time and would not be solved until the bigger, brawnier 'Atlas' axle was adopted for Escort in the 1970s.

*Roger Clark on a rare snow-free special stage of the 1966 Monte Carlo rally. He and his car, NVW 243C, were placed fourth on the road but were then disqualified because the organisers invented a 'lighting infringement' of the regulations.*

## Competition Record

| | | |
|---|---|---|
| 1966 Monte Carlo | Roger Clark | 4th (then disqualified) |
| 1966 Swedish | Roger Clark | DNF |
| 1966 Circuit of Ireland | Brian Melia | 2nd |

| REGISTRATION NUMBER | ENGINE SIZE | MODEL TYPE |
|---|---|---|
| **MNO 761C** | **1558cc 4-cyl 2OHC** | **LOTUS CORTINA MK I** |

Immediately after Boreham had built up the new 'NVW' cars for 1966, they followed up by completing a brand-new red-painted Group 2 car (which had been previously registered), which was destined for a short, colourful and rarely successful career in Vic Elford's hands. Vic once told the author that this was one of the Boreham-prepared cars which convinced him that the time had come for him to move to another team.

Its first event, in February 1966, was the Rallye dei Fiori (the forerunner of the Rally San Remo), which was held in the Italian mountains above San Remo, to the east of Monte Carlo. The combination of Elford, co-driver David Stone and Lotus-Cortina put up an impeccable show, but after the event the Italian scrutineers uncovered a mistake in the car's homologation papers, this being a simple mis-type of the number of gear wheel teeth inside the gearbox, and promptly disqualified the car.

Things went better for the same team on the Tulip rally, which followed in early May, for the car was ideally specified (and Elford was well-prepared) for an event with so many speed hillclimbs and all-tarmac surfaces. BMC's Mini-Cooper 1275S was now approaching its full maturity and was just able to outpace the Lotus-Cortinas, the result being that Vic finished second overall, a mere 45 seconds off the pace behind Rauno Aaltonen's Mini-Cooper S. Vic's engine suffered a difficult-to-locate misfire, only later discovered to be due to

*Vic Elford's new-for-1966 Lotus-Cortina, MNO 761C, looked as if it had won the Rallye dei Fiore in February but the scrutineers disqualified it for a homologation infringement.*

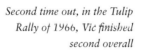

*Second time out, in the Tulip Rally of 1966, Vic finished second overall*

what *Autosport*'s report called a 'split main carburettor jet'.

Unhappily, things got worse again on the Greek Acropolis rally. This was an event where the Cortina's well-proven toughness produced a 1-2 result (Bengt Soderstrom and Roger Clark as listed elsewhere), but it should have been a 1-2-3 finish if Elford's now legendary bad luck had not struck again. On a rough and tough rally (and in spite of not carrying out any practice for the event), Elford started well and was always up with the leaders, but after about one third of the event, when he had taken over the lead, his car suffered a clutch failure after the mechanics completed a gearbox change, and

thereafter had to tackle every standing start by leaving the car in first gear after he had switched off and using the starter motor to get things moving again!

In the end, and while leading the entire event after Hopkirk's Mini-Cooper S had been penalised for 'illegal servicing', he was disqualified for taking a detour from the official route to avoid a tight uphill hairpin where the clutchless car might have been immobilised. Disgusted, and increasingly unhappy with his fortunes in the Ford works team, Elford made sure that he never again came into contact with this car, which therefore fades from the works rally scene.

### Competition Record

| | | |
|---|---|---|
| 1966 Rallye dei Fiori | Vic Elford | 1st (then disqualified) |
| 1966 Tulip | Vic Elford | 2nd |
| 1966 Acropolis | Vic Elford | Disqualified |

| REGISTRATION NUMBER | ENGINE SIZE | MODEL TYPE |
|---|---|---|
| **NNO 821C** | **1558cc 4-cyl 2OHC** | **Lotus Cortina Mk I** |

Here was one of two real rarities – effectively a works Lotus-Cortina rally car that was actually prepared by a racing team. Along with a sister car, NNO 822C, this beautifully-detailed Group 1 example was built-up and run by Alan Mann Racing specifically to compete in the 1966 Monte Carlo Rally.

"Shortly before the 1966 Monte Carlo Rally," Alan Mann wrote in his autobiography, "Walter Hayes got in touch with me confidentially and said that in his opinion things were getting rather slack. In his words, he wanted me to sharpen things up a bit by running a couple of Lotus-Cortinas in the

Monte, so we entered Ljungfeldt and Procter." Because this all happened 50 years ago, the principal characters involved at the time have passed on, so the author can only surmise that, having recently appointed Henry Taylor as his Competition Manager, Hayes was not happy with Boreham's recent record. On the other hand he was still mightily impressed by Alan Mann Racing's performance in winning the European Touring Car Championship in 1965.

Having taken advice from Boreham as to what was and was not allowed by the newly-revised FIA Group 1 regulations, AMR built up two all-new cars at its Byfleet HQ. Mechanically, and by definition, they had to be the same as the works cars, but of course they were painted in that startling red-and-gold colour scheme which had become familiar on the race circuits in 1965.

In addition, as Group 1 regulations restricted cars to using only two extra driving lamps, the AMR cars were equipped with massive rectangular driving lamps mounted high on the nose of the bonnet; it was apparently Bo Ljungfeldt's advice which led to them being placed there. Significantly, however (and unlike the other works cars for the event), single-filament quartz halogen headlamps were not used, which meant that a normal dipping mechanism could be retained, and there were no scrutineering problems.

Peter Procter, the versatile race driver, rally driver (and ex-Olympic standard racing cyclist), who had many successes to his name, was engaged to drive NNO 821C, and was setting a good pace in the first part of the event (it was still 12th with the final night's stages still to run), but on the first batch of special stages there was trouble when a spark plug shed an electrode and damaged a piston, after which the motor was only running on three cylinders. Later, it began to misfire more badly as more and more of a new type of Castrol R engine oil was consumed, piston rings began to gum up, and in the end all compression was lost.

Was this car ever used again? Not as a rally car, but who knows if it eventually donated itself, or parts of itself, to the ever-growing fleet of AMR race cars?

For the 1966 Monte, Ford contracted Alan Mann Racing to prepare two new Group 1 Lotus-Cortinas, and because of the strict regulations, which only allowed two auxiliary driving lamps, AMR chose these huge projectors to light the way. Driven by Peter Procter, this car, NNO 821C, held up well until an engine problem intervened and retirement eventually became necessary.

| Competition Record | | |
|---|---|---|
| 1966 Monte Carlo | Peter Procter | DNF |

| REGISTRATION NUMBER | ENGINE SIZE | MODEL TYPE |
|---|---|---|
| **NNO 822C** | **1558CC 4-CYL 2OHC** | **LOTUS CORTINA MK I** |

This, the second of the two right-hand-drive Group 1 cars built up by Alan Mann Racing to compete in the 1966 Monte Carlo rally, was allocated to Bo Ljungfeldt (who had so nearly won the Monte for AMR in 1964 in one of Ford-USA's gargantuan 4.7-litre Falcons). Mechanically identical to the sister car of Peter Procter, it eventually expired with the same engine maladies. But not without a fight. Early in the event, where snow and ice on the stages meant that front-wheel-drive cars seemed to have an advantage, Ljungfeldt battled hard and consistently against the works Mini-Coopers of Timo Makinen and Rauno Aaltonen. After the rest halt in Monte Carlo, and with only the final night's stages to run, Ljungfeldt was third overall, a mere 18 seconds behind Aaltonen's Mini (and ahead, incidentally, of Roger Clark's works car).

Work done by Castrol back in their laboratories in the UK had seemed to solve the misfiring problems from which his and team-mate Procter's cars suffered so terminally, but in the end it was all in vain when Ljungfeldt also dropped out; his

Bo Ljungfeldt drove one of the two Alan Mann-prepared Group One Lotus-Cortinas, NOO 822C, in the 1966 Monte Carlo rally.

team suggested that the engine had finally let go, but the media insisted that he had crashed in the region of the infamous Col du Turini.

That was the last we saw of that car until it reappeared, miraculously repaired, to be driven in full Group 2 condition by Boreham's usual co-driver, Brian Melia, on the Gulf London of June 1966. On this occasion, however, it was apparently prepared away from Boreham, at Alec Lobb's garage in Braintree, and so only tenuously carried the title of works car. All historic records have been lost, but it may even have been sold off by Alan Mann Racing by that time. Early in the event, in one of the fearsomely fast stages in north Yorkshire, Melia put it off the road, where it suffered a bent and leaking front-suspension strut, and within 12 hours it arrived at a control in Co. Durham on the end of a tow-rope, complete with a smashed rear differential, so retirement was inevitable.

| Competition Record | | |
|---|---|---|
| 1966 Monte Carlo | Bo Ljungfeldt | DNF |
| 1966 Gulf London | Brian Melia | DNF |

## THE MK II CARS

No sooner had Bengt Soderstrom's Mk I car been sent off to compete in (and win) the Swedish rally of February 1967, than the works team at Boreham completed the fleet of brand-new Mk II GTs, and a new-old Mk I Lotus-Cortina, to take part in the East African Safari. Details of the career of those GTs has already been included in Chapter 3.

Now it was time for a concentrated of programme of building, developing, and competing with Mk II Lotus-Cortinas to get under way, with much of the on-going development to be concentrated on the refinement of the Tecalemit Jackson (TJ)

fuel injection system which was homologated for use in those cars. It was at this time that much of the routine engine supply was carried out by BRM in Lincolnshire.

Design of the Escort Twin-Cam was also under way by the autumn of 1967, so before the end of the year the Mk 2 Lotus-Cortina was already beginning to look like yesterday's car.

However, even before we go on to analyse the fortunes of each works Lotus-Cortina Mk II, the last-ever event tackled by the works cars, the 1968 London-Sydney Marathon, merits special study.

### London-Sydney 1968 – Ford's big disappointment

Ford started the London-Sydney Marathon as hot favourite but their campaign ended in chaos and disarray. Although Roger Clark's Lotus-Cortina led the event until two days from the end, first the twin-cam engine, then the rear axle of his Mk II let him down, and he had to settle for 10th.

When it was originally announced in 1968, a Marathon rally from London to Sydney in Australia sounded like the answer to a question that no-one had ever bothered to ask. Works teams like Ford were already busy enough, their budgets were already spoken for, and drivers used to driving flat-out for four or five days did not warm to the idea of taking 24 days to reach the other side of world.

It all began, they say, at a lunch in the *Daily Express* building towards the end of 1967. Looking to gain favourable publicity for his newspaper, the proprietor of the *Daily Express*, Sir Max Aitken, got together with Jocelyn Stevens and Tommy Sopwith, to create a motoring event which the *Express* could sponsor. Why not, they said, organise a transcontinental motor rally from London to Sydney in Australia?

Launched in January 1968, the scope of the event startled everyone. The route covered 10,070 miles, there would be 14 driving days without scheduled rest halts between the start in London and Bombay in India. From there the P & O ship

*Chusan* was to take the surviving cars to Fremantle (near Perth) for the final 3,000-mile dash across Australia to Sydney. Starting on 24 November, and ending on 17 December, it would be a straightforward test of crew endurance and reliability – with a tight time schedule and high speeds.

At first, Ford was reluctant to get involved, and Walter Hayes's first plan was to support just two British Fords (1600Es) and two Taunus 20MRS types from Germany. This changed gradually into four works and three supported Lotus-Cortinas and three Taunuses, while Ford-Australia entered three large V8-engined Falcon GTs. The main opposition came from BMC's front-wheel-drive 1800s, the works Citroen DS21s, and a Hillman Hunter from Rootes/Chrysler.

John Davenport and Gunnar Palm surveyed the London-Bombay route in a Lotus-Cortina (the re-shelled UVW 924E of 1967), while Bill Barnett and Gunnar Palm surveyed the Australian section, which would involve 70 hours of flat-out motoring in searing heat. Preparation of works cars – VVW 506E (Clark), YVW 4F (Eric Jackson), CTC 26E (Bengt Soderstrom) and VPI 77 (Rosemary Smith, entered by Ford-Ireland) – did not begin until September, and there were always worries about engine durability, for petrol quality would be unpredictable until the cars reached Australia.

When Roger Clark came to write his autobiography *Side-*

*From the right, Bengt Soderstrom, Gunnar Palm, Ove Andersson, Roger Clark, Yvette Pointet, Rosemary Smith, Eric Jackson and Ken Chambers, all ready to start the 1968 Marathon.*

*ways to Victory* in the 1970s he commented: "It wasn't the flat-out endurance test some people had prophesied, and though there wasn't an official night stop between London and Bombay we certainly didn't go short of sleep. I reckon that by the time we rolled in to Bombay, I had had more good sleep than I normally get, and most of it in beds too. We slept on the cross-channel boat, in beds in Turin, Belgrade (about 11 hours), Istanbul and Sivas, and all of this was before we had been given a single hard-working competitive section."

Well before that, however, the team's stars had begun to hit trouble. Ford effectively lost two competitive Lotus-Cortinas before the Iron Curtain was breached, for Peter Harper's car (not officially a works car, and prepared by Tecalemit-Jackson, the fuel-injection specialists in Plymouth) had suffered a failed water pump, which led to the engine boiling and a head gasket failing, while Bengt Soderstrom's car suffered a broken engine cam follower and eventually ran out of time.

At first there was a long, publicity-worthy but exhausting trundle through France, Italy, and Yugoslavia to Turkey. Then came the re-start from Sivas, where cars were faced with the first challenge in which they had to be driven flat-out – flat-out, that is, for three hours – for Erzincan, knowing that they would certainly lose time. The racers were hoping not to lose much, but the amateurs (or 'tourists' as they were also de-

scribed) were simply hoping to survive.

The distance along the shorter, mud-afflicted route was 175 miles, and the target time was 2 hours 45 minutes, but no-one really expected to beat that. Not even rally-favourite Roger

*Those were the days before works teams began using vans for service support, so team mechanics like Norman Masters (left) and Terry Samuell filled their Cortina estate cars to the brim before setting off. The Lotus-Cortina in the foreground is one of the London-Sydney team cars.*

*Home from home. The comfortably kitted-out interior of a works Lotus-Cortina, ready for the London-Sydney Marathon of 1968.*

After the drama, the dust, the speeds, and the exhaustion of the first half of the Marathon, an enforced rest on board the P & O ship *Chusan* was a complete contrast. This graceful old ship, which was already 18 years old, was on its regular scheduled voyage, this time the difference being that 72 rally cars, their crews, and a number of team bosses and media crews, were all on board. The cars were securely locked away below decks, and there was no chance of working on them while the ship was at sea.

This was the point at which the Australian crews, who, frankly, had been humiliated by the pace of the Europeans in the first half of the event, started spreading tall stories about the horrors of what was to come. Harry Firth, Ian Vaughan and Bruce Hodgson (all of them in works Ford-Australia Ford Falcon GTs) were the worst offenders, all of them forecasting that the Europeans would be blown away by what they were about to experience in the 67 hour/3,000 mile dash across their continent, and that the Australian 'experts' would leave them well behind. This was, of course, a classic wind-up, and although the Falcons duly pulled up to third, fifth and eighth before the end, they were still outpaced by the European cars and crews.

It was shortly after a high-profile start from Perth, in Western Australia, to Lake King, where Clark was once again on time when almost all others were losing out, that the event suddenly threw itself into high drama. On its way to Quorn the engine in Clark's Lotus-Cortina broke a valve and damaged a piston. Although the Ford mechanics immediately cannibalised Eric Jackson's sister car to repair Clark's (with a complete head change), he was nevertheless 14 minutes late at Quorn and dropped to third place. Jackson's car retired at that point. The Staepelaere/Lampinen Ford Taunus now led the event.

In film script terms the chase was now on. Clark's Lotus-Cortina regained eight minutes and second place at Brachina, Cowan's Hunter moved up to fourth, but the leader board looked stable, though Lucien Bianchi's Citroen took over the lead. Then, north of Murrindal (close to Melbourne) Clark's car suddenly broke its rear axle, appeared to be stranded, and could only get going again after a complete axle had been begged from a local in a (non-Lotus) Cortina who was passing by. Roger and Ove then lost nearly 100 minutes getting it changed, and finally fell right out of contention.

More drama then ensued, for this left Bianchi's Citroen DS21 in the lead, with the German Taunus close behind him. Then, on the tight 42-minute section to Hindmarsh Station, Staepelaere put the Taunus off the road, breaking a steering tie rod, and lost nearly three hours before repairs could be made. So it was all over and Citroen had won – or had they? As *Autosport*'s reporter saw it, "As the cars came down from the mountains towards Nowra, and a quiet Sunday afternoon drive towards Sydney, [Bianchi] handed the driving over to

Clark in the Lotus-Cortina made it on time, losing 6 minutes (later he said he could have gone a bit quicker...), with the Staepelaere/Lampinen Taunus 20MRS back on 14 minutes. The Hunter lost 21 minutes.

Next, the long drag across Afghanistan to Kabul – 23hr 33 minutes was scheduled, but many crews were up to 10 hours *early* in reaching the capital. This was to be a non-competitive sector (at least, that is what the organisers intended), yet more than half the entry lost time and slipped even further out of contention, while quite a number did not make it that far at all. It was on this sector that Rosemary Smith's Lotus-Cortina struck trouble when her engine blew a piston. Tony Fall's works BMC 1800 broke its steering linkage, and Terry Hunter's well-fancied Porsche 911 broke its engine. Not only that, but Dieter Glemser's German Ford engine broke its camshaft drive, while Rauno Aaltonen's BMC 1800 broke its front suspension.

When the cars reached Bombay, hours early in spite of the huge and inquisitive crowds which surrounded them at every minor hold-up, Ford's enormous effort looked to be paying off. Roger Clark was comfortably in the lead, Staepelaere's Taunus was close behind, and Eric Jackson's car was in 9th.

## Position on arrival in Bombay

| | | |
|---|---|---|
| 1 | Ford Lotus-Cortina (R. Clark/O. Andersson) | 11 mins penalty |
| 2 | Ford Taunus 20MRS (G. Staepelaere/S. Lampinen) | 20 |
| 3 | Citroen DS21 (L. Bianchi/J-C. Ogier) | 21 |
| 4 | BMC 1800 (P. Hopkirk/A. Poole/A. Nash) | 22 |
| 5 | BMC 1800 (R. Aaltonen/H. Liddon/P. Easter) | 24 |
| 6 | Hillman Hunter (A. Cowan/C. Malkin/B. Coyle) | 27 |
| 7 | Ford Falcon GT (Aus) (H. Firth/G. Hoinville/G. Chapman) | 29 |
| 8 | BMC 1800 (E. Green/J. Murray) | 30 |
| 9 | Ford Lotus-Cortina (E. Jackson/K. Chambers | 31 |
| 10 | Ford Falcon GT (Aus) (B. Hodgson/D. Rutherford) | 36 |

Ogier so that he could snatch a bit of sleep before the inevitable pomp and ceremony of the finish. Then it happened: with Ogier powerless to do anything about it, two youths in a Mini collided with the Citroen and pushed it off the road. Bianchi was trapped inside the wrecked car for 20 minutes while help – summoned by Paddy Hopkirk, who had to drive back along the road to warn a group of spectators about the accident – came in the form of some cutting equipment".

This meant that the Hillman Hunter, and its intrepid crew of Andrew Cowan, Brian Coyle and Colin Malkin, had pulled off a quite unexpected victory in the world's most highly publicised transcontinental rally. At the finish, in front of a 10,000 crowd at the Warwick Farm race track near Sydney, every car and its crew looked grubby and exhausted, though this was quite excusable.

For Ford it had been a huge disappointment. First Clark, then Gilbert Staepelaere, might have won the event, but no fewer than four of the seven supported Lotus-Cortinas – Clark, Harper, Rosemary Smith and Bengt Soderstrom – suffered engine-related failures. For manager Henry Taylor, his team, and in particular Roger Clark, this was a shattering blow. Walter Hayes had to reassure Clark that Ford still loved him, and that it would never happen again. Nor did it – 18 months later, when Hannu Mikkola won the World Cup Rally, it would be in a 'Kent'-engined Escort.

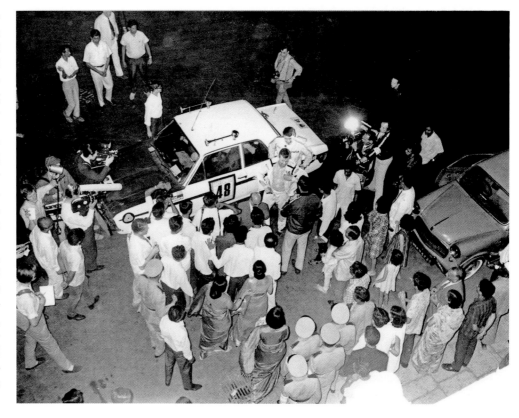

*Just before arrival at the Bombay control of the London-Sydney Marathon, Roger Clark's leading car VVW 506E pauses so that the crew can give interviews.*

## Final Positions

| | | |
|---|---|---|
| 1 | Hillman Hunter (A. Cowan/C. Malkin/B. Coyle) | 50 |
| 2 | BMC 1800 (P. Hopkirk/A. Poole/A. Nash) | 56 |
| 3 | Ford Falcon GT (Aus) (I. Vaughan/R. Forsyth/J. Ellis) | 62 |
| 4 | Porsche 9111S (S. Zasada/M. Wachowski) | 63 |
| 5 | Ford Falcon GT (Aus) (B. Hodgson/D. Rutherford) | 70 |
| 6 | BMC 1800 (R. Aaltonen/H. Liddon/P. Easter) | 71 |
| 7 | Ford Taunus 20MRS (H. Kleint/G. Klapproth) | 91 |
| 8 | Ford Falcon GT (Aus) (H. Firth/G. Hoinville/G. Chapman) | 114 |
| 9 | Citroen DS21 (R. Neyret/J. Terramorsi) | 125 |
| 10 | Ford Lotus-Cortina (R. Clark/O. Andersson) | 144 |

| REGISTRATION NUMBER | ENGINE SIZE | MODEL TYPE |
|---|---|---|
| **TVX 880E** | **1558cc 4-cyl DOHC** | **LOTUS CORTINA MK II** |

*Bengt Soderstrom drove TVX 880E on its first-ever rally, the 1967 Gulf London. The car was also due to take part in the 1967 RAC rally but it was cancelled immediately before the start*

The third works car to appear at the start of the three-day Gulf London of 1967 (Manchester to Manchester, by way of Wales, Scotland, Kielder and the classic Yorkshire stages) was new for that event, and like Roger Clark's sister machine (UHK 327E), its engine was fitted with the still-developing Tecalemit-Jackson fuel injection system. Bengt Soderstrom started well in this event and on the first day was within striking distance of his team-mate Ove Andersson, whose car, UVW 924E, would eventually win, and he was always on the leader board, but a driveshaft broke at a critical uphill section of a special stage and immobilised the car.

This was its only appearance as a works car, for although it was scheduled to take part in the 1967 RAC rally, this event was cancelled at short notice.

### Competition Record

| 1967 Gulf London | Bengt Soderstrom | DNF |
|---|---|---|

**BOREHAM IN 1967**

When Ford began its 1967 motorsport programme at Boreham there were no plans to start work on an Escort project but this developed during the year and immediately changed the tone of Ford's motorsport ambitions. Originally the main thrust of the programme was to prepare for the launch of the Lotus-Cortina and Cortina GT Mk II models, to carry on refining the chosen TJ fuel-injection system as a performance-raising option, and to use the new models in rallies and saloon car races. As in 1966, too, Group 5 Anglias were intended to feature in saloon car racing, though the cars would all be prepared away from Boreham (at Broadspeed in Birmingham and Superspeed in Romford, Essex).

In the first half of the year much work centred on building new Cortinas for rallying. No fewer than eight cars (including a complete set of six for the East African Safari) were produced, and a lot of time was spent on the development of TJ fuel-injected versions of the eight-valve Lotus-Ford Twin-Cam engine. At the end of the year six Mk II Lotus-Cortinas were set to tackle the RAC rally, but the event was cancelled (due to the worsening Foot & Mouth disease outbreak) on the night before its scheduled start.

The first Escort Twin-Cam prototype was not completed until the autumn, with a further three cars built before the end of 1967.

*Bengt Soderstrom in TVX 880E exits a Welsh stage of the 1967 Gulf London Rally. The Jaguar E-Type 2+2 parked alongside the arch was actually the car being used by the author to follow this high speed/high mileage rally.*

| REGISTRATION NUMBER | ENGINE SIZE | MODEL TYPE |
|---|---|---|
| **UVW 924E** | **1558CC 4-CYL DOHC** | **LOTUS CORTINA MK II** |

Not only did this early example of a works Lotus-Cortina Mk II, originally resplendent in Saluki Bronze paintwork, have a long and distinguished career at Boreham, but it also gave the author a great deal of personal pleasure. The reason is that, in the summer of 1967 when it was a still relatively new works machine, it was loaned out to *Autocar* magazine for a full test and for performance figures to be taken. I was one of the two staffers (Geoffrey Howard was the other) who had the privilege of 'owning' the car for several days in 1967. In this way it was possible to learn, in depth, just what had already gone into the evolution of these cars.

Along with cars currently being completed at Boreham for Roger Clark and Ove Andersson to drive on other events, UVW 924E was effectively a further developed derivative of the Mk I Lotus-Cortinas which had performed so well in 1966. The monocoque 'platform' was the same as before, which meant that the running gear, suspension and steering (left-hand-drive on this car) were all well-known quantities, as were the fat magnesium-alloy Minilite road wheels and Goodyear tyres. It was only the two-door bodyshells which were new and unproven, as was soon to become obvious when the new cars experienced rough treatment on rough rallies.

Those were the days, incidentally, when roll cages had not been standardised (they were still frowned upon, in fact, by the scrutineers because they 'added unnecessary strength to existing structures'), when there was not even a bracing strut across the engine bay linking the two front suspension turrets, and when drivers sometimes preferred lap belts instead of three-point or event full-harness fitments. As originally built, UVW 924E had what looked like a normal Lotus-Cortina engine, but one which revved to 7500rpm and developed about 160bhp. The rear axle ratio was 4.70:1, which resulted in a top speed of a rev-limited 97mph, with 0-90mph in 21.1sec compared with 30.9sec for a standard road car.

In May 1967, when new, and in its lustrous Saluki Bronze, it took Bengt Soderstrom to third place in the Acropolis rally, close behind Paddy Hopkirk's winning Mini-Cooper S and Ove Andersson's Lancia Fulvia HF. Because it survived this rough, tough and incredibly dusty event in such good condition, it was immediately allocated to Soderstrom to compete in the Jant rally in Sweden, and following this foray it was hurried back to the UK to be hastily refurbished, and to be driven by Ove Andersson in the Gulf London rally, where it was one of three full works cars (UHK 327E, for Roger Clark and TVX 880E for Bengt Soderstrom being the others).

Right from the start of this incredibly long event (Manchester

*UVW 924E started life as a Lotus-Cortina Mk II works rally car in 1967, here seen on the way to winning the Gulf London rally. It was later given a new bodyshell and gave invaluable service as Ford's route survey car for the 1968 London-Sydney.*

*Bengt Soderstrom (left) and Gunnar Palm ready to start the 1968 London-Sydney Marathon.*

103

to Manchester, 3 days and nights on the road, with no night halt, 47 finishers from 120 starters) Andersson was competitive, the battle being between this Lotus-Cortina and two Swedish-prepared Porsche 911s of Bjorn Waldegard and Ake Andersson. By the time the cars reached Newton Stewart, the two Porsches were well ahead of the Lotus-Cortina, but both the German coupés hit trouble in 'killer' Kielder, both needed time-absorbing delays to rectify suspension damage, and the result was that the Cortina moved smoothly into the lead, which Andersson and his co-driver John Davenport never lost.

By this time the bodyshell was getting tired, so the car was re-shelled, the intention being that it should reappear with a brand-new white/green spear style in November for Bengt

Soderstrom to drive in the 1967 RAC rally. For that event it was fitted out with TJ fuel injection and went through pre-event scrutineering without dramas, but was then foiled by the cancellation of the event at 12 hours notice due to the continuing spread of bovine foot-and-mouth disease which made the running of it quite impractical.

Only weeks later, in January 1968, the same car/team combination, still with a fuel-injected engine, started the Swedish rally (which would normally have been run off in February but was moved so that it would not clash with the winter Olympics), and to everyone's surprise they ran on Swedish Goodrich (*not* Goodyear) winter tyres. This was a 52 special stage event in which surfaces were packed snow or sheet ice, so the Lotus-Cortinas struggled to be competitive against front-wheel-drive Saabs and rear-engined Porsche 911s. Even so, Soderstrom was equal to all the Saabs though unable to match Bjorn Waldegard's Porsche, and after being third at the half-way rest halt he finally took an excellent fourth place behind that Porsche and two works Saab V4s.

Thereafter this car was not used again in a rally, but was invaluable as a test machine before the London-Sydney Marathon and was also used to survey the London-Bombay section of that event.

## Competition Record

| | | |
|---|---|---|
| 1967 Acropolis | Bengt Soderstrom | 3rd |
| 1967 Jant (Sweden) | Bengt Soderstrom | 3rd |
| 1967 Gulf London | Ove Andersson | 1st |
| Bodyshell then scrapped, and a 'new/old' car created around a new shell. | | |
| 1967 RAC | Bengt Soderstrom | Rally cancelled |
| 1968 Swedish | Bengt Soderstrom | 4th |
| 1968 London-Sydney Marathon | Test then route survey car | Not entered |

*UVW 924E had already had a busy life as a rally car in 1967, but was then given a new bodyshell and used as the reconnaissance car for the London-Bombay section of the London-Sydney Marathon of 1968, when John Davenport and Gunnar Palm shared the driving.*

| REGISTRATION NUMBER | ENGINE SIZE | MODEL TYPE |
|---|---|---|
| **UHK 327E** | **1558CC 4-CYL DOHC** | **LOTUS CORTINA MK II** |

New for the Gulf London marathon of July 1967, this car was prepared for that event in FIA Group 5 form, and was fitted out with Tecalemit-Jackson fuel injection, for which the Boreham works team, if not Roger Clark himself, had high hopes. It was not an installation that gave Roger much encouragement, for when he first saw it, before the start of the Gulf London, "I was appalled. The injection was... a system that was supposed to be cheap and simple; what it actually meant was that there were lots of little things buzzing and whirring around under the bonnet. There were pipes, belts, wires, pumps, nozzles – you name it... It was not my idea of a good rally car at all.

"The engine never gave any extra usable power in the special stages, and when an oil pipe split and leaked all the sump's contents into the middle of Dovey forest I can't say I was sorry. I never did come to terms with 'things that go whirr in the night.'"

Roger found it difficult to extract the best result from this car, and on the very first evening of the Gulf London, which started from Manchester airport, in the Dovey forest the car burst an oil pipe in the fuel injection system, which soon ruined the engine. Surprisingly the author has not managed to find a single image of this car on that event, either at pre-event scrutineering or in the stages themselves.

This was the one and only time that a car carrying this identity competed in works motorsport, though it was all set to compete in the 1967 RAC rally, which was cancelled on the night before the start of the event.

**Competition Record**

| 1967 Gulf London | Roger Clark | DNF |
|---|---|---|

| REGISTRATION NUMBER | ENGINE SIZE | MODEL TYPE |
|---|---|---|
| **UVX 566E** | **1558CC 4-CYL DOHC** | **LOTUS CORTINA MK II** |

This, thought to be the first works Lotus-Cortina Mk II rally car to be completed, was prepared in the spring of 1967, soon after the model was announced (that was in March 1967) and as soon as it could be homologated. At the time Boreham was fully committed to a big programme with this new model, for work on what became the Escort Twin-Cam was still only at the 'why don't we?' stage, which had been discussed at length by team boss Henry Taylor and planner Bob Howe. Not a single prototype for that new model yet existed, and it would be months before such a significant development came to fruition.

UVX 566E was one of the fleet of increasingly sophisticated cars which Boreham completed in 1967, and it made its first public appearance in the Scottish rally of June 1967, driven by Roger Clark. As personally witnessed by the author, there were scores of special stages in a four-day event held in dry and dusty Scotland, and this was a daunting challenge for any new model, especially as it had to face other fully fledged works cars from, BMC, Rootes, Saab and Triumph, but Roger Clark never flinched from the challenge.

Running in what we might call 'standard' forestry-stage

*This brand new Lotus-Cortina Mk II, UVX 566E, won the 1967 Scottish rally outright with Roger Clark at the wheel...*

Lotus-Cortina condition, the new car had the latest 'No-Spin' limited-slip differential and 6.0in. magnesium Minilite wheels shod with the latest Goodyear tyres. A second such car, incidentally (TVX 880E) had originally been entered for Bengt Soderstrom to drive, but this machine was not yet finished

*...and here it is in full flight through a hot and dusty special stage. Its sister car UVX 565E was the unsuccessful FVA-engined race car that Boreham was developing at the time.*

and would appear the following month in the Gulf London.

Clark did not lead from the start, holding second place close behind Tom Trana's works Saab V4 at the Grantown overnight halt, and he later suffered several punctures, but he soon took the lead. He had only one significant problem (and I now quote from my own *Autocar* report): "A nasty little stage near Inverness boasted one really vicious jump, whose landing place dealt several sump shields a really grievous blow. So hard did the leading Lotus-Cortina land that it kinked the body a little in the scuttle region, and made the door fittings very tight for the rest of the rally."

Because the green paint spear along the flanks showed evidence of this distortion, thereafter it became known as 'The Banana'. Yet Clark did not back off at all, set a series of fastest times as the event progressed, and in spite of having to have work done on a damaged exhaust system he eventually pulled out more than five minutes on Lars-Ingvar Ytterbring's works Cooper S.

Suitably refurbished, de-kinked (and with a reinforced bodyshell after the Scottish), only three weeks later the same car then tackled the incredibly long, tough, and gruelling Gulf London. On this occasion it was loaned out to British Champion Tony Chappell, a Ford main dealer from South Wales who normally used a privately-prepared Lotus-Cortina of his own. He was competitive until his car suffered a broken driveshaft and then went off the road soon afterwards, after which he put the car on its side in the Chirdonhead stage of the Kielder complex, where it languished for more than one-and-a-half hours. Amazingly (and this is a measure of the way that the rally managed to eliminate all but 47 finishers) he eventually got going again, and finished in a brave seventh place.

The car was in a sorry state by then, so as Boreham was now full of later-specification Lotus-Cortinas and work on the Escort Twin-Cam project was getting more intense it was pensioned off.

| Competition Record | | |
|---|---|---|
| 1967 Scottish | Roger Clark | 1st |
| 1967 Gulf London | Tony Chappell | 7th |

| REGISTRATION NUMBER | ENGINE SIZE | MODEL TYPE |
|---|---|---|
| **UVX 611E** | **1558CC 4-CYL DOHC** | **LOTUS CORTINA MK II** |

Graham Hill certainly drove UVX 611E at the Bagshot rough-road proving grounds when training in Mk II Lotus-Cortinas before the '67 RAC rally in which he was due to compete. However, all the evidence is that it was no more than a lightly-modified test/press car, complete with sump guard and Minilite alloy wheels, which had no other motorsport history. It does not figure in any other Boreham activities before or after that particular October day in Surrey.

| REGISTRATION NUMBER | ENGINE SIZE | MODEL TYPE |
|---|---|---|
| **CTC 23E** | **1558CC 4-CYL DOHC** | **LOTUS CORTINA MK II** |

In the spring of 1967 Ford revealed its new Lotus-Cortina Mk II and, as described in greater detail in Chapter 7, registered a batch of factory-owned cars with 'CTC ...E' plates. CTC was not, however, an Essex number but it was an acronym for Cortina Twin Cam, which made it all worthwhile.

CTC 23E was allocated to one of the first batch of works cars to be prepared at Boreham, and after originally appearing at some TV rallycross events it was made ready for Roger Clark to drive in the 1967 RAC rally. Like other team cars in that event it ran in FIA Group 5 condition and was fitted with TJ fuel injection, but we will never know how it would have fared because the event was cancelled on the night before the start.

Still factory-fresh, therefore, it was entered for the snow-bound Swedish rally of January 1968, but as driver Roger Clark was suffering from influenza during the event and showed no signs of improving, he retired part way through.

Months later, when Ford was preparing for the London-Sydney Marathon, Walter Hayes decided to loan a car to the British Army Motoring Association, for Captain David Harrison and Lieutenant Martin Proudlock to drive. This was prepared by the crew themselves, but with a total works kit of parts supplied, and although it was not officially a works car it stood to gain complete support if time could be found for it at service points where the Boreham team was in evidence. Because they started from No. 90, clearly they might be low down in the me-

*Capt. Harrison starts out on the London-Sydney in CTC 23E.*

chanics' priorities if time was tight. The fuel-injection system which the car had used in Roger Clark's hands was abandoned in favour of the conventional twin-choke Weber installation. Like all the other Boreham-specified cars, it was effectively prepared to a 'Safari-plus' specification, which is to say that the bodyshell was stiffened up wherever possible, the engine tune was part-way between road-car and full European Group 2 spec., and the transmission and back axle ratios were standard except that a limited-slip differential was fitted.

By what one might whimsically call 'Marathon standards – which means that the car hit at least one wild animal along the way and went off the road more than once – it had a relatively trouble-free run. Although Captain Harrison had a steady run to Turkey, he then lost 48 minutes on the tight Sivas-Erzincan section, no fewer than 206 minutes before the Kabul (Afghanistan) control, and a further 17 minutes on the Kabul-Sarobi section. Yet he struggled on to Bombay, where he was placed 45th overall. The car was still relatively fit during the dash across Australia, but there was one time-consuming delay due to the car going off the road, for he lost another 324 minutes in total, but still managed to reach Sydney in 30th position.

This BAMA team never saw the car again after the finish. Capt. Harrison believes it was scrapped in Australia rather than returned to the UK. This had been a very brave effort by a crew who had never before tackled such a long and arduous event.

*CTC 23E was originally intended for Roger Clark to drive in the 1967 RAC rally, when it had TJ fuel injection fitted, but that event was cancelled just before the start. Weeks later Roger drove it in the 1968 Swedish rally but was suffering from influenza and had to retire. Later it was re-prepared, reverted to Weber carburettors instead of TJ injection, and was lent to Capt. David Harrison of the British Army to contest the 1968 London-Sydney Marathon, where he finished in a creditable 30th place.*

**Competition Record**

| | | |
|---|---|---|
| 1967 TV rallycross events | Roger Clark/Graham Hill | Various, unplaced |
| 1967 RAC | Roger Clark | Rally cancelled |
| 1968 Swedish | Roger Clark | DNF |
| 1968 London-Sydney marathon | Loaned to Capt. David Harrison, BAMA | 30th |

| REGISTRATION NUMBER | ENGINE SIZE | MODEL TYPE |
|---|---|---|
| **CTC 26E** | **1558CC 4-CYL DOHC** | **LOTUS CORTINA MK II** |

Although this works rally car carried an early 1967 registration number (like CTC 23E it was one of the original Lotus-Cortina Mk II press/launch cars), it had no competition career until it was prepared for the London-Sydney Marathon of 1968, when as a completely refurbished machine it was allocated to Bengt Soderstrom and Gunnar Palm. This crew had been among the most successful of all Ford works drivers in recent years.

Technically the car was almost the same as the one driven by Roger Clark and Eric Jackson, and it looked likely to be among the front runners throughout. "I did all the recces for the team," Gunnar told me, "I did London to Bombay with John Davenport, then Perth to Sydney with Bill Barnett, though we broke the car's steering half-way across the Australian desert and had to reverse for 26 miles."

Unhappily, on the event itself there were mechanical problems almost at once: "On the rally, after only two days, the Lotus-Cortina broke a cam follower, and we had to buy a replacement from a private owner in Italy. We had a mechanic flown to Milan to make the repair, lost 12 hours waiting, drove flat out to Belgrade, and made up all the time. Then we passed into Turkey, and a piston hit a valve." The phlegmatic Soderstrom shrugged it off and made for the nearest restaurant, then a plane back to Stockholm. The car was eventually rescued and returned to the UK, while Gunnar carried on with the remnants of the support team to the end.

Gunnar then joined forces with Ove Anderson for the next three years, then Hannu Mikkola for three years after that, and added stellar successes such as the 1970 World Cup and the 1972 East African Safari to his CV along the way.

As to the car, there were no more works events for it to do, so it was sold off.

*Bengt Soderstrom, partnered by Gunnar Palm, in CTC 26E close to Big Ben on the first day of the London-Sydney Marathon. Unhappily the engine of their Lotus-Cortina went sick in Italy.*

**Competition Record**

| | | |
|---|---|---|
| 1968 London-Sydney Marathon | Bengt Soderstrom | DNF |

| REGISTRATION NUMBER | ENGINE SIZE | MODEL TYPE |
|---|---|---|
| **VPI 77 (REGISTERED IN IRELAND)** | **1558CC 4-CYL DOHC** | **LOTUS CORTINA MK II** |

The appearance of a Republic of Ireland registration number in this listing is easily explained, for although prepared as a works entry at Boreham, the car was nominally owned by Ford-of-Ireland, and the principal driver was Dublin-resident Rosemary Smith. As an extremely successful rally driver (she won the Tulip rally outright in 1965, for instance) Rose-mary been faithful to the Rootes Group/Sunbeam works team throughout the 1960s and earlier-Cortina period, but found herself without a drive in 1968 as their works team slimmed down considerably. After Rootes decided to enter only one car (a Hillman Hunter) in the London-Sydney Marathon, she readily accepted an offer from her native Ford organisation, and joined forces with Frenchwoman Lucette Pointet, who normally rallied in a Citroen DS.

Although Rosemary had not previously rallied a Lotus-Cortina she was used to powerful machines, including the works Sunbeam Tiger, and she soon settled into this new right-hand-drive car from Boreham. Unpenalised up to the control at Sivas, in Turkey, she then lost 45 minutes on the long and tough section to Erzincan in Eastern Turkey. Pressing on, the car then blew a piston on the run in towards Kabul in Afghanistan, lost more than three hours at that control, and was then immobilised for ages while the piston, complete with its connecting rod, was removed. So they limped on with a three-cylinder Lotus-Cortina.

64th on arrival in Bombay – only eight other crews were behind them – they nevertheless found time to have the engine further patched up by the Ford mechanics before carrying on from Fremantle in the Australian section. It was typical of this driver that, although she always looked pin-neat and feminine, she also had amazing toughness and resilience. In the next few days she kept the ailing machine going (it had serious suspension problems, and the clutch packed up on the very last section), lost time only where the majority of competitors also did so, and ended up 48th of the 56 survivors.

*Rosemary Smith in the Boreham-built, but Ford-of-Ireland supported, Lotus-Cortina VPI 77 getting started in the London-Sydney.*

| Competition Record | | |
|---|---|---|
| 1968 London-Sydney Marathon | Rosemary Smith | 48th |

| REGISTRATION NUMBER | ENGINE SIZE | MODEL TYPE |
|---|---|---|
| **VVW 506E** | **1558CC 4-CYL DOHC** | **LOTUS CORTINA MK II** |

Although this car later achieved notoriety as the one which blew its engine in Australia with Roger Clark well on his way to winning the London-Sydney Marathon outright, it was not new for that event. First completed in 1967, it was originally allocated as Ford's 'publicity' entry in the RAC rally of that year, where it was to be driven by F1 World Champion Graham Hill, with regular team driver David Seigle-Morris as his co-driver. Hill had practiced seriously at Bagshot before the event, including rolling a test car and complaining of a broken windscreen (broken it was, along with much else!). For the rally itself, this new car was entered in FIA Group 5, with a number of non-homologated items in the specification.

As is well known, the rally was cancelled just 12 hours before it was due to start due to the unstoppable spread of bovine Foot-and-Mouth disease over countryside which the rally would have covered. As a consequence Hill never got his works Cortina drive, and (although this was his aim) could not prove that he was just as fast as Jim Clark had been in 1966. Instead, he and David Seigle-Morris shared the car in a rallycross event at Lydden Hill circuit in Kent before it went back into hibernation while Boreham began its build-up of the Escort Twin-Cam programme in 1968.

It was not until the late summer of 1968 that work began again on the car, to prepare it to what we might call long-distance/Safari-type standards, so that it could take part in the London-Sydney marathon, which was due to start in late November. There is no doubt that when that event finally got under way, Roger Clark and his co-driver Ove Andersson were hot favourites to win and to lift the £10,000 first prize.

In the first ten days everything went very much according to plan, for although there were no planned night halts there were only two long high-speed sections to be tackled. Roger won both of these stages and led the event at Bombay, where the cars were loaded on the *SS Chusan* for the long voyage to Fremantle in Western Australia.

Following the re-start from Fremantle (the Indian Ocean port for Perth), Clark led off as the leading car and was expecting to reach the control at Quorn with at least two hours to spare when it happened. To quote Roger: "Suddenly there was a bang from the engine, a clattering noise, and we only had three cylinders.... I suspected something serious. All I could do was crawl on and hope for the best." After teammate Eric Jackson had stopped to ascertain the damage (see the YVW 41F entry), the stricken car struggled on and reached its service workshops at Port Augusta, where the team soon discovered that a valve had broken and damaged a piston. As is now known, team co-ordinator Bill Barnett took the decision to commandeer the head from Eric Jackson's otherwise healthy car, and finally sent the car on ahead in a vain chase.

Roger drove very rapidly, even by his own other-worldly levels, and began to regain positions, but all was then lost when, less than 24 hours from the end, there was another disaster as the differential bolts sheared. The pantomime surrounding Roger's finding of a spectator/local fisherman who would 'lend' him an axle from his own Cortina has often been told – and suffice it to say that it was another two hours before that change could be made. The result was that the much-overworked car finally finished 10th and, incidentally, the only Lotus-Cortina on the leader-board. It was the last time it would be used as a works rally car.

*With the competition numbers on the doors blanked off to meet local traffic laws in Western Australia, Roger Clark's Lotus-Cortina is driven from the docks at Fremantle to the official Perth re-start control.*

## Competition Record

| | | |
|---|---|---|
| 1967 RAC | Graham Hill | Rally cancelled |
| 1967 Lydden Hill rallycross | Graham Hill and Roger Clark | |
| 1968 London-Sydney Marathon | Roger Clark | 10th |

| REGISTRATION NUMBER | ENGINE SIZE | MODEL TYPE |
|---|---|---|
| **YVW 2F** | **1558CC 4-CYL DOHC** | **LOTUS CORTINA MK II** |

During the 1960s, Nick Brittan progressed from being an impecunious club race driver to an astute, thrusting PR man/publicist, who also established himself as a competent race car driver in cars like the 'Green Bean' Anglia, and fast little Rallye Imps produced by the Fraser team for the Chrysler factory.

It was his high profile, and his ability to bring a good story, if not results, to an event, which encouraged Ford to loan him a so-far-unrallied Lotus-Cortina for the London-Sydney Marathon. For Nick, and for Ford, this was a big leap in the dark, for the car itself had no rally record (it had started life as a fleet/demonstration car), Nick's co-driver was his wife Jenny, who had no motorsport experience at all, while Nick himself was about to tackle his very first serious rally.

Starting just a few minutes behind the rally favourite – Nick at No. 56, Roger Clark No. 48 – he could perhaps hope to dog the master's footsteps on the transport sections,

*Nick and Jenny Brittan had the use of this Boreham-built Lotus-Cortina, YVW 2F, for the 1968 London-Sydney Marathon. Jenny is driving in this gentle study taken on Westminster Bridge in London.*

but had no hope of being competitive where flat-out motoring was needed. It did not take long (by this marathon's standards) to prove that point. Although he was on time as far as Turkey, this, according to rally correspondent John Sprinzel, is what happened after that: "About 100 miles outside Sivas the Ford Lotus-Cortina driven by the Brittans hit a horse, and they had to drive the remainder of the stage with freezing rain lashing through the broken screen. They lost a lot of time getting a replacement, and had to miss the Teheran control, which gave them an automatic 24 hour penalty. Nick, a determined if not expert rally driver, would have liked to struggle on, but soon concluded that there was no point in struggling all the way to Sydney and finishing 'down among the dead men', so the car was withdrawn at the Kabul control."

The car was never again used by the factory, and accordingly leaves this story.

---

**Competition Record**

| 1968 London-Sydney Marathon | Nick Brittan | DNF |
| --- | --- | --- |

---

| REGISTRATION NUMBER | ENGINE SIZE | MODEL TYPE |
| --- | --- | --- |
| **YVW 41F** | **1558CC 4-CYL DOHC** | **LOTUS CORTINA MK II** |

---

Well ahead of the start of the London-Sydney Marathon, Eric Jackson's entry was looked on as Ford's 'banker' for the entire event, because this was a 10,000-mile marathon, Eric and his co-driver Ken Chambers were both seasoned long-distance trek experts, and these two heroes had already completed much of the mileage (in the reverse direction) when tackling 'round-the-world in 40 days' (as detailed in Chapter 4 on Corsairs).

Although originally built a year before preparation began, YVW 41F had led a blameless and stress-free life as a road car before 1968. Jackson and Chambers had no difficulty in keeping up with the schedule on the immensely long road sections, and a total of 31 penalty minutes on the two long stages which took place before the cars reached Bombay meant that they were handily placed at ninth.

The sprint ('sprint'? There was still 3,000 miles to go!) started well, and Eric calculated that they were already up to sixth place, when suddenly they came upon Roger Clark's stricken car (VVW 506E) at the side of the road, with an engine which was making horrible noises and was clearly in big trouble. Although they were powerless to help on the spot, Jackson and Chambers then took note of the problem, gave what encouragement that they could, and rushed off to the next control at Quorn to warn Bill Barnett, Mick Jones and Ken Wiltshire of the problem.

As noted in the description of VVW 506E's career, the result was that the complete cylinder head assembly of Jackson's car was removed to be fitted to Clark's car, which was still in the lead at that time. This immobilised the Jackson car and caused its immediate retirement.

Rallying legend, circulated by Ford at the time, was that Jackson had freely donated his car's head and opted for retirement 'for the greater good', but in later years Eric insisted, and still does insist, that he had no choice in the matter. In

*This was the packed start of the London-Sydney Marathon from Crystal Palace in south London, with Ford's Eric Jackson in YVW 41F about to roll off the start ramp.*

view of what happened to other cars in the last two days of the event, Eric was convinced that his hitherto healthy Lotus-Cortina could have finished in the top three, even possibly win the event.

Like other Ford works cars used on this Marathon, it was not used on any future event.

---

**Competition Record**

| 1968 London-Sydney Marathon | Eric Jackson | DNF |
| --- | --- | --- |

| REGISTRATION NUMBER | ENGINE SIZE | MODEL TYPE |
|---|---|---|
| **WVX 306F** | **1558cc 4-cyl DOHC** | **LOTUS CORTINA MK II** |

This one-event wonder (at least, in Boreham works terms), painted in dark green and carrying acres of Gulf Oil sponsorship, appeared only on the 1968 Swedish rally, but had not been seen before this nor would it ever be seen again. Originally prepared at Boreham for entry in the 1968 Safari rally, a change of priorities dictated by work on the Escort Twin-Cam mean that it was diverted to the Swedish instead, and like the sister cars on the same event (UVW 924E and CTC 23E) it had TJ fuel injection.

Unhappily, on an early stage close to the start at Karlstad, the throttle linkage collapsed, and although it was soon repaired it collapsed yet again (on a lengthy 100km special stage), stranding the car and bringing its rally to a close. It was not seen again as a works rally car.

*The very last works Lotus-Cortina built for use in Europe, WVX 306F, which was driven briefly by Ove Andersson on the Swedish rally of January 1968. It featured fuel injection, which was not a success as a linkage failure caused the car to retire on an early special stage.*

**Competition Record**

| 1968 Swedish | Ove Andersson | DNF |
|---|---|---|

| REGISTRATION NUMBER | ENGINE SIZE | MODEL TYPE |
|---|---|---|
| **WWC 465F** | **1558cc 4-cyl DOHC** | **LOTUS CORTINA MK II** |

The last and most enigmatic works Mk II of all was prepared in 1967/68 as a 'Safari-type' of development car but never appeared on a single event. It was vitally important to Ford's on-going efforts, however, as it was used extensively as a test car for many on-going projects at Boreham, including what became the team's final use of Lotus-Cortinas, in the London-Sydney Marathon of November 1968.

Before then, however, the same identity (WWC 465F) had appeared on the first definitive Escort Twin-Cam prototype, which was built in the autumn of 1967 and which appeared in photoshoots in December 1967/January 1968. Although no written records now survive to confirm this, it is almost certain that it was the original donor car that enabled Mick Jones and Ken Wiltshire to assemble the first Escort Twin-Cam.

**Competition Record**

| 1967 | Test/component car for 1968 Escort Twin-Cam project |
|---|---|
| 1968 | Test car for London-Sydney Marathon project |

No actual starts in major competitions.

*In preparing for the London-Sydney Marathon of 1968, Boreham built up an all-can-do test car, WWC 465F, which had previously been central to the development of the original Escort Twin-Cam model. These shots were taken at the Bagshot facility in the summer of 1968.*

## WORKS MK II RALLY CAR PERFORMANCE – AN *AUTOCAR* ROAD TEST

In July 1967 Ove Andersson and John Davenport drove a works Lotus-Cortina Mk II (UVW 924E, in Saluki Bronze) to outright victory in the gruelling Gulf London rally, covering hundreds of miles of rough Forestry Commission special stages in three days and nights without a single night halt. After an event-long battle with two Swedish-built Porsche 911s, UVW 924E won outright. Only 47 of the 120 starters completed the event.

Within a week of this famous victory, and after no more than a quick service, a wash, and a look-see back at Boreham, this hard-worked and frankly somewhat creaky car was lent to *Autocar* magazine for the 'Given the Works' performance test treatment, where the lucky drivers were technical editor Geoff Howard and myself. The account of that test, which was carried out in a hot July week, in central London, on the public highways and at the MIRA proving grounds near Nuneaton, covering no less than 630 miles, was published in a three-page feature in the issue of 14 September 1967.

Geoff Howard wrote: "It was a hot and sticky day when I arrived at the seclusion of Boreham airfield where the test track and competition department are housed. The car was left-hand-drive and exactly as it finished the rally". We were told: "No real rev limit but *please* don't burst the engine, and watch out for the odd characteristics of the limited-slip diff".

It was odd to find that the car was equipped only with lap-strap seat belts. The car seemed quite content to deal with commuting traffic in London (*Autocar*'s offices were then just south of the Thames, close to Waterloo railway station. The engine idle speed was set at 1,000rpm and between us we set a self-imposed upper rev-limit of 7500rpm. The engine delivered about 150bhp, and had been prepared by BRM, though at this time it was clearly somewhat tired after its ordeal. Complete with twin-choke Weber carburettors (the TJ fuel-injection system had not been fitted to this car) and an exhaust system which had taken a real battering on the rough special stages, the car emitted the sorts of noises which sent Howard into raptures: "The crescendo of mechanical whine, throb and beat as the revs build up, which drops momentarily when gears are switched and then continues in a different key, is something which has to be experienced. An American magazine once described it as something to make a grown man scream with ecstasy and I can't think of a better way of putting it, although I just became flushed and tingled inside. The limited-slip differential was deliberately slack to give some flexibility and insulation from vicious torque reversals. It made the most alarming crunch each time it freed, like someone standing on a wine glass."

As far as most enthusiasts are concerned, however, it is the performance figures which tell most of the story. These were taken at MIRA by Howard and the author on a warm, dry day, the car still running on the special Goodyear rough-surface special tyres and Minilite wheels on which it had finished the Gulf London Rally. Here are the relevant figures, along with a comparison with a standard Lotus-Cortina press car (CTC 25E) which the magazine had just tested in August 1967:

| | Works rally car (UVW 924E) | Standard road test car (CTC 25E) |
|---|---|---|
| Maximum speed in gears (mph) | 4.70:1 final drive | 3.78:1 final drive |
| Top | 97 | 104 |
| 3rd | 75 | 83 |
| 2nd | 57 | 58 |
| 1st | 42 | 39 |
| | | |
| Acceleration from rest (secs) to | | |
| 30mph | 3.7 | 3.6 |
| 40mph | 5.0 | 5.6 |
| 50mph | 6.9 | 7.9 |
| 60mph | 9.4 | 11.0 |
| 70mph | 12.1 | 14.9 |
| 80mph | 16.3 | 20.1 |
| 90mph | 21.1 | 30.9 |
| 100mph | - | 44.0 |
| Standing start quarter mile | 17.1 | 18.2 |
| | | |
| Top gear acceleration (secs) | | |
| 10-30mph | - | 10.0 |
| 20-40mph | 9.4 | 10.0 |
| 30-50mph | 7.7 | 9.8 |
| 40-60mph | 7.8 | 10.6 |
| 50-70mph | 7.5 | 12.4 |
| 60-80mph | 7.5 | 15.4 |
| 70-90mph | 8.7 | 18.7 |
| 80-100mph | | 23.2 |

# CHAPTER 6:
# SAFARI, THE BIGGEST CHALLENGE

Of all the great rallies being run in the 1960s, the one most feared by all the serious works teams was the East African Safari. At that time Britain still had a thriving Empire in which the three adjoining countries of Kenya, Uganda and Tanzania provided an important market. Ford, like every other European car manufacturer, wanted more than a reasonable share of that market, and saw promotional events like the Safari as an opportunity to show off their wares, especially as the regulations demanded the use of standard-specification cars (later these would officially become 'Group 1').

Right from the start of what was originally called the Coronation Safari in 1953, there was support for the Kenyan Ford importers (Hughes Ltd of Nairobi). Local motor trader Vic Preston and DP Marwaha won the event outright in a Ford Zephyr in 1955, and full works teams (and considerable factory support 'on the ground') followed in the next few years.

No sooner had the Cortina been launched than Ford began to prepare or enter full-blown factory teams, at first in 1963 Cortina Supers, later Cortina GTs, and finally Lotus-Cortinas. Sometimes these were 'official' team entries, with European-based drivers, and sometimes they were Boreham-prepared but entered and run by Peter Hughes's business in Nairobi, with the very best of local drivers. On every occasion they were competitive, and in six years, 1963 to 1968 inclusive, there was one outright victory, three second places, three third places, four class wins and three Manufacturers' team victories, a formidable record by any standards.

The following is the year-by-year summary of that period.

## Works Cortinas on Safari in 1963

Although Ford entered a large team of cars in the 1963 Safari rally – Anglia 105Es, Zephyrs and Cortinas – this was not a successful expedition, and has almost been brushed away by Ford into the shadowy archive of their motorsport past. It is worth recalling, however, just how hard they tried to win this, their first visit to the Safari with Cortinas, for it was one of the most difficult events ever promoted, with only seven finishers (of whom Peter Hughes's works Anglia 105E finished a storming second overall).

Because they had to be entered before the Cortina GT was even announced, and certainly before it even approached sporting homologation, the cars prepared and entered were two-door Cortina Supers, with the 1.5-litre engine, but not the GT engine tune. The badging on the cars, as seen in the event, confirms this. Those were the days, too, when the Safari was run for strictly FIA-regulated Group 1 cars, which meant that almost no homologated extras could be used either.

The works Cortina Supers only ever competed in this single event – the Cortina GT was homologated in April 1963. The cars were prepared at Lincoln Cars in Brentford (Boreham was still being built), and were driven by Pat Moss, Peter Riley, Anne Hall and Bo Younghusband – three works drivers and a local.

The cars were all registered locally in Kenya on arrival (which explains the KHL ... number plate sequence), and were not re-imported to the UK for further rallying after the event.

This was probably the most punishing of all Safaris, for although the time schedule was extended to ensure at least a few finishers, only seven cars of the 84 starters completed the event. None of the four Cortinas finished, although they had looked extremely competitive until well beyond half distance. The event started, finished and had its rest halt at Nairobi in Kenya, but also visited Uganda and Tanganyika (now Tanzania), and covered 3180 miles. All sections were on public 'roads', the set average speeds sometimes being well over 50mph and quite impossible to meet. Conditions varied from boiling hot to warm torrential rain, and mud was one of the biggest obstacles.

Pat Moss eventually crashed her car, as did Anne Hall, while Peter Riley's struck the hidden ramp of a culvert. There was much licking of wounds after this debacle. Better preparation would be needed to make the Cortina competitive in Africa, and when Boreham opened up in the autumn of 1963 that failing would speedily be rectified. When an equally massive team invaded East Africa at Easter in 1964 the result was a total triumph.

| REGISTRATION NUMBER | ENGINE SIZE | MODEL TYPE |
|---|---|---|
| **KHL 871** | **1498CC 4-CYL OHV** | **CORTINA SUPER** |

For local man Bo Younghusband, the chance to take a works drive in a Cortina was accepted with great speed, even though he had not rallied such a car before, and the fact that it was not going to be very fast did not deter him. Local knowledge, the driving 'bushcraft' which could only be gathered by having much previous experience, all helped enormously, the result being that by the time the cars returned to Nairobi after the original 36-hour northern loop Younghusband was in second place overall, headed only by Erik Carlsson's amazing two-stroke Saab.

Later, in the southern loop, Carlsson's Saab had to retire, and for the moment this put Younghusband's Cortina in to the lead (closely followed by his team-mate and rival Peter Hughes in an Anglia 105E). Only 23 cars were still running – surely the storybook miracle could not be achieved on this, the Cortina's first Safari? Sadly it could not. During the night, on the long drag back towards Nairobi from Dar-es-Salaam on the Tanganyika coast, the Cortina holed its sump, dumping all the oil and destroying the engine. The last of the works Cortinas, therefore, was eliminated.

*Bo Younghusband about to set off on the 1963 Safari in his Cortina Super, KHK 871.*

**Competition Record**

| 1963 East African Safari | Bo Younghusband | DNF |
|---|---|---|

| REGISTRATION NUMBER | ENGINE SIZE | MODEL TYPE |
|---|---|---|
| **KHL 484** | **1498CC 4-CYL OHV** | **CORTINA SUPER** |

Peter Riley's first Safari in a works Cortina started well, even though his car shed most of its exhaust system at one stage (Peter Garnier of *Autocar* later described it as coming up a long uphill section "in a great cloud of dust, its silencer gone and the car sounding wonderful").

Helped along by the advice of his local Kenyan co-driver, he was nevertheless holding on to seventh place at the halfway halt and – most important to the publicists – the team was currently holding the lead in the Manufacturers' Team Prize.

Unhappily, on the southern loop Riley's car suffered several misfortunes, first when the front suspension was bent by a major impact. Later the car went off the straight-and-narrow and hit a large section of a concrete culvert, which destroyed the front suspension and immobilised the machine for good – and broke a bone in co-driver David Markham's foot too. Retirement was inevitable. The car was not seen again in International motorsport.

*Peter Riley was only a member of the works team for one season, 1963. Here he is seen in the wild country of the Safari in KHL 484.*

**Competition Record**

| 1963 East African Safari | Peter Riley | DNF |
|---|---|---|

| REGISTRATION NUMBER | ENGINE SIZE | MODEL TYPE |
|---|---|---|
| KHL 487 | 1498CC 4-CYL OHV | CORTINA SUPER |

This was to be Pat Moss's first-ever outing in a Cortina, and although pre-event hopes were high, there was no doubt that the Super, with only about 60bhp, and with raised suspension to improve the ground clearance, was a great come-down from the 200bhp Austin-Healeys she had been more used to driving in the BMC rally team. Pat was as grittily determined as usual, but things did not start well on the first night when the Cortina slid off a muddy track and needed a quick tow from Anne Hall's sister car to make it mobile again. Pat returned the compliment some hours later, then once again went off the road – it was going to be that sort of rally.

As was later noted in Pat's biography *Harnessing Horsepower*, after the rest halt in Nairobi there was a third excursion near Mbulu, when the car slid sideways down a bank in the dark and subsided quite gently on to its roof. This time the roof had flattened (there were no roll cages in rally cars at that stage), the glass had all shattered, it was raining hard, and even with the help of some local farmers the battered machine, once recovered, would not start. Retirement, a welcome hot bath and some breakfast seemed to be the best option, which Pat and Anne Riley duly took. As for the car, as far as is known that was the end of its short and ignoble works rallying career.

*Pat Moss joined the team at Boreham for the 1963 rally season. Here she is with Ann Riley about to start the 1963 Safari in her Cortina Super, KHL 487.*

*Pat Moss, in KHL 487, fraternising with a local Kenyan boy when training for the 1963 Safari.*

**Competition Record**

| 1963 East African Safari | Pat Moss | DNF |
|---|---|---|

| REGISTRATION NUMBER | ENGINE SIZE | MODEL TYPE |
|---|---|---|
| KHL 488 | 1498CC 4-CYL OHV | CORTINA SUPER |

In 1963, no question, Anne Hall thought she had a point to prove, for although she had previously been the acknowledged 'leading lady' in the Ford team for some time, the arrival of Pat Moss (who was being paid handsomely) in 1963 made her situation difficult. Even so, she started the Safari with high hopes, as she had figured well in previous outings, and within hours she provided help to Pat by pulling her Cortina out of a muddy ditch near the Ugandan border. Anne kept plugging on, and at the halfway halt back in Nairobi she was in fourth place overall.

Everything went well after the re-start, until not even the car's sump guard could protect the engine, the sump pan was punctured, and lengthy repairs needed to be made. Teammate Peter Riley stopped and offered a tow to the nearest garage where Ford mechanics could provide assistance, and somehow or other the machine kept going, with Anne looking set to win the Coupe des Dames competition. Finally, on the last glutinous night, the Cortina became bogged down once again, could not be retrieved and (in picturesque Safari language) became 'Time Barred'.

*Anne Hall ready to start the 1963 Safari from Nairobi in KHL 488.*

*Anne Hall, here seen in the 1963 Safari in the works Cortina Super, had been a regular in the team for some years but was soon supplanted by Pat Moss.*

*Louise Cardwell takes her turn to drive Anne Hall's Cortina Super in the 1963 Safari. This was the only occasion on which Ford used Cortina Supers, which had been prepared at Lincoln Cars.*

**Competition Record**

| 1963 East African Safari | Anne Hall | DNF |
|---|---|---|

## Safari – Works victory in 1964

Ford's victory in the 1964 East African Safari, using Group 1 Cortina GTs, was so remarkable that it deserves individual study, especially as development of these cars was still at an early stage. As team co-ordinator Bill Barnett once commented, "It was really 'blacksmith engineering' at that time – first we would improve the engines, then modify the gearboxes, but we continued to blow up rear axles … and once we'd sorted that out, the drivers would be back, demanding more power."

Those were the days in when the East African Safari was still the world's most important rally, covering more than 3000 miles in five days, with only one peaceful overnight halt. . The roads were so awful, and the schedule speeds so high that special stages were simply not necessary. Rougher than any other, hotter, more unpredictable, and sometimes downright dangerous, it was the ultimate challenge. Heavy rain could fall with little notice, dirt tracks could become quagmires, and river crossing could become impassable. Not only that, but jay-walking elephants could be a real problem.

It is easy to forget just how standard the cars had to be. Appendix J Group 1 rules applied which, in theory at least, meant that near-showroom condition models had to used. It all depended on how much had already been homologated – and there's no doubt that the hand-prepared body shells were much stiffer and more robust than those which Dagenham was churning out every day. Fittings such as twin fuel tanks (there was an extra Cortina-estate tank behind the rear seat) and wide-rim steel wheels had somehow slipped into the homologation papers for 'standard' showroom cars.

Difficult to believe, maybe, but those Safari-winning works cars probably had no more than 85bhp, used drum brakes at the rear, and had difficulty in getting extra strong rear leaf springs past the scrutineers. To ensure more protection from the awful tracks, front and rear suspensions were lifted just as far as possible, and knobbly tyres were always specified. An enormous effort went into waterproofing the engines – this, as we shall see, being justified by the results. Puny one-inch diameter roll-over hoops were fitted in the cabin but did not add much to bodyshell rigidity.

Since the cars had to be shipped out to East Africa rather than airfreighted, the six brand-new two-door Cortina GTs had to leave Britain in January, which explains why there wasn't time for Ford to take part in many European events during the winter of 1963/64. Visually these cars showed off Ford's hard-won trade support deals, which included Total for petrol, Castrol for oil and Dunlop for tyres.

Unregistered when they left the UK, they acquired a sequence of Kenyan numbers, KHS 595 to KHS 600, once they arrived. Kenyan Import and Export regulations were very strict, which explains, maybe, why the identities don't look familiar, and why we never saw them back in European afterwards.

Ford already had a great record in the Safari, so picking a competitive driving team was no problem. Of the six, three were British (Vic Elford, Henry Taylor and John Sprinzel), and three were Kenyan-domiciled (Peter Hughes, Mike Armstrong and Bo Younghusband). All three Kenyans had previous Safari success behind them, Peter Hughes having finished second in an Anglia 105E in 1963. Although John Sprinzel and Peter Garnier both had much rally experience, this was their first-ever Safari together. Sprinzel had Fleet Street connections, and Garnier was *Autocar*'s Sports Editor, so this was effectively a 'media' car.

Where local expertise was needed – knowing where to push and where to cruise, how to find grip on slippery surfaces, and how to cope with deep water and flash floods – local drivers like Peter Hughes might be unbeatable. Where ultra-fast driving and sheer on-the-limit bravery were needed, then it was the Europeans, particularly Vic Elford and Henry Taylor, who would figure highly. Betting men looked wisely at the Henry Taylor/Jack Simonian combination, for Taylor was a fast Brit, and Simonian was not merely a local co-driver but a fast and capable driver too.

Although Boreham had a new Competition Manager, Alan Platt, in 1964, it was co-ordinator Bill Barnett who masterminded the build-up to the event. Standard Cortinas were sent out to the event for drivers to practice, the unofficial 'distance' awards going to Peter Hughes and John Sprinzel, who claimed to have spent three weeks out in the bush, completing the most difficult sections at least nine times. "Because Sprinzel's co-driver, Peter Garnier, couldn't find the time," Barnett recalls, "I surveyed the entire Safari route with Sprinzel, which

*This group shot in Nairobi shows how serious Ford was about winning the Safari in 1964 in Cortina GTs. Do not get too excited by the display of rally cars at the front, for KHS 599 should be carrying a different Competition Number, as should KHS 595 alongside it. All would be settled before the start, however.*

was an ideal way of settling all the service points … All in all I spent six or seven weeks in Africa."

For Ford this was the biggest and most important entry that the Cortina GT would ever make. Frustrated by the regulations – no matter what improvements were feasible, the rules made sure they were illegal – they could only rely on preparation, the mechanics' expertise, and attention to detail. Peter Ashcroft, Bill Meade and Mick Jones were all among the new boys at Boreham and in the years which followed they were always proud of what had been achieved.

It wasn't the heat that was going to hurt the Cortinas but the battering they would receive. If the rains came, local drivers could be trusted to tiptoe their way through the floods, but where it was dry the bodyshells, dampers and wheels could all be expected to suffer. This was where Ford's local experts, like Vic Preston and Peter Hughes, were so valuable. Back at Boreham, Rally Engineer Jack Welch and his team were still learning about the Cortina structure (earlier cars had already coped well with the Acropolis and Spa-Sofia-Liège rallies in 1963), but the locals could now add their own knowledge. Heavy duty tyres, they insisted, were more important than ultimate grip, high ground clearance was vital, and a high-mounted auxiliary driving lamp would be invaluable.

Nothing was left to chance. Ford put in more intensive practice than they had ever previously carried out. The cars were as strong as possible. The most expert crews had been hired. The service back up – six Cortina estate cars, each with a Boreham crew on board, and a chartered Cessna light aircraft – was as comprehensive as possible. Everything, though, depended on the weather, for in East Africa at Easter-time the rainy season was likely to arrive with real ferocity. This time around it was to be an early Easter, so would it rain? Let's just say that at the pre-event drivers' briefing a Kenyan meteorological expert walked up to the platform carrying an open umbrella above his head! The point was taken.

Tactics? As far as Ford was concerned, there were no tactics and no team orders. Vic Elford was already convinced that he was the fastest rally driver in the world and was out to prove it, Peter Hughes wanted to improve on his second place in 1963, and team-leader Henry Taylor wanted to make his point to all his other team mates. The rally team, in any case, was aching for a victory – any victory – so a morale boost was needed. Their most recent Ford outright win had been by Gerry Burgess's Zephyr in the RAC rally of 1959. More than four years on, and following the move from Lincoln Cars in Brentford to the new buildings at Boreham, another win was overdue.

Right away, on the gruelling northern loop, it was clear that the weather and driver problems, more than mechanical frailty, could stop the Cortinas. First to suffer was John Sprinzel, whose appendix chose that day to flare up; difficulty in urging the Cortina to climb a steep and slippery hill didn't help. Even so, when the field reached Kampala, the leading Cortinas were first, second, fourth and fifth, with local heroes Mike

*A pre-Safari briefing meeting, held at the Hughes premises in Nairobi under the guidance of Rally Co-ordinator Bill Barnett (closest to the camera). John Sprinzel is to Bill's left, Peter Hughes to Sprinzel's left, and that is Vic Elford across the table, pencil in hand.*

Armstrong and Peter Hughes up front.

When the 62 survivors reached Nairobi, all six Cortinas were still running – the top four placed 1-2-5-6 – with Mike Armstrong leading and with Erik Carlsson's Saab and Lucille Cardwell's Mercedes-Benz 220SEb still in the hunt. Only Vic Elford's car, with damaged suspension, had suffered badly.

Then came the second, southern loop, down to Dar es Salaam on the coast and back, where the floods were extensive and the rivers were in spate. Hours, not minutes, could be lost if a crew was unlucky, and many were. Taylor's and Elford's cars both ended up stranded in floods at one point, while Sprinzel's car went off the road once too often and shattered its steering. Henry Taylor's car broke a MacPherson strut,

*Members of Ford's winning team surround KHS 600, winner of the East African Safari in 1964. Among the personalities present were Peter Ashcroft (blue shirt), and (left to right behind the car) Jack Welch, Bill Barnett, Leon Baillon, Vic Elford, Peter Hughes (on the roof), Bill Young, Mike Armstrong and EC Bates. Team boss Alan Platt is in the dark suit in front of Armstrong.*

then a driveshaft, and was forced out.

Before the cars got back to Nairobi, bush-master Peter Hughes had overtaken Mike Armstrong, who was also overtaken by the remarkable Carlsson/Saab 96 combination, but four Cortinas made it to the finish. Not only had two thirds of the team survived (when only a quarter of the rest of the field made it), but they had performed magnificently. They took outright victory and 1-2-3-4 in their capacity class, and lifted the much coveted Manufacturers' Team trophy too.

Writing about his experiences in *Autocar* a few weeks later, Peter Garnier described this as a 'Jumping Jackpot', and no-one disagreed with him. It would be eight more years, with the talents of the Escort RS1600 and Hannu Mikkola, before Ford repeated the trick.

This was the make-up of the six-car team:

| Competition No | Crew | Registration |
|---|---|---|
| 2 | M P Armstrong/E C Bates | KHS 596 |
| 4 | P Hughes/W Young | KHS 600 |
| 3 | B Younghusband/P R Hechle | KHS 599 |
| 7 | H Taylor/J Simonian | KHS 597 |
| 10 | V Elford/L Baillon | KHS 595 |
| 14 | J Sprinzel/P Garnier | KHS 598 |

### Final Results

| | | |
|---|---|---|
| 1. | Ford Cortina GT (P Hughes/W Young) | 63 minutes penalty |
| 2. | Saab 96 (E Carlsson/G Palm) | 74 minutes |
| 3. | Ford Cortina GT (M P Armstrong/E C Bates) | 78 minutes |
| 4. | Mercedes-Benz 220Sb (Lucille Cardwell/Jill Lead) | 151 minutes |
| 5. | Ford Zodiac Mk III (V Preston/E R Syder) | 161 minutes |
| 6. | Peugeot 404 (B Shankland/K Kassum) | 164 minutes |

V Elford/L Baillon (Cortina GT) finished tenth overall

Manufacturers' Team Prize: Ford (P Hughes, M Armstrong and V Elford)

| REGISTRATION NUMBER | ENGINE SIZE | MODEL TYPE |
|---|---|---|
| **KHS 595** | **1498CC 4-CYL OHV** | **CORTINA GT MK I** |

*Vic Elford and Leon Baillon ready to roll off the ramp to begin the 1964 Safari in KHS 595.*

This was Vic Elford's first attempt to conquer the new challenges of the East African Safari and he was determined to drive steadily and put up a good show. In Vic's own words, "We might well have had a much better result but for the fact that way up in the Northern Territories, towards Ethiopia, I broke a steering arm on the car and as a consequence had to drive for about 100 miles with steering on one wheel only". He had been seventh at the time, and after that had to struggle to stay on terms; being stuck in deep water at one point after the Nairobi rest halt did not help.

*Vic Elford (left) and his local co-driver Leon Baillon before the start.*

**Competition Record**

| 1964 East African Safari | Vic Elford | 10th |
|---|---|---|

| REGISTRATION NUMBER | ENGINE SIZE | MODEL TYPE |
|---|---|---|
| **KHS 596** | **1498CC 4-CYL OHV** | **CORTINA GT MK I** |

Mike Armstrong, one of the experienced Kenyan drivers in this formidable six-car Cortina team, got off to a good start from Nairobi and, especially as he was running No 2, had virtually a clear run at most of the natural obstacles in the early stages. By the time the event reached Kampala, in Uganda, on Good Friday, he was already leading the rally, and held this position until he got back to the Nairobi rest halt.

In the second half of the event, Armstrong was gradually overhauled by team-mate Peter Hughes's Cortina and by Erik Carlsson's front-wheel-drive Saab, but soon settled into third place and held it to the end.

*Mike Armstrong in action in the 1964 Safari with his GT, KHS 596, on its way to third place. He was also a member of Ford's winning team on the event. Was this a posed picture? Total, after all, was the company's fuel sponsor at the time.*

**Competition Record**

| 1964 East African Safari | Mike Armstrong | 3rd |
|---|---|---|

| REGISTRATION NUMBER | ENGINE SIZE | MODEL TYPE |
|---|---|---|
| **KHS 597** | **1498cc 4-cyl OHV** | **CORTINA GT MK I** |

Henry Taylor was established as Boreham's leading and most successful driver of the time in 1964, but was not expected to challenge the local Kenyans for supremacy in this Safari. Nevertheless, aided by local man Jack Simonian (who would later drive Mk II GTs in the 1967 Safari) he was well placed after the first two days of the event. A long soak in impassable water after Nairobi didn't help, nor did a crash into seemingly impenetrable scrub later on. The end came in the last 24 hours when they took a disastrously long (and wrong) detour, then the front suspension broke, then the rear axle – and that was it.

*Team captain Henry Taylor (left) and Jack Simonian with KHS 597 ready for the start of the 1964 Safari.*

*John Sprinzel (left) and Henry Taylor in front of Taylor's GT.*

**Competition Record**
| | | |
|---|---|---|
| 1964 East African Safari | Henry Taylor | DNF |

| REGISTRATION NUMBER | ENGINE SIZE | MODEL TYPE |
|---|---|---|
| **KHS 598** | **1498cc 4-cyl OHV** | **CORTINA GT MK I** |

This was an ill-starred entry from the beginning, for although John Sprinzel was a seasoned competitor it was his first Safari, his first works drive for Ford, and as a Fleet Street-supported entry he also had Peter Garnier (Sports Editor of *Autocar*) as his co-driver. Sprinzel had a grumbling appendix before the start of the event, Garnier had not had a chance to do any re-connaissance and the two had never previously done a major rally together, so all in all they needed luck to make it through.

That luck did not materialise, for in the mixed dry and muddy conditions they got thoroughly stuck and lost a lot of time on the first day of the event. In spite of his worsening state of health, Sprinzel kept plugging on (he was always a very determined sportsman), even after a major electrical problem when the voltage regulator fell off its mounting and had to be jury-rigged for the car to get back to Nairobi and the mid-event halt. Delays due to floods and to going off the track added to their misery, and it was only the efforts of the team mechanics that kept them going at all.

Later, a combination of rally traffic jams in awful sections, flood water and – ultimately – another accident, all added up, and with an immobile car whose steering was irretrievably broken retirement was inevitable. It was only then that the stubbornly redoubtable Sprinzel was persuaded to go to hospital to have his appendix removed.

*John Sprinzel (at the wheel) and Peter Garnier (Sports Editor of Autocar) at speed at an early stage on the 1964 Safari. Before the end of the event KHS 598 looked much less smart than this!*

*Peter Garnier, John Sprinzel's co-driver, was known to be a keen sailor, but being stranded in a deep waterhole during practice was presumably above and beyond the call of duty!*

### Competition Record
| | | |
|---|---|---|
| 1964 East African Safari | John Sprinzel | DNF |

| REGISTRATION NUMBER | ENGINE SIZE | MODEL TYPE |
|---|---|---|
| **KHS 599** | **1498CC 4-CYL OHV** | **CORTINA GT MK I** |

Bo Younghusband, like Peter Hughes (in KHS 600), was an experienced Safari driver when he started the 1964 event in this works Cortina GT, and he soon settled into fourth place behind two of his team mates. Using all his bushcraft, Younghusband kept going until the last day, still among the top few runners, when the Cortina suffered a broken throttle linkage, which the intrepid Kenyan 'repaired' by jamming the throttle wide open with a rubber band and carrying on ginger-ly with diligent use of the ignition switch. At least he had the satisfaction of being one of the four works Cortinas to make it to the finish.

### Competition Record
| | | |
|---|---|---|
| 1964 East African Safari | Bo Younghusband | 4th in Class, 15th Overall |

| REGISTRATION NUMBER | ENGINE SIZE | MODEL TYPE |
|---|---|---|
| **KHS 600** | **1498CC 4-CYL OHV** | **CORTINA GT MK I** |

Peter Hughes was not only a driver with a formidable Safari record (he had finished second in an Anglia 105E in 1963, for instance) but was also the head of the company which imported Fords in Kenya. He was lucky enough to start the 1964 event from No 3, was already established in second place by the time the event reached Kampala, and held on to that place (behind team-mate Mike Armstrong) all the way back to Nairobi.

Once Hughes passed Mike Armstrong he was in a lead which he never looked like losing again, and although he had to fight off a determined charge from Erik Carlsson's Saab, he held on to win. Only 21 cars from the original 94 starters made it to the end, and Ford was also delighted to win the Manufacturers' Team prize.

*After the event, the spoils. The 1964 Safari-winning GT (KHS 600) looked filthy, but the trophies were sparkling, and both Peter Hughes (left) and his co-driver Bill Young were happy to dress up for the occasion.*

**Competition Record**

| 1964 East African Safari | Peter Hughes | 1st |
|---|---|---|

### 1965 – 'Works-blessed' private entries

This was a year in which Boreham was much involved at home in the changeover from works Cortina GTs to works (leaf-spring) Lotus-Cortinas, so a decision was made to build Cortina GT cars to East African specification for the Safari, send them out to Nairobi, and entrust Peter Hughes and Hughes Ltd with the task of running the cars in the event.

These cars were all driven by Kenyan experts – Peter Hughes, Vic Preston, Mike Armstrong and Jack Simonian. It was an ultra-tough Safari which was finally won, against all the odds, by Joginder and Jaswant Singh in their ageing Volvo PV544. For Ford, however, the good news was that Vic Preston took third place and Mike Armstrong ninth (those two cars winning their capacity class too). For many hours Peter Hughes and Jack Simonian had also been well up on the leader board until, toward the end of the event, both were forced to retire, Hughes with a broken driveshaft.

## 1966 – A private effort by Hughes Ltd

This was a year in which Ford influence was almost entirely absent, so the Ford effort, concentrated on Cortinas, was entirely supported by Hughes Ltd. The drivers included Peter Hughes himself, Jack Simonian and Vic Preston. Hughes drove a leaf-spring Lotus-Cortina, reputedly the first to be imported into Kenya.

As the event progressed, Simonian's GT had to retire with a very sick engine, but the other two stalwarts kept going, running as high as second (Vic Preston) and third (Hughes) for much of the time, being led only by Bert Shankland's rugged Peugeot 404. Finally it was Preston who took second place, while Peter Hughes's Lotus-Cortina slipped back to fourth

overall. The unexpected bonus came at the end, when it was realised that Ford might, just might, win the Manufacturer's Team Prize if H Smith's privately-prepared Cortina GT could be persuaded to reach the finish.

The miracle (which involved much skullduggery, if not outright cheating) was that the car, which had expired almost 40 miles from the finish in Nairobi, was somehow pushed, towed and heaved, and then finally persuaded to crawl under its own just-surviving power to reach the chequered flag. The reward was that Smith's car not only took third in class but also helped Ford to lift that much-coveted Team Prize yet again.

*Peter Hughes drove this Lotus-Cortina, KKR 3, in the 1966 Safari*

## 1967 –A big works effort with Mk II GTs and two Mk I Lotus-Cortinas

This was an occasion, observed by the author, when Ford mounted its biggest effort so far on this East African classic event. Not only did Ford produce four brand new two-door Cortina GTs and a Mk I Lotus-Cortina, but they also supported Vic Preston's Lotus-Cortina entry in his own Mk I Lotus-Cortina, while London's *Weekend Telegraph* magazine pitched in at a very late stage to enable John Sprinzel to use a four-door Mk II GT locally-prepared by himself and Boreham mechanics.

This was the first Safari to allow FIA Group 2 cars to be entered, and Ford had worked hard on their Cortinas to make

them not only as strong as possible but also more powerful than usual. The twin-choke side-draught Webers of the Mk I had not been homologated for the new car, so the GTs' engines had been thoroughly reworked and 99bhp was claimed. The latest (2000E-type) gearboxes were fitted, along with 5.5in Lotus-Cortina-type road wheels. Because of the limited time available for preparation, the *Weekend Telegraph* car was running with standard running gear.

Roger Clark, tackling his first-ever Safari, must have thought that all his birthdays had come at once, as he was

*This group shot was taken before the start of the 1967 Safari, where Ford entered four new Cortina GT Mk IIs, supported a fifth car for John Sprinzel (back of this group), and provided a Lotus-Cortina (KKR 455) for Roger Clark.*

accompanied by his friend (and very capable driver) Gilbert Staepelaere, and he had a new Lotus-Cortina of the Mk I type (the Mk II had not yet been homologated) built to the very well-proven rough-road specification that had been so successful in 1966 when Bengt Soderstrom had won the RAC rally in a sister car. 135bhp was claimed, and this car, along with Vic Preston's year-old machine, was expected to be one of the fastest in the event.

Ford came so very close to winning this event, for the last

works car was eliminated only hours from the finish when Jack Simonian, in the lead, hit an impala, killing the unfortunate animal and pitching his car off the road. It all started from Nairobi in an encouraging fashion, with Bengt Soderstrom's car (KKR 453) leading the way. Halfway through, when the cars had already been on the road for 32 hours and 1650 miles, Jack Simonian's car was third and the other Cortinas were all in the top ten.

It was then that the drama gradually unfolded. Soderstrom, running first on the road, plunged into a trench and could not be recovered. For a time it looked as if Vic Preston's Lotus-Cortina (which had already done some previous rallying) might win. Then Simonian also had an accident. For Ford, which had needed a special budget even to compete in this event, it was really no consolation that team cars took third, sixth and seventh, and also won the Manufacturers' Team Prize, or that privateer Vic Preston was second overall.

*Safari characters in 1967: Bill Barnett, team boss Henry Taylor, and driver Jack Simonian, who so nearly won the event.*

| REGISTRATION NUMBER | ENGINE SIZE | MODEL TYPE |
|---|---|---|
| KKR 451 | 1498CC 4-CYL OHV | CORTINA GT MK II |

As he was not only a previous winner but was also the proprietor of the Hughes importing organisation, Peter Hughes took over what was nominally the 'lead car' (in other words, the one with the lowest of five consecutive local registration numbers). His was one of the four identically-specified and brand-new Cortina GT Mk IIs.

He drove steadily (by his standards) to be fifth upon arrival in Dar-es-Salaam, and dropped further to eighth before his car nosed into his own garage's workshops for service before the overnight halt in Nairobi. Seventh in Kampala, and finally up to third on arrival at the finish, Hughes had done everything which could be expected of him. It tells us

much about his performance that in the second part of the event he left Nairobi 31 minutes adrift of Shankland's Peugeot 404, which won, and ended the event just 25 minutes behind. Not only that, but in conjunction with Jack Simonian and Lucien Bianchi he was a member of the winning Manufacturers' Team.

*Peter Hughes completed a carefully-controlled drive in the 1967 Safari by taking third place in this Cortina GT Mk II, KKR 451*

| Competition Record | | |
|---|---|---|
| 1967 East African Safari | Peter Hughes | 3rd |

| REGISTRATION NUMBER | ENGINE SIZE | MODEL TYPE |
|---|---|---|
| **KKR 452** | **1498CC 4-CYL OHV** | **CORTINA GT MK II** |

Local hero Jack Simonian, who was not only an accomplished driver and co-driver but a close friend and associate of Peter Hughes, shared this car with Peter Huth, who would himself come very close to winning the Safari in the following year.

Ninth after the first night's running, but only 16 minutes adrift of the lead, Simonian then had an inspired spell, pulling right up to third at the halfway halt. Soderstrom's crash after the halt (see KKR 453, below) then elevated Simonian to second place, after which he upped his pace and passed Shankland's Peugeot into the lead.

The drama then developed another twist, for after Simonian left Nakuru, on the eastern slope of Mount Kenya, he rushed over one brow near Thompson's Falls and struck a fully-grown impala buck. The Cortina finished up on its side in the bush, and much time was lost before the battered machine could be extricated by a breakdown truck. The front suspension was deranged, one wheel was keeled over at an odd angle, and the result was a delay of more than an hour, dropping Simonian back to sixth place.

*After rally leader Bengt Soderstrom had crashed his GT, Jack Simonian came very close to winning the 1967 Safari in KKR 452, but in the end he had to settle for sixth place.*

| Competition Record | | |
|---|---|---|
| 1967 East African Safari | Jack Simonian | 6th |

| REGISTRATION NUMBER | ENGINE SIZE | MODEL TYPE |
|---|---|---|
| **KKR 453** | **1498CC 4-CYL OHV** | **CORTINA GT MK II** |

Bengt Soderstrom and Gunnar Palm started the 1967 Safari as firm favourites, not only because they had a Cortina GT Mk II which was thought likely to win, but because within the last few months Bengt had won both the British RAC and the Swedish rallies, both of them in Lotus-Cortinas.

Starting first on the road, Bengt had a great advantage over all his rivals because he was not having to drive into dust clouds stirred up by cars ahead. This and his natural pace behind the wheel meant that he was comfortably in the lead by the time the cars reached Dar-es-Salaam on the coast of the Indian Ocean after the first day. Even so, at half-distance back in Nairobi, his lead over Bert Shankland's Peugeot 404 was only eight minutes.

Unhappily, only 90 minutes after the re-start on Easter Saturday evening the Cortina GT crashed. As the author commented in his *Autocar* report, "Soderstrom's Cortina plunged headlong into a culvert that was being rebuilt and whose warning signs were missing. Crews had been warned of this hazard at a drivers' briefing and an exact mileage from the last control given; there was a short detour that rally cars were to take".

It took more than two hours to get the car dragged out, when it was found to have deranged front suspension and a bent propshaft. Retirement, however delayed, was inevitable. Many years later a re-creation of this car, looking asnew and immaculate, went on show at various classic events in Germany.

*Looking immaculate when being checked over by Boreham mechanics before the start of the 1967 Safari was Bengt Soderstrom's Cortina GT Mk II, which was eliminated in a crash when leading the event.*

**Competition Record**

| 1967 East African Safari | Bengt Soderstrom | DNF |
|---|---|---|

| REGISTRATION NUMBER | ENGINE SIZE | MODEL TYPE |
|---|---|---|
| **KKR 454** | **1498CC 4-CYL OHV** | **CORTINA GT MK II** |

Here was a multi-national crew who got this drive as a reward for the sterling work they had both done in privately-prepared Ford rally cars in Europe. Lucien Bianchi was Belgian, Henri Greder was French, and they had already sampled Fords as diverse as Cortinas, GT40s and Falcons.

For them the event started well. By the time they reached Dar-es-Salaam the two were handily placed in fourth position, led only by Soderstrom's sister car and two Peugeot 404s. Unfortunately their car then suffered an accident which damaged the steering, and their navigational equipment stopped working, but they were still sixth at half-distance. Although they produced as gritty a performance as expected, Bianchi and Greder suffered bad luck again in the second part of the event when their rear axle began to make awful noises and, though the mechanics did their best, nothing could be done about it on the roadside. The duo kept on going, and it was only after the finish that they discovered that one of the axle tubes had actually bent.

They struggled to the end in seventh place, but at least had the pleasure of being involved in Ford's Team Prize success, the other two members of course being Peter Hughes and Jack Simonian.

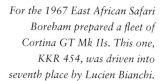

*For the 1967 East African Safari Boreham prepared a fleet of Cortina GT Mk IIs. This one, KKR 454, was driven into seventh place by Lucien Bianchi.*

| Competition Record | | |
|---|---|---|
| 1967 East African Safari | Lucien Bianchi | 7th |

| REGISTRATION NUMBER | ENGINE SIZE | MODEL TYPE |
|---|---|---|
| **KHZ 33** | **1498CC 4-CYL OHV** | **CORTINA GT MK II** |

At this stage in his career John Sprinzel saw himself as an elder statesman of rallying, but factories were often sympathetic to his talents because he had strong links with the British national press. On this occasion it was not until the last week or so that he did a deal with the London *Weekend Telegraph* magazine (who financed the running of the car), found a local co-driver in Jim Wilson, liberated a four-door GT from Hughes's local stocks in Nairobi, and along with Boreham mechanics spent three days turning it into a standard Group 1 rally car, with all the appropriate factory livery. A two-door car, incidentally, was apparently not available at such short notice.

Although never on the pace, Sprinzel plodded on gamely, refusing to let his co-driver take the wheel at any point. Finally, just eight controls from the end, he retired, completely exhausted.

| Competition Record | | |
|---|---|---|
| 1967 East African Safari | John Sprinzel | DNF |

| REGISTRATION NUMBER | ENGINE SIZE | MODEL TYPE |
|---|---|---|
| **KKR 455** | **1558CC 4-CYL DOHC** | **LOTUS-CORTINA MK I** |

This was Roger Clark's very first Safari but he started as a strong contender, mainly because of the strong successes he had already achieved with Lotus-Cortinas in Europe. Ford sent him out as the hare to lead all the hounds on this event, and teamed him up with Gilbert Staepelaere of Belgium, who had already had much success in Europe in Belgian-prepared Lotus-Cortinas. The car, was one of the very last Mk I Lotus-Cortinas to be manufactured and used in a rally, for the new Mk II had only recently been announced and was not yet homologated for use in motorsport.

Let Roger Clark tell his own story of what happened: "Even if we did finish nowhere, I could never have been bored. First of all we broke a half-shaft, then the dynamo stopped working, and next the rear dampers punched their way through the bodywork. Later on a marshal gave our route card away to another competitor at a busy checkpoint, and then an engine mounting collapsed. No, it wasn't my year, was it".

*Even though the Mk I Lotus-Cortina had already dropped out of production, in 1967 Boreham built up KKR 455 for Roger Clark to drive in the 1967 Safari. All manner of mechanical traumas caused him to retire. Roger's co-driver on this event was Gilbert Staepelaere.*

**Competition Record**

| 1967 East African Safari | Roger Clark | Completed the course |
|---|---|---|

### 1968 - A final 'might-have-been'

Ford's last involvement with Cortinas in the 1968 Safari was a low-profile affair compared with previous years – and indeed was a much lower-profile entry than had been planned towards the end of 1967. Originally the intention had been to send a complete team of Lotus-Cortina Mk IIs, but by the end of the year it became clear that the launch of the still-secret Escort Twin-Cam, and the rushed build-up of a number of works rally cars, press and demonstrator cars, and the first few 'customer' competition cars, would keep Boreham far too busy, for they would have to take precedence in the first weeks of 1968.

Therefore the idea of sending Roger Clark, Ove Andersson and Bengt Soderstrom was abandoned. Clark's car was never built, the one intended for Ove Andersson was diverted to compete in Sweden during the winter. This left only one new car, a Group 2 Lotus-Cortina for Bengt Soderstrom, locally registered KMA 800, to make the trip to Kenya at Easter time. It did not appear in the official entry list as a works car but as being entered by Bengt Soderstrom himself, in the same way that four other very purposeful-looking locally-built Lotus-Cortinas all had private entrants' names in the lists, even if people had seen several of them being prepared in the Hughes Ltd workshops in the weeks leading up to the event.

However, although Ford went to a lot of trouble alerting enthusiasts to the detail preparation which went into a modern Safari car, it was all in vain. Bengt started from No 4 but the wet conditions soon hampered him and his equally distinguished rivals. Within hours of the start, competitors encountered bridges which were down, roads which had been washed away, and seemingly endless mud out in the bush.

By the time the already depleted field reached Kampala, in Uganda, Soderstrom was in fifth place, and within hours of turning to make the return journey to Nairobi he had taken the lead. After Nairobi, the Lotus-Cortina was then overtaken by local drivers among the 21 survivors, the car soon suffered a spate of electrical problems, and retirement came at the Himo control, south of Nairobi.

Ford was devastated by this loss, and not even a stirring fight by privateer Peter Huth, whose Hughes-prepared Lotus-Cortina finally took second place after leading at one point, could bring a smile back to their faces. Only seven cars finished the event, and this was the last time a works Cortina figured in the starter's list of the Safari.

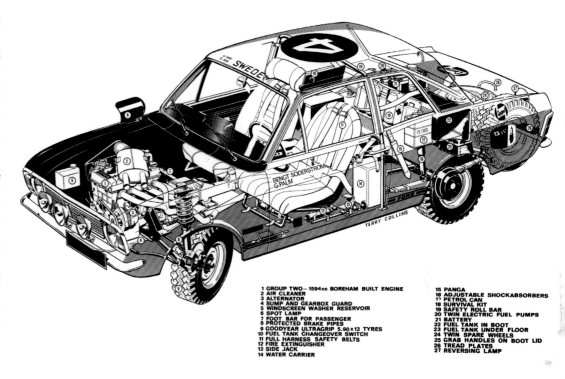

1 GROUP TWO— 1594cc BOREHAM BUILT ENGINE
2 AIR CLEANER
3 ALTERNATOR
4 SUMP AND GEARBOX GUARD
5 WINDSCREEN WASHER RESERVOIR
6 SPOT LAMP
7 FOOT BAR FOR PASSENGER
8 PROTECTED BRAKE PIPES
9 GOODYEAR ULTRAGRIP 5.90×13 TYRES
10 FUEL TANK CHANGEOVER SWITCH
11 FULL HARNESS SAFETY BELTS
12 FIRE EXTINGUISHER
13 SIDE JACK
14 WATER CARRIER
15 PANGA
16 ADJUSTABLE SHOCKABSORBERS
17 PETROL CAN
18 SURVIVAL KIT
19 SAFETY ROLL BAR
20 TWIN ELECTRIC FUEL PUMPS
21 BATTERY
22 FUEL TANK IN BOOT
23 FUEL TANK UNDER FLOOR
24 TWIN SPARE WHEELS
25 GRAB HANDLES ON BOOT LID
26 TREAD PLATES
27 REVERSING LAMP

*When Ford set out to win the Safari in 1968, they issued this pre-event cutaway drawing of what went into Bengt Soderstrom's works car. This was almost the final fling for works-prepared Lotus-Cortinas...*

*...and this was Jack Simonian and Peter Hughes trying their best to win in this privately-prepared sister car.*

# CHAPTER 7:
# MK I CORTINA GT AND LOTUS-CORTINA IN RACING

When Ford started out to turn the Cortina into a race and rally winning machine, they rapidly developed a clear policy regarding works cars. The factory itself, through the new Boreham Competition Centre, would concentrate on rallying, whereas the motor racing side – Touring Car Racing in particular – would always be carried out by consultants or by Lotus. This explains why it was Jeff Uren and Alan Mann who provided the early successes in 1963, why Team Lotus soon joined in, and why Alan Mann and Team Lotus made much of the running in the next four seasons.

Cornish-born Jeff Uren's Willment-backed team started the process in a 1963 season which included campaigning their Cortina GTs, a Lotus-Cortina and even a massive Ford Galaxie, all from the same team. Before then, Jeff had already become British Saloon Car Champion in 1959 (in a self-prepared Ford Zephyr), and spent a short period (in the pre-Walter Hayes period at Lincoln Cars) as Ford's Competitions

*The 1963 Willment team regularly appeared in the British Saloon Car Championship with three Cortina GTs and the massive Ford Galaxie, and here is the line-up at Silverstone in May.*

Manager, before being asked to run a team of Ford Falcons in the 1963 Monte Carlo.

Even before then, in September 1962, he sat down with John Willment, who was about to open a Ford main dealership in Twickenham, the result being the setting up of the legendary Willment motor racing division. As Jeff once told the author:

"John said that I could run the team for him. 'Between us,' John suggested, 'we can get a lot of publicity, and we can have a bit of fun too.'"

The original plan was to run Lotus-Cortinas, but this model was delayed, so the emphasis turned to preparing a team of Cortina GTs instead.

"Maybe we couldn't beat the Jaguar 3.8s. But we would have to beat the Rapiers and Riley 1.5s, and I thought the new Cortina GT could do that. So I went along to see Walter Hayes at Ford, and asked for three Cortina GTs, plus £10,000 and a quantity of spare parts.

"Walter asked me, 'Do you think you can win classes with the GT?' I said yes, *and* that we could win the Championship too. I told him I could find the drivers.

"He pondered, then said, 'Your reputation in the company has preceded you. You've always delivered everything you said you could do – you've ruffled feathers along the way, but you've always done it. Yes, I will back you.'"

So, with three cars – quite unproven when the deal was done – Jeff set out to win the British Touring Car Championship, but first he had to sign his drivers.

"I wanted Jack Sears to drive for me, but he said he had retired from racing. So I decided to call Jack! We were also talking about bringing a Galaxie across from the USA, and I also mentioned this when I talked to him.

"'Jack,' I asked him, 'are you interested in winning the British Touring Car Championship this year?'.

"'What in?' he replied."

"In two cars," I told him, "in the Cortina GT – and a Galaxie."

"'I don't know anything about these cars. Do you think it could be done?, he asked me.

"Well, I told him it could be done, and that he could do it."

For Jeff, and for the Willment team, the result could not have been better. Starting from scratch at Oulton Park early in 1963, the newly formed team started winning. Outright victories for the Galaxie and a series of class wins for the Cortina GTs meant that Jack Sears became Champion in the eleven-event series, and that the Willment name became famous. Although there were three cars, all of them white with red striping for recognition purposes, and although all three usually turned up at race meetings, only two cars were raced on a habitual basis – FOO 229 and FOO 230. Impressive pictures exist of the Willment team, complete with a 7-litre Galaxie, lined up in a race event paddock during 1963.

"But we didn't have much time to prepare. We raced the Cortina GT immediately after its announcement – the day afterwards – and won the class. The opposition simply couldn't believe this, so they protested, and the cars were stripped. They were perfectly legal, of course, and for the rest of the season we were 'clean'.

"Preparation? Spike Winters, who had been employed by John Willment for a long time, was the engine man. Spike and I worked on the chassis – I had learned a lot about spring rates and damper settings by then – and we started with just three mechanics, one of whom was Ken Brittan. I had no secretary, no separate office, nothing. And we only had the cars for just three weeks before the first race!"

The Willment team, managed by Jeff Uren, had not only performed better than anyone had dared to hope, *and* had won the Touring Car Championship, but they were not given the chance to run fully-supported works-backed Lotus-Cortinas in 1964, that honour going to Team Lotus instead.

"Even so, for 1964 Walter gave us two cars, in fact, and we used twin-cam engines which had been built by Spike Winters. Team Lotus used BRM-prepared engines, and had Jim Clark as their lead driver, but we managed to beat them occasionally".

Because these cars were apparently not road registered, and because it was Team Lotus which ran the 'official' works cars in the 1963-66 British Championship, they have not been covered in this survey beyond 1964.

## Alan Mann Racing

Then there was the European effort. By 1962 Alan Mann (running under the Alan Andrews banner at that time) had become a successful Ford dealer on the South coast, so for his 1963 racing he had high ambitions. As he once commented: "I went to see Ford's competitions manager, Syd Henson, and tried to get hold of a Lotus-Cortina, but the car was late, so instead he offered help with a Cortina GT. Most of Ford's money was going into John Willment's cars, for Jack Sears, but he offered me a spare engine and some bits as long as we built our own car. Walter Hayes put a bit of money in too. So we built a car. I was quite good at preparing engines, flowing

*Alan Mann, team boss/team owner of Alan Mann Racing, whose expert organisation provided European Championship-winning Lotus-Cortinas in 1964, 1965 and 1966 – a near-unbeatable record.*

### ALAN MANN

From 1964 to 1969, Alan Mann ran one of the most successful racing teams in the UK. Whether it was with Lotus-Cortinas, Falcons, Mustangs or Escorts, his company Alan Mann Racing always produced the most immaculate machinery, and usually reliable too.

Alan Mann himself was a car salesman who tried motor racing but decided that he was never going to beat Stirling Moss and wisely drew back from full-time driving. Instead he set up a garage business which specialised in buying and selling racing cars, then moved to revitalise a Ford dealership near Brighton, and set up AMR in 1962. His first efforts were with Anglias and Zodiacs, from 1963 they raced Cortina GTs, and in 1964 Ford's Walter Hayes gave him the job of racing Lotus-Cortinas in Europe.

Although he could be almost invisible at the circuits – you rarely saw Mann waving his arms around, and he never seemed to raise his voice – his team was always amazingly effective. Operating from modest premises in Byfleet, Surrey, he had the sort of super-skilled mechanics who could turn ordinary Fords into winners, which maybe explains why the Monte Falcons of 1964 and the Mustangs which dominated the Tour de France were so effective. As if he was not already busy enough, his business also managed the team of Ford-engined AC Cobras which won the World Sports Car Championship in 1965, and he also built some of the lightest and best GT40 development cars in motor racing.

He campaigned Lotus-Cortinas extremely successfully from 1964 to 1968, after which he produced the world's best Escort Twin-Cams. Latterly, much of the engineering and new-design work was carried out for him by Len Bailey, who had an office at Byfleet, and it was Len who was mainly responsible for the design of the sleek and lovely F3L racing sports car, which was the first two-seater to use the DFV F1 engine. Alan makes the point that AMR only originally got two engines for two F3L cars, and that they never did get a spare engine throughout an unsuccessful 1968 season.

Unhappily Mann did not get on with Ford's new boss, Stuart Turner, so at the end of 1969 his contracts with the company were not renewed. This was the point at which AMR was closed down (Frank Gardner took over the premises and some of the workforce), and Mann moved on to the next part of his life, which was to run a helicopter leasing business. Later he also purchased Fairoaks airfield, near London, and expanded his aerospace interests. By the 2000s he had been reunited with some of the cars that had made him famous, and he even bought back one or two of them.

*Testing, testing. Goodwood in 1965, with Graham Hill explaining a point to (left to right) Alan Mann, Sir John Whitmore, a technician from FAVO, and Henry Taylor.*

heads and so on – we got our camshafts from Cosworth – and I got Jimmy Blumer to drive it. We were usually as quick, or nearly as quick, as the Willment cars."

Blumer's works-supported car won its class in two races, and was always in there, fighting against the Willment-prepared GTs, so Mann's reward came at once.

"Towards the end of that season it all took off big-time, Ford-America were launching the Cortina in America, there was to be a 12-hour race sponsored at Marlboro, in Maryland, not far from Washington DC. Ford were sending the two Willment cars, and they thought it sensible to send an extra car, so I was invited to take ours along. Ford-USA would find all the mechanics, and they would pay for everything. I needed another driver to go with Jimmy Blumer, so I approached Henry Taylor. Well, the Cortinas finished first, second and third in that race.

"This is where I met the American who supplied the mechanics – proper NASCAR mechanics – a man called John Holman, who came to mean a lot to me. We sat down to talk about changing wheels – it was a 12-hour event, don't forget – and in Europe, at the time, we thought a two-minute stop was pretty good. John asked about jacking and number of wheel-nuts. He insisted on jacking from the side and in the end, with refuelling as well, his pit stops took about 24 seconds!"

This event ranks as the Cortina's very first major international success. The Sears/Olthoff (Willment) car averaged

53.0mph to win on the very tight 1.7-mile circuit, while the second-placed Blumer/Taylor machine (prepared by Alan Mann's team) finished close behind. But it wasn't easy. To quote from *Autosport*, "The Fords...went like the devil between pit stops, these being endless and varied. The Cortina of Jimmy Blumer/Henry Taylor, which had led for much of the distance, dropped back to second, suffering from acute fuel starvation."

Ford's joy was completed by a local Falcon Sprint finishing third overall, and by the third Cortina finishing tenth. Ford's Cortina sales campaign in the USA could not possibly have got off to a better start.

In the meantime, Alan's two self-prepared/self-developed Lotus-Cortinas had astonished everyone with their reliability in the ETC (European Touring Car) Challenge, where Sir John Whitmore won five events outright and only missed out on the Championship by a weird points-scoring systems which favoured class-winning Minis. As Alan later commented in his own autobiography (*Alan Mann – a Life of Chance*): "We did feel unhappy not to have won the Championship that year, thanks to what we felt was a very odd system of scoring points, but that's history. Our cars only lost one race in that season, and that was the round at Monza, the final event in the series. For some reason, there in the heart of Italy, the Alfas were going much quicker than they went anywhere else that year."

Strictly speaking, but let us not split too many hairs in discussing it further, these AMR cars arguably should not count as full-blown works cars because: "We built our own cars, all the time, everything. There was no input from Ford, little guidance, and none from Lotus. Team Lotus never offered any help, nothing at all, and I never asked for any. Our cars were very different from theirs – you won't see pictures of John Whitmore's cars with the front wheels waving in the air, but Jim Clark's cars did that all the time."

"We did all our own rebuilds, and we had good budgets to run the team. We didn't have drawing boards, we did no drawing at all, we just used experience and careful preparation. I did a lot of the test driving. I think that sorting out the chassis was part of the battle, and we had a completely different set-up from theirs. But the Cortina was never a particularly easy car to drive, not compared with the Falcons or Mustangs anyway.

"Incidentally, I always preferred the old A-bracket cars. We made a few modifications to make them work but they were abandoned for all the wrong reasons in 1965. We stiffened up the aluminium diff casings internally and ours never cracked, they were perfect.

"You had to have a discipline over preparation and rebuilds, most parts had to be changed – lifed – very regularly, then they were perfectly reliable. John Whitmore, well, he was amazingly fast and very predictable. He could get down to a lap time in four or five laps, that's all he needed."

Even with the so-called 'fragile' A-frame Lotus-Cortinas the team's performance in 1964 had been so successful that there was never any doubt that the programme would be repeated in 1965, and this time they were fully backed by Ford. Just as competitive as before, from mid-season the team used new leaf-spring cars, Sir John Whitmore was coming to the peak of his form, and the red-and-gold cars totally dominated the European series.

The legendary AMR racing colours were devised after the pit crew had difficulty in identifying their cars from the mass of other Lotus-Cortinas (all of them white with green spears along the flanks) in the Nurburgring 6-Hour race of 1964. The trouble was that "all the Lotus-Cortinas looked the same" At the time Alan was driving a Ferrari as his road car, so he used the famous Rosso Red, the gold being a fine contrasting colour which, as every Escort enthusiast now knows, costs a fortune to replicate. However, to confuse matters, this livery was not immediately applied to all the cars, and even in the spring of 1965 it was still possible to see an AMR race car in white/green. Archive pictures prove this.

However, there was never any doubt as to the way these cars were built, maintained, and driven. To quote *Autosport*'s seasonal survey at the end of 1965: "Sir John Whitmore was outstandingly successful, his Alan Mann Lotus-Cortina proving to be both fast and reliable... Sir John won not only because he had a well-prepared car, and good team management, but because he simply out-drove the opposition."

"But we always had trouble with the Alfas at Monza," Alan remembered, "and the BMWs at the Nurburgring."

He also remembered John Whitmore's speed and consistency, reminding me that he only ever damaged one car. "I only had to ask him to drive quickly once. We were at Spa in the 24 Hour race with the Lotus-Cortinas, we knew we couldn't last twenty-four hours – a Lotus-Cortina, come on! – but as Mercedes-Benz were there with a full works team, I wanted to wind them up. So I told John, 'Your job here is that you've got a grandstand full of people, Belgian TV, everything – go out and lead the Mercedes cars'. He did a great job, passing and re-passing, leading the race, and the crowd loved it. But he only lasted about six hours"

Even so, Alan carried on running Lotus-Cortinas in the European Touring Car Challenge which were competitive, as ever, but found the competition much hotter in 1966 than it had been in 1965, for Alfa Romeo had homologated the super-light Giulia GTA model and spent huge amounts of money on their programme. Yet the Whitmore-Mann-Lotus-Cortina combination won four of the ten events outright.

## Team Lotus

As far as factory-backed cars are concerned, the Team Lotus story spans five years, 1963 to 1967, but it all took time to mature. It was typical of Lotus, and Colin Chapman in particular, that he did not accept the idea of running 'fac-

tory-owned' cars with Essex registration plates in 1964, but always made sure that the team cars, the 'BJH' series – were locally registered in Middlesex, as the Lotus factory where the race cars were prepared was then based at Cheshunt, a few miles north of London.

The early Lotus-Cortinas proved to be depressingly fragile race cars, but somehow Team Lotus made them work, up to a point. Indeed, once the A-frame/coil spring suspended Lotus-Cortina made its first racing appearance, it caused a sensation. To quote Paddy McNally of *Autosport*: "The Gold Cup meeting at Oulton Park [in September 1963] saw the first International debut of the then recently-homologated Lotus-Cortinas. Although not the outright winners, they were tremendously impressive, and finished third and fourth behind the Ford Galaxies of Dan Gurney and Graham Hill."

The Lotus-Cortinas were still only running with 145bhp. For 1964, not only would Team Lotus get the job of running a British Championship effort, but F1 stars Jim Clark and Peter Arundell usually found time to drive the cars. Because of their front-wheel-waving antics in the corners, BJH 417B, BJH 418B and BJH 419B became famous, and well-loved by Ford enthusiasts.

The story of season is easily told. Jim Clark started all eight rounds in the BRSCC series, won every class, every time, and even threw in three outright victories as well. Nothing could have been more emphatic than this. Once again, to quote McNally: "The works Lotus-Cortinas were well prepared and exceedingly fast, proving capable of winning a race outright if the Ford Galaxies absented themselves for any reason. Initial-

*Just to prove that Team Lotus built three separate Lotus-Cortina race cars in 1963, and that there was no cloning, this was the transporter which delivered them all to Snetterton for the BTCC race in 1963. In that race, 168 RUR was driven by Trevor Taylor. Whatever happened in later life to the registration number worn by the transporter?*

*Two famous ex-Team Lotus Lotus-Cortina race cars reunited after many years: 166 RUR, closest to the camera, was an original 1963 model, while KPU 396C was from 1966.*

For 1965 the Team Lotus cars were even faster than before, because BRM (with a development team led by Mike Hall, who would later move to Cosworth and would design the all-conquering Ford-Cosworth BDA engine) took on the race-engine development contract, pushing up peak horsepower figures for the slightly over-bored 1594cc units to about 150bhp at 7000rpm; because of homologation restrictions, they were still obliged to use standard-type Weber carburettors.

Something of a mystery still surrounds the fact that the three 1965 (C reg.) machines used as Team Lotus race cars all definitely reached maturity in high season with leaf-spring rear suspension. Did they actually start the year with that system, even though road cars were still being built with the original A-frame layout and the new suspension did not officially become available on road cars until June 1965? Contemporary photographs of early-season outings are inconclusive, and after more than 50 years memories have become 'selective' too. Let us just say, therefore, that the 'same' cars – JTW 496C, JTW 497C and (just occasionally) JTW 498C – were usually driven by Jack Sears and Jim Clark, were demonstrably even faster than in 1964, and were just as exciting to watch.

Lotus-Cortinas always won their 2-litre capacity class, with Jim Clark and Jack Sears winning three times each. Jim also won two events outright – once at Goodwood and once at Oulton Park, the latter by default following the disqualification of the Mustang which actually finished first. Once again, to quote Patrick McNally in *Autosport*: "They were superbly controllable if a little heavy on the tyres... Once their cars were sorted out, Clark and Sears between them broke just about every class record, lapping at fantastic speeds. They even won outright at International Goodwood on a wet track while the [4.7-litre] Mustangs floundered. In the final race at Oulton Park they were hard on the Alan Brown Mustang's tail right to the finish".

For 1966 the scene changed considerably, for Championship regulations were altered and the cars were able to run to FIA Group 5 regulations, which gave almost unlimited freedom for mechanical improvement. The British Team Lotus cars – the 'PHK...D' team cars – therefore ran with coil spring/wishbone front suspension, 160bhp at first (with carburettors) and later with 180bhp fuel-injected BRM-tuned engines, along with cast magnesium road wheels.

In a ten-event season, one or other of these cars won outright three times, and always won the 2-litre capacity class. Not only Jim Clark (all three race victories, and five class wins) and Peter Arundell, but also Sir John Whitmore and Jacky Ickx, all drove the team cars. Chopping and changing drivers meant that Championship points were sometimes squandered, but Team Lotus easily lifted the Makes title. In 1966 the only cars which could beat them in a straight fight were other Fords, either the 7.0-litre Galaxies or the 4.7-litre Mustangs and Falcons.

ly these cars suffered from under-steering characteristics induced, as much as anything, by the steering geometry, which might be criticised. But much development work was done in the steering department, and when fitted with thick anti-roll bars the cars were very rapid, even though their tendency to lift the front wheels made them unstable."

They were, indeed, a whole lot more sophisticated than the cars of their more powerful rivals, much lighter than any of them, and with a great deal better balance and 'chuckability', Jim Clark always making the most of this characteristic.

*Because KPU 396C was fitted out to FIA Group 5 in 1966, a very non-standard independent front suspension was employed.*

First of all, the exploits of the barely-developed Cortina GTs, as prepared and run by the Willment and Alan Mann Racing teams, should be described. Please note that because these events are being described after a time lapse of more than 50 years, and because John Willment, Jeff Uren and Alan Mann are no longer with us – the Willment racing records in particular being long dispersed – it has not been possible to assemble completely audited, event-by-event and incident-by-incident coverage of every individual Cortina GT's race career. The author apologises for certain gaps which are evident.

For the record, however, these were the dates and locations of the 1963 British Touring Car Championship at which (except for the first race, at Snetterton, which took place before they were homologated) both these teams habitually entered cars:

| | |
|---|---|
| 30 March 1963 | Snetterton |
| 6 April 1963 | Oulton Park |
| 15 April 1963 | Goodwood |
| 27 April 1963 | Aintree |
| 11 May 1963 | Silverstone |
| 3 June 1963 | Crystal Palace |
| 20 July 1963 | Silverstone (F1 GP meeting) |
| 5 August 1963 | Brands Hatch |
| 14 September 1963 | Brands Hatch |
| 21 September 1963 | Oulton Park |
| 28 September 1963 | Snetterton |

One or other of the Cortina GTs described below won its capacity class at every one of the races from 6 April onwards.

| REGISTRATION NUMBER | ENGINE SIZE | MODEL TYPE |
|---|---|---|
| FOO 173 | 1498cc 4-cyl OHV | CORTINA GT MK I |

Ford main dealer David Haynes (from Maidstone and a very competent 'gentleman racer') drove this car in the International Trophy race at Silverstone in May so well that he finished second in his class behind Jimmy Blumer's AMR Cortina GT, even defeating his team mate Frank Gardner who was deputising in Jack Sears's usual car.

Unhappily, David then rolled the car at Brands Hatch in the International event held during August – an escapade captured vividly on camera in *Autosport* – which brought its regular front-line racing career to a close. Thereafter Willment concentrated on its other two cars, FOO 229 and FOO 230, though FOO 173 was repaired (re-shelled, more likely) and raced again in lesser events later in the year. Not only that but it was used, in parallel with a massive Willment Galaxie, in Shell motorsport adverts of the period.

*FOO 173 was the very first of the Willment-prepared GTs to go motor racing in 1963. Jimmy Blumer is at the wheel. This car was later severely damaged in a racing accident at Brands Hatch.*

| REGISTRATION NUMBER | ENGINE SIZE | MODEL TYPE |
|---|---|---|
| FOO 229 | 1498cc 4-cyl OHV | CORTINA GT MK I |

Although its sister car, FOO 230, performed so well in the *Motor* Six-Hour race (see below), there was no such luck for this car in the same race, where David Haynes and Les Leston had to retire it with a deranged clutch mechanism. Back on form for the British GP meeting, it then provided David Haynes with second place in its capacity class.

On its return from the USA at the end of 1963, its career as a quasi-works GT race car was over, and it drops out of this story.

FOO 229, a Willment-prepared GT, at Aintree in April 1963.

Traffic jam at Crystal Palace in mid-1963, with a Jaguar 3.8 leading all three of the Willment GTs, of which FOO 229 was momentarily in the lead.

### Competition Record

| | | |
|---|---|---|
| *Motor* Six-Hour race, Brands Hatch | David Haynes/Les Leston | DNF |
| Marlboro 12 Hour Race (USA) | Dave Clark/Curtis Taylor | 10th Overall |

| REGISTRATION NUMBER | ENGINE SIZE | MODEL TYPE |
|---|---|---|
| **FOO 230** | **1498cc 4-cyl OHV** | **CORTINA GT MK I** |

First time out at Oulton Park in April 1963 in a 52-mile race, in a new car which cannot possibly have had more than 90bhp, Jack Sears started steadily (there were six Jaguar 3.8s up front) and had to deal with the Rapiers and Alan Hutcheson's Riley 1.5 before finally taking a storming fourth place behind three Jaguars. It was an exciting start to what promised to be an enthralling programme. A week later, Sears did it again in the St Mary's Trophy race at Goodwood, where he beat Blumer by 24 seconds in just 10 laps, then repeated the dose in the Aintree 200 event. Sears missed out on the next round, where he was drive the gargantuan Willment-entered Galaxie instead, but Frank Gardner deputised competently, finishing third in his class.

According to the entry lists, Jack Sears should have been driving a Galaxie in the *Motor* Six-Hour race of July, but a last minute dispute over this car with the eligibility Scrutineers saw him and Bo Ljungfeldt back in the more familiar Cortina GT, FOO 230, instead. Run off in awful wet weather conditions, this proved to be a lucky weekend for the Cortina GT, which kept going when other cars span or drowned out.

*Two Willment GTs (FOO 229 and FOO 230), together with the unregistered Alan Mann Racing Cortina GT, all crossed the Atlantic in the Autumn of 1963 to compete in the 12 Hour race at the Marlboro circuit...*

**IT'S A CLEAN SWEEP FOR CORTINA GT IN AMERICAN TRACK DEBUT!**

★ English Ford Cortina GT's win 1st and 2nd place overall in SCCA-sponsored Marlboro competition—a grueling 12-hour endurance race

★ Winning Cortina GT completes 381 laps . . . a new track record

★ Three Cortina GT's finish 1-2-4 in their class

★ Cortina GT's take team prize

★ One-third of entries fail to finish . . . All Cortina GT's complete race

★ Cortina GT wins Index of Price and Performance Award . . . a handicap-based category that indicates best value in price class

★ Wins Mechanic's Award—real proof of its reliability and easy maintenance

★ Ninth victory in nine starts for Cortina GT in world-wide competitions

*English Ford*

*Sparrow's 3.8-litre-engined Jaguar has to fight hard to stay ahead of David Haynes driving the Willment GT FOO 230 at Brands Hatch in 1963.*

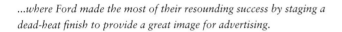

*...where Ford made the most of their resounding success by staging a dead-heat finish to provide a great image for advertising.*

Finishing fourth, but later promoted to third when the leading Jaguar was post-event disqualified, it also won the Index of Price category in what had been a phenomenal performance by this determined team. Only two weeks later, having drawn breath, this indefatigable machine then took sixth place, and its class win, at the British GP support race, this time with Bob Olthoff behind the wheel.

On its return from the USA at the end of 1963 its career as a quasi-works race car was over, and accordingly it drops out of this story, except for one intriguing final appearance. At the end of the British 1964 series, there was a real oddity of an entry, for a Willment Lotus-Cortina, nominally registered 230 FOO (not FOO 230 and not a Cortina GT), raced at Oulton Park, the last big event of the year. The author has no credible explanation for this.

*FOO 230, whether driven by Jack Sears or (here) Frank Gardner, was always competitive in the 1.6-litre class of the British Saloon Car Championship of 1963. Its principal non-Ford competition came from Alan Hutcheson's Riley 1.5.*

## Competition Record

| | | |
|---|---|---|
| BRSCC 6-Hour race, Brands Hatch (ETC) | Jack Sears/Bo Ljungfeldt | 3rd |
| Marlboro 12 Hour Race (USA) | Jack Sears/Bob Olthoff | 1st |

| REGISTRATION NUMBER | ENGINE SIZE | MODEL TYPE |
|---|---|---|
| **NOT REGISTERED** | **1498CC 4-CYL OHV** | **CORTINA SUPER, LATER GT** |

Driving Alan Mann's new bronze-coloured Cortina (a 1500 Super which was rapidly upgraded to GT specification), Jimmy Blumer turned up at Oulton Park in April 1963 with little hope of providing a good result. In the event, he went off in an early lap, took time to get back on the tarmac, and finished up a whole lap behind Sears's Willment car. It was the same story at Goodwood a week later, where Blumer finished second in class behind Sears, and it was again the same story in the Aintree 200 meeting a couple of weeks later.

His first day 'in the sun' came in May, at the International Trophy venue at Silverstone, where he not only won his class, but took sixth place in this race behind Sears's Galaxie and several 3.8-litre Jaguar Mk IIs. This car was always competitive, if not quite (and very marginally so) as rapid as the Willment/Sears GTs – nowhere more so that at the rain-soaked *Motor* 6-Hour race where Blumer and Taylor tiptoed around while others spun off all around them.

There were just two more outings in July and August (Blumer taking second in class to a Willment car at Brands Hatch in August) before (along with the Willment team), Mann was invited to send this hard-working car out to North America to tackle the Marlboro 12 Hour race. As already noted in the preamble to this Chapter, the result truly endeared Alan Mann's team both to Ford-UK, and to the prestigious Holman & Moody organisation in the USA, for the car took second place overall, very close indeed to the Willment car which won the race.

Only weeks later the car was taken to compete in the Double 500 miles race at Bridgehampton in New York state, where it really did not have a chance to be competitive as the event was open to sports cars.

Brought out of retirement for the Spa 24 Hour race of 1964, the GT was running well, if not shatteringly fast, for hours before the engine began to boil and that was that.

---

**Competition Record**

1963 British Saloon Car Championship — Jimmy Blumer started seven races, won the 1.5-litre class twice, and twice took second place in that class.

In addition:

| | | |
|---|---|---|
| 1963 *Motor* Six-Hour Race (ETC) | Jimmy Blumer/Henry Taylor | 10th Overall |
| 1963 Marlboro 12 Hour Race (USA) | Jimmy Blumer/Henry Taylor | 2nd Overall |
| 1963 Double 500 Bridgehampton Race (USA) | Henry Taylor | 8th in first race, 11th in second race. |
| 1963 BRSCC Brands Hatch 'Boxing Day' | Alan Mann | 1st |
| 1964 Spa 24 hours | Roy Pierpoint/Tony Hegbourne | DNF |

---

| REGISTRATION NUMBER | ENGINE SIZE | MODEL TYPE |
|---|---|---|
| **166 RUR** | **1558CC 4-CYL DOHC** | **LOTUS-CORTINA MK I** |

Along with 168 RUR, this was one of the first two Lotus-Cortina race cars to appear after homologation was achieved on 1 September 1963. Driven by Jack Sears at Oulton Park in the International Gold Cup meeting three weeks later, it immediately set a fastest record lap in the 2-litre category, though as this was only a 50-mile race there were few reasons to doubt the A-frame rear suspension's performance at the time. Sears and his colleague Trevor Taylor (in 168 RUR) had qualified on the front row, and apart from the thunderous

7-litre Galaxies ahead of them they were never challenged. In the end Sears took third place behind the Galaxies, just four seconds behind Dan Gurney's winning car.

Soon after this appearance, the car was sold off to the Ford company in the USA, where it carried on a praiseworthy career, but otherwise it drops out of this story.

*Front end detail of 166 RUR, as built in 1963. This looks almost entirely standard, but look carefully and you can see the engine oil cooler tucked in behind the grille.*

*Neat, tidy, and anonymously liveried, would you recognise this as a Team Lotus race car on the public highway?*

| Competition Record | | |
|---|---|---|
| 1963 Oulton Park | Jack Sears | 3rd/1st in Class |

*The spartan driving compartment of 166 RUR.*

*For 166 RUR, Team Lotus made virtually no changes to the original A-frame rear suspension, except for stiffer springs and dampers.*

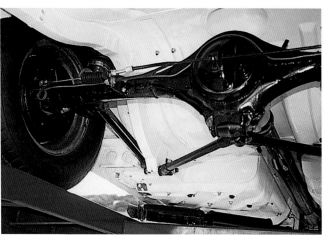

| REGISTRATION NUMBER | ENGINE SIZE | MODEL TYPE |
|---|---|---|
| **167 RUR** | **1558cc 4-cyl DOHC** | **LOTUS-CORTINA MK I** |

One week after the Team Lotus cars had made their debut at Oulton Park, the team cars, including 167 RUR for the first time, appeared at Snetterton in the saloon car race which accompanied the Three Hour race meeting. Jim Clark, who had not apparently set foot in a race-prepared Lotus-Cortina before this event, immediately found that he loved 167 RUR and was faster than Trevor Taylor, while Jack Sears stepped back to drive the Willment/Uren Lotus-Cortina.

The result of this 36 minute race was predictable, with Jack Brabham's 7-litre Galaxie winning the event outright, but with Jim Clark in 167 RUR taking second place, very closely followed (in a staged finish?) by Trevor Taylor in 168 RUR.

Like the other 'RUR' cars, this machine was not used again in a British or European motorsport programme.

### Competition Record
| 1963 Snetterton | Jim Clark | 2nd/1st in Class |
|---|---|---|

| REGISTRATION NUMBER | ENGINE SIZE | MODEL TYPE |
|---|---|---|
| **168 RUR** | **1558cc 4-cyl DOHC** | **LOTUS-CORTINA MK I** |

*Team Lotus Cortina race cars had the special fuel tank and the dry sump oil tank in the boot. Spare wheels were not carried.*

Along with 166 RUR, this was one of the first two Team Lotus Lotus-Cortina cars to start a race after homologation had been achieved. At the International Gold Cup Trevor Taylor qualified just 0.2 seconds behind Sears, out-dragged him off the starting grid, but soon settled down into fourth place (team orders?) and ended the race 0.2seconds behind the sister car. It was the same story at Snetterton a week later, except that it was Jim Clark who led Taylor across the line.

Like the other 'RUR' cars in this story, this particular car was not used again as a works Ford in British or European events.

### Competition Record
| 1963 Oulton Park | Trevor Taylor | 4th Overall |
|---|---|---|
| 1963 Snetterton | Trevor Taylor | 3rd Overall |

| REGISTRATION NUMBER | ENGINE SIZE | MODEL TYPE |
|---|---|---|
| 780 BOO | 1558CC 4-CYL DOHC | LOTUS-CORTINA MK I |

As stated in the introduction to this Chapter, some works or works-blessed Lotus-Cortinas raced without their registration plates on show; alternatively the plates had been removed or the cars were never registered for road use. This no doubt confirms why 780 BOO (an Essex, i.e. factory, registration plate dating from 1963) was seen only once and raced only once, under the Willment banner. Since other Willment-prepared cars raced in 1964 but sometimes carried no registration plates, this car might (but who knows, now that all records have been lost?) be one of them.

Used for the first and only time in 1963 following homologation, the Willment Lotus-Cortina raced at Snetterton at the 'Three Hour' meeting, where Jack Sears was almost on a par with Jim Clark and Trevor Taylor in the Team Lotus cars. During the race all three Lotus-Cortinas were close together, and when the flag dropped Sears's car took fourth place overall, a performance which helped clinch his overall achievement as Saloon Car Champion for 1963.

### Competition Record

| 1963 Snetterton | Jack Sears | 4th Overall |
|---|---|---|

| REGISTRATION NUMBER | ENGINE SIZE | MODEL TYPE |
|---|---|---|
| BJH 417B | 1558CC 4-CYL DOHC | LOTUS-CORTINA MK I |

Because this particular car (in spite of the rumours there definitely was only one BJH 417B) was usually driven by Jim Clark, and because it was invariably at the front of races, or at least battling for the lead with the Galaxies (which won five of the season's eight British Touring Car Championship races), it got most of the attention from historians and photographers, who almost seem to have ignored its sister cars.

Clark had become F1 World Champion for the first time in 1963 (driving Lotus 25 and 33 single-seaters), yet somehow managed to find time in his 1964 calendar to start all eight British Touring Car Championship races, the first being held at Snetterton in March, the eighth and last at Oulton Park in September. In that concentrated period he won three races outright – at Oulton Park (twice) and at Crystal Palace – and won his (2-litre) capacity class on every other occasion, including three second overall places.

The first victory almost came by default, for at Oulton Park in April Clark had settled into second place behind Jack Sears's mighty 7.0-litre Galaxie when the Galaxie suddenly lost its brakes and span off into instant retirement. Similarly, at Crystal Palace in May, the Galaxie was in the lead before it blew a tyre and ceded victory to the Lotus-Cortina.

With Jim Clark on F1 duty for Lotus at the British GP at Brands Hatch (a race which he won), Lotus 'borrowed' Sir John Whitmore from Alan Mann Racing to drive BJH 417B. In a race for which the monstrous Galaxies were not eligible

*In 1964 the combination of Team Lotus, Lotus-Cortina BJH 417B and Jim Clark was virtually unbeatable, for they won their category wherever they competed. Jim was third overall on this occasion at Silverstone in May.*

(Appendix J Group 2 regulations applied), the Lotus-Cortinas (particularly the Team Lotus and John Willment cars) were totally dominant. To no-one's surprise Sir John took the lead as the cars streamed off the start line and held on to win the 20-lap race quite comfortably.

Only two races were left before the end of the series, with Clark finishing second to Jack Sears's Galaxie at Brands Hatch in August and winning at Oulton Park on 19 September. At Oulton Park, however, the Galaxie was leading the race after six laps but then suffered ignition failure and the engine died.

For BJH 417B, therefore, 1964 was a racing season which could hardly have been bettered, but the car was soon out of the limelight, as new Team Lotus cars (JTW 496C amd JTW 497C) would take over in the following year.

*Sir John Whitmore drove BJH 417B to outright victory at Brands Hatch in July 1964 in the support race for the British F1 GP, and that is Jackie Stewart in BJH 419B behind him.*

## Competition Record

| | | |
|---|---|---|
| 1964 Snetterton | Jim Clark | 2nd, 1st in Class |
| 1964 Goodwood | Jim Clark | 2nd, 1st in Class |
| 1964 Oulton Park | Jim Clark | 1st |
| 1964 Aintree | Jim Clark | 3rd, 1st Class |
| 1964 Silverstone | Jim Clark | 3rd, 1st in Class |
| 1964 Crystal Palace | Jim Clark | 1st |
| 1964 Brands Hatch (British GP meeting, non-Championship event) | Sir John Whitmore | 1st |
| 1964 Brands Hatch | Jim Clark | 2nd, 1st in Class |
| 1964 Oulton Park | Jim Clark | 1st |

| REGISTRATION NUMBER | ENGINE SIZE | MODEL TYPE |
|---|---|---|
| **BJH 418B/BJH 419B** | 1558CC 4-CYL DOHC | LOTUS-CORTINA MK I |

It has not been entirely possible to accurately identify which of the two 'second-string' Team Lotus Lotus-Cortinas tackled which particular BTCC round in 1964, so the author has considered them both together. Whereas BJH 417B (see above) tackled every round, one or other of 418B and 419B was always used in support.

Although demonstrably capable of wining touring car races, BJH 418B/419B never had the privilege of beating their more famous sister car BJH 417B. The cars raced together throughout the year, originally driven by Peter Arundell, but

following his F2 accident other drivers were invited to step in.

The season started badly, with engine trouble at Snetterton, but after that one car often managed to slot in behind Clark and 417B. Although one assumes that the the cars were mechanically identical to Clark's, the driving talent was not always equal to his, which may explain Arundell's placing behind Clark at Goodwood, and Sir John Whitmore's placing at Oulton Park. Arundell was in his accustomed place (staring at 417B's exhaust pipe) at Aintree, and again at Silverstone and Crystal Palace in May.

Unhappily, Arundell was then very badly injured in an F2 single-seater race at Rheims in July, which meant that he could no longer race the second-string car. Fortunately he survived, but he was out of motor racing for some months. Jackie Stewart (still not yet into his F1 career) deputised at Brands Hatch in the British GP support racer, where he held on to second (to 417B) for much of the race before spinning on a greasy drizzle-affected Clearways corner, dropping to third behind Jack Sears in a rival John Willment car. The last two races of the season, at Brands Hatch and Oulton Park, were a disappointment for stand-in driver Mike Spence, especially as he rolled the car in its final appearance – that, in fact, being the only serious damage suffered by a Team Lotus saloon car during the season.

*For the first half of 1964 BJH 418B was usually driven in saloon car races by Peter Arundell.*

*Arundell took fifth overall in BJH 418B at Silverstone in May 1964, two places behind Jim Clark in sister car BFH 417B.*

## Competition Record

| | | |
|---|---|---|
| 1964 Snetterton | Peter Arundell | DNF |
| 1964 Goodwood | Peter Arundell | 3rd |
| 1964 Oulton Park | Sir John Whitmore | 3rd |
| 1964 Aintree | Peter Arundell | 4th |
| 1964 Silverstone | Peter Arundell | 5th |
| 1964 Crystal Palace | Peter Arundell | 2nd |
| 1964 Brands Hatch (non-British Championship race) | Jackie Stewart | 3rd |
| 1964 Brands Hatch | Mike Spence | DNF |
| 1964 Oulton Park | Mike Spence | DNF |

| REGISTRATION NUMBER | ENGINE SIZE | MODEL TYPE |
|---|---|---|
| **BTW 297B** | **1558CC 4-CYL DOHC** | **LOTUS-CORTINA MK I** |

*Brands Hatch in 1964, in the 6-Hour race which Sir John Whitmore and Peter Procter won overall in BTW 297B. Using the sister car, BTW 298B, Henry Taylor and Peter Harper were second.*

When the season opened at Zolder in Belgium, *Autosport*'s Paddy McNally wrote glowingly of the two AMR cars: "The two Alan Mann Lotus Cortinas walked all over the opposition... Sir John Whitmore and Henry Taylor took an immediate lead, and the outcome was never in doubt." Only Jack Sears's 7-litre Ford Galaxie was faster, so there was no bitterness about being beaten and, in what looked like a staged finish, Sir John finished just ahead of Henry Taylor.

Four weeks later the two AMR race cars (there were no spares) contested the gruelling 6-Hour Touring Car race held on the full Grand Prix circuit at Brands Hatch, where they outpaced all the opposition including not only the works Mercedes-Benz cars of Eugen Bohringer and Herbert Linge but also all the various 3.8-litre Jaguar Mk IIs which had been expected to set the pace. Sir John Whitmore's car proved to be a full two seconds a lap quicker than any of the Jaguars, and both the cars completed 168 laps, though there were worries towards the end that the rear axles were both beginning to leak oil.

Only a week later BTW 297B tackled the Mont Ventoux hill climb in France, but the A-frame assembly came awry part way up the hill, inflicting some damage to the underside of the shell and making sure that the car could not complete the climb. A massive rebuild was needed at the Ford main dealer's premises in Grenoble before the car could then be transported to Germany for the Nurburgring Six-Hours.

For 1964 Alan Mann prepared two brand-new A-frame Lotus-Cortina race cars, engineered and maintained in his own workshops but financed by Ford and other trade sponsors. BTW 297B was always driven by Sir John Whitmore, who had distinguished co-drivers (Peter Procter, Tony Hegbourne and Jack Sears) for the truly long-distance events. Like the Team Lotus cars, these machines had engines giving about 145bhp.

On that occasion, and partnered by Tony Hegbourne, Sir John finished second behind Eugen Bohringer's winning Mercedes-Benz 300SE. With the other AMR car close behind,

**Competition Record**

| | | |
|---|---|---|
| 1964 Zolder race (ETC) | Sir John Whitmore | 1st in Class, 2nd Overall |
| 1964 Brands Hatch 6 Hours (ETC) | Sir John Whitmore/Peter Procter | 1st |
| 1964 Mont Ventoux hill climb (ETC) | Sir John Whitmore | DNF |
| 1964 Nurburgring 6-Hours (ETC) | Sir John Whitmore/Tony Hegbourne | 2nd |
| 1964 Karlskoga Kanonloppet (ETC) | Sir John Whitmore | 1st |
| 1964 St. Ursanne hillclimb (Switzerland) (ETC) | Sir John Whitmore | 1st |
| 1964 Zandvoort (ETC) | Sir John Whitmore | 3rd |
| 1964 Timmelsjoch, Austria, hillclimb (ETC) | Sir. John Whitmore | 1st in Category |
| 1964 Budapest (Hungary) Nagydij (ETC) | Sir John Whitmore | 2nd |
| 1964 Monza (ETC) | Sir John Whitmore | DNF |
| 1965 Monza, Coppa Europa (ETC) | Sir John Whitmore | DNF |
| 1965 Mont Ventoux hill climb (ETC) | Sir John Whitmore | 1st |
| 1965 Nurburgring 6-Hours (ETC) | Sir John Whitmore/Jack Sears | 1st |

*Sir John Whitmore driving BTW 297B on his way to winning the Brands Hatch Six Hour race of 1964.*

*BTW 297B and BTW 298B on the start line before the beginning of the 1964 Brands Hatch 6-Hour race, where the two AMR-prepared cars finished first and second overall.*

it was Paddy McNally's commented, "The Alan Mann Lotus Ford Cortinas driven by Sir John Whitmore/Tony Hegbourne and Henry Taylor/Peter Harper were magnificent. They could no doubt have disputed the lead but common sense prevailed and they contented themselves with just winning their class."

It was this event, Alan Mann said, that persuaded him to evolve a unique colour scheme for his cars, for up to that time all the current Lotus-Cortina race cars seemed to be white with the characteristic Lotus green spear along the flanks. Within weeks the team (but not the cars entered for the Spa 24 Hour event) had trialled the red/gold livery that made the Alan Mann cars so distinctive and easy to identify in the coming years, though the conventional white/green spear scheme still appeared on some of their cars until the middle of 1965. To aid instant recognition if both team cars passed the pits in close proximity, Sir John's cars tended to have four or five vertical white stripes painted under the grille.

By this time the cars, the drivers and the team had settled into a thoroughly professional and successful combination, so Sir John continued to build up victories and high placings with great regularity. So after his car had sprinted away into the lead of the Zandvoort Trophy race everyone, including Alan Mann, was shocked to see that the engine went on to three cylinders and seemed to lose most of its oil – but at least the team's new boy, Jacky Ickx, stayed loyally behind him in the other car and ushered him over the line to win the class.

After a rather relaxing class win in the Timmelsjoch hill-climb in Austria, and another good class win in Budapest just a week later, the team then had time to settle down to get the two cars ready for the final event of the ETC, the Coppa Europa at Monza. It was not a happy result for them, however, for quite against the experience of earlier in the season they

found themselves thoroughly outpaced by the works Alfa Romeos (which were, need one say, Italian in an Italian motor race). It all happened a long time ago, and I think most people would be correct to suppose that Alfa Romeo were running cars which did not comply with the limitations of Group 2 regulations. Normally the Alfas would run with 1.6-litre engines, but it was known that a 1.75-litre version of the twin-cam engine was already under development. Alan Mann himself once said, "We could never catch those Alfas at Monza and, although we could not be sure, we always suspected they had pretty big engines."

Perhaps the fates were already lined up against this Lotus-Cortina, for the Italian scrutineers had queried the AMR cars' homologation details, and – of all things on an October afternoon in Northern Italy – there was an outbreak of carburettor icing. Blown away by what seemed likely to be illegally-tuned Alfa Romeos, AMR were probably relieved (if irritated) when the car succumbed to gearbox trouble later in the event.

Now we come to one of motorsport's oft-recurring posers, for in the first part of the 1965 season this identity (BTW 297B) reappeared, and most successfully too, but on a white/green car which had the wider-grille/Aeroflow bodyshell! Not only that, but Alan Mann's autobiography notes, "By 1965 all our cars from the previous season had already gone. We prepared all-new cars yet again, and the racing Lotus-Cortinas went back to the simpler leaf spring rear suspension". All well and good, except that the leaf-spring Lotus-Cortina was not officially announced and homologated until June 1965, by which time the new/old 'BTW' cars had already completed three European Touring Car Championship races without protests being raised.

Rather than muddy the waters even more, I have piously listed the new/old cars' achievements under their old/freshly-applied identities.

Whatever car this was, it first competed in the Coppa Europa race at Monza in March 1965, which was using the banked circuit layout, and was well up with the leading Alfas until mid-race before the BRM-tuned engine faltered and blew itself asunder. That was the low point of the entire season, for it then unleashed outright victories in the Mont Ventoux hillclimb (cutting no less than 44 seconds from the previous record). Only one week later it travelled to tackle the prestigious Nurburgring 6-Hour race and won outright with Sir John Whitmore teaming up with Jack Sears and staging a near dead-heat finish with the team's Mustang.

At this point BTW 297B finally disappeared from the AMR scene, to be replaced by one of the startlingly attractive red-and-gold 'KPU ...' cars which quite dominated the rest of the season. But was the new car merely the old car with a different identity and (later) a new paint job? Because it all happened half a century ago, we will never know.

| REGISTRATION NUMBER | ENGINE SIZE | MODEL TYPE |
|---|---|---|
| **BTW 298B** | **1558CC 4-CYL DOHC** | **LOTUS-CORTINA MK I** |

As already noted (see BTW 297B above), this was the second brand-new Lotus-Cortina race car to come from the Alan Mann Racing stable in 1964 and, although it never actually won a long-distance race, it was always competitive and often finished closely behind Sir John Whitmore, who drove the sister car BTW 297B throughout the year.

This explains why BTW 298B finished behind Sir John at Zolder for, although it was never explained, team orders were clearly being imposed. As indeed they were at Brands Hatch four weeks later, when this car finished dutifully just a few cars' lengths behind the winning Lotus-Cortinas as the cars crossed the line. Then, on the Mont Ventoux hillclimb event which followed in the south of France just a week later, this car won the event outright, following the breakdown of BTW 297B.

Another week later, the two cars started the Nurburgring 6-Hour race and eventually finished strongly in second (BTW 297B) and third (BTW 298B) places. Then, with Henry Taylor otherwise engaged on Spa-Sofia-Liège duty (see Chapter 3, 888 DOO), a promising youngster, Jacky Ickx, was to drive the second AMR car at Zandvoort, where he impressed everyone with his pace and duly finished behind Whitmore's ailing sister car.

In the rest of the season Ickx performed well at the Timmelsjoch hillclimb and again in Budapest, though Henry Taylor had no luck at Monza where first his car also suffered from carburettor icing and then had a broken brake pipe which immobilised it.

For 1965 there was a new/old car, still using the old BTW 298B registration number (see the BTW 297B entry above for a technical/quasi-legal explanation), which Henry Taylor first drove at Monza, where it retired abruptly when the engine burst as it came around the flat-out banked section. A fast ascent of the Mont Ventoux hillclimb then restored the team's spirits, though it all went wrong at the Nurburgring 6-Hour race when the car suffered intermittent fuel starvation. At a subsequent stripdown, several lengths of toilet paper were found to have been stuffed into the petrol tank and, as Alan Mann commented, "Sabotage was suspected".

After this busy career, this particular identity was retired.

## Competition Record

| | | |
|---|---|---|
| 1964 Zolder (ETC) | Henry Taylor | 2nd in Class |
| 1964 Brands Hatch 6-Hour (ETC) | Henry Taylor/Peter Harper | 2nd |
| 1964 Mont Ventoux hillclimb (ETC) | Henry Taylor | 1st |
| 1964 Nurburgring 6-Hours (ETC) | Henry Taylor/Peter Harper | 3rd |
| 1964 Karlskoga, Sweden (ETC) | Henry Taylor | 2nd |
| 1964 Zandvoort, Holland (ETC) | Jacky Ickx | 4th |
| 1964 Timmelsjoch hill climb, Austria (ETC) | Jacky Ickx | 2nd in Class |
| 1964 Budapest, Hungary (ETC) | Jacky Ickx | 13th |
| 1964 Monza (ETC) | Jacky Ickx | DNF |
| 1965 Monza (ETC) | Henry Taylor | DNF |
| 1965 Mont Ventoux hillclimb (ETC) | Peter Procter | 3rd |
| 1965 Nurburgring 6-Hours (ETC) | Henry Taylor/Peter Procter | 25th |

| REGISTRATION NUMBER | ENGINE SIZE | MODEL TYPE |
|---|---|---|
| **BTW 299B/BTW 300B** | **1558CC 4-CYL DOHC** | **LOTUS-CORTINA MK I** |

Carrying their by-now familiar livery of white with red striping on the bonnets, the 1964 Willment Lotus-Cortinas were always competitive in the British Touring Car Championship. The season started well, for at Snetterton it was only Jim Clark's Lotus-Cortina which was ahead of them, this performance being repeated at Goodwood two weeks later. Only one of the cars started at Oulton Park, and did not finish, but things were more satisfactory at Aintree in April when Frank Gardner was always close behind the two 'official' Team Lotus cars; on that occasion, Bob Olthoff's Willment car had to retire with suspension problems.

At Silverstone in May it was Olthoff who was in the third Lotus-Cortina to finish, while at Crystal Palace it was Gardner's turn to chase the Team Lotus cars home. The non-Championship race at Brands Hatch (it was a support race for the British F1 GP) was a real showpiece for all Lotus-Cortina runners, but although Sir John Whitmore took the victory in BJH 417B, Jack Sears was a fine second in the fastest of the Willment cars (the one usually driven by Gardner).

A fine performance by Olthoff at Brands Hatch (second in his class, behind Jim Clark's car) and by Boley Pittard at Oulton Park brought these two cars' season to an end.

*In 1964 the Willment team prepared and ran two A-frame Lotus-Cortinas (BTW 299B and BTW 300B) with considerable success. This was Frank Gardner leading Bob Olthoff at Silverstone.*

## Competition Record

(both cars, registration not always apparent but listed where certain)

| | | |
|---|---|---|
| 1964 Snetterton | Bob Olthoff | 4th |
| | Frank Gardner | 5th |
| 1964 Goodwood | Frank Gardner | 4th |
| | Bob Olthoff | 5th |
| 1964 Oulton Park | Bob Olthoff | DNF |
| 1964 Aintree | Frank Gardner | 5th |
| | Bob Olthoff | DNF |
| 1964 Silverstone | Bob Olthoff (BTW 300B) | 6th |
| | Frank Gardner (BTW 299B) | DNF |
| 1964 Crystal Palace | Frank Gardner | 3rd |
| | W.Brausch Niemann | DNF |
| 1964 Silverstone (non-BTCC event) | Jack Sears | 2nd |
| | Bob Olthoff | DNF |
| 1964 Brands Hatch | Bob Olthoff | 2nd |
| 1964 Oulton Park | Bob Olthoff (carrying 230 FOO) | 2nd |
| | Boley Pittard | 4th |

Note: According to an interview once given to the author by project manager Jeff Uren, the Willment team did not enjoy even quasi-works support with Lotus-Cortinas in 1965, so their detailed performance is not listed here. One of the cars, BTW 299B, did not appear in 1965 (it had probably been sold off), but BTW 300B, driven by Frank Gardner, was still demonstrably competitive. During the touring car race season Gardner finished third on one occasion, fourth four times, and fifth just once.

| REGISTRATION NUMBER | ENGINE SIZE | MODEL TYPE |
|---|---|---|
| **EHK 489B** | **1558cc 4-cyl DOHC** | **LOTUS-CORTINA Mk I** |

*AMR prepared two cars to compete in the Spa 24-Hour Saloon Car race in 1964, where Sir John Whitmore fought for the lead for several hours before the engine of this Lotus-Cortina EHK 489B expired.*

At the request of Ford-of-Belgium (and, one presumes, with some financial support), AMR was persuaded to prepare two additional Lotus-Cortina race cars to compete in the legendary Spa 24 Hour race. These were completely different from the cars which Alan Mann was already running in the 1964 European Touring Car Championship. Mann himself had no illusions, convinced that a Lotus Cortina could not complete the 24 hour flat-out race in Belgium. So he briefed his drivers accordingly and sent them out to lead the race if possible until the cars expired.

EHK 489B was driven by Sir John Whitmore and the Australian Frank Gardner. After Sir John had put the new car on pole ahead of Bohringer's Mercedes-Benz 300SE, he set out on a head-to-head race for as long as possible, but after less than three hours racing the car's clutch began to fail, and although it kept going it was not thought worth trying to make a repair. Mann, the drivers and the Belgian crowds had loved it, but that was that; it was all over within six hours.

### Competition Record
| | | |
|---|---|---|
| 1964 Spa 24 Hours (Belgium) | Sir John Whitmore/Frank Gardner | DNF |

| REGISTRATION NUMBER | ENGINE SIZE | MODEL TYPE |
|---|---|---|
| **EHK 490B** | **1558CC 4-CYL DOHC** | **LOTUS-CORTINA MK I** |

This, the second of the specially-prepared-for Spa cars, was driven by Henry Taylor and Peter Harper, who were becoming regular driving partners, Although never as dramatically fast as the sister car, these two experienced drivers kept the car going for hours longer, and it was only an enforced dynamo change that dropped it to sixth place. Unhappily, the engine then let go at the unsocial hour of 3.30am, so Mann's gloomy prognostication had been fulfilled.

*EHK 490B was specially built to tackle the Spa 24-Hour Saloon Car race, where it was driven by Henry Taylor and Peter Harper, but the engine blew before the halfway point was reached.*

**Competition Record**

| 1964 Spa 24 Hours, Belgium | Henry Taylor/Peter Harper | DNF |
|---|---|---|

| REGISTRATION NUMBER | ENGINE SIZE | MODEL TYPE |
|---|---|---|
| **JTW 496C** | **1558CC 4-CYL DOHC** | **LOTUS-CORTINA MK I** |

Team Lotus produced three new works cars for 1965 British Championship racing, these all apparently being leaf-spring cars (before the road car version had even been launched) with BRM-tuned engines producing more than 150bhp. Initially they struggled for pace against the now privately-entered Willment cars (so was the BRM tuning as effective as claimed?), but they soon became regular class leaders when driven by Jim Clark, Jack Sears and occasionally Sir John Whitmore.

The season began badly for Jack Sears at Brands Hatch in March, when he spent much time fighting with Roy Pierpoint's Ford Mustang for the lead but in the end suffered a front-wheel puncture and had to retire. He was no luckier at Oulton Park, where the car had to be parked with ignition failure after the car-to-car barging that took place.

There was ill-fortune at Snetterton, too, where both team

151

## Competition Record

| | | |
|---|---|---|
| 1965 Brands Hatch | Jack Sears | DNF |
| 1965 Oulton Park | Jack Sears | DNF |
| 1965 Snetterton | Jack Sears | 6th |
| 1965 Goodwood | Jack Sears | 2nd |
| 1965 Silverstone | Jack Sears | 3rd |
| 1965 Crystal Palace | Jack Sears | 3rd |
| 1965 Silverstone (non-BTCC race) | Jack Sears | 3rd= |
| 1965 Brands Hatch | Jack Sears | 3rd |
| 1965 Oulton Park | Jack Sears | 2nd |

*This paddock shot at Oulton Park in 1965 shows just how relaxed the pre-race scene could be in those days. Jack Sears (centre, facing the camera) finished second in JTW 496C.*

cars came together on the very first lap of the race, which meant that Sears had to visit the pits for 496C's bodywork to be cleared of the front wheel, but he then persevered to make it home in sixth place. Nine days later, at a Goodwood event where the weather was awful (there was a hailstorm before the BTCC race was due to start), the race distance was shortened to a mere five laps. Sears got away in second place immediately behind his team mate Jim Clark and held that to the end.

Silverstone in May, on the other hand, was run in ideal dry conditions, and although not even the Team Lotus cars could match the pace of the Mustangs they put up a spectacular show, and Jack Sears in 496C led his team mate Mike Spence home in third place. With Jim Clark back for the Crystal Palace race the positions were reversed, Sears finishing close behind his team mate and neither car able to catch Pierpoint's leading Mustang.

It was really the same story in the non-BTCC race at Silverstone in July, except that there were two 4.7-litre Mustangs at the head of the field, and that Jack Sears and his temporary team mate Sir John Whitmore crossed the finishing line in a dead heat for third place. Later in the summer Sears must have been thoroughly fed up with the sight of Mustang rear ends, for two such cars led him across the line at Brands Hatch.

At Oulton Park in September, in the last BTCC race of the 1965 season, Jack Sears finished third on the road but was subsequently promoted to second place (behind Jim Clark's sister car) after the Mustang which finished first was disqualified on a scrutineering technicality.

| REGISTRATION NUMBER | ENGINE SIZE | MODEL TYPE |
|---|---|---|
| **JTW 497C** | **1558CC 4-CYL DOHC** | **LOTUS-CORTINA MK I** |

Although Jim Clark clearly enjoyed racing a Lotus-Cortina just as much in 1965 as he had in 1964, his world-wide racing calendar was now so full that he could not start every race, which explains why 'his' car (JTW 497C) was sometimes driven by other guests. It all started badly for him at Brands Hatch in March when this car was badly damaged in a practice crash and JTW 498C had to be substituted instead. In that race the stand-in car led handsomely, and spectacularly from the start but faltered after only seven laps when its front wheels seemed to come loose, and only two laps later one of those wheels pulled off its studs, and the car had to be abandoned.

Jim was not then available for the next race at Oulton Park, which explains why Sir John Whitmore took his place using the 'team spare' (498C). Jim Clark and 497C were re-introduced at Snetterton, but it all went wrong on the very first lap when his car collided with Jack Sears (in 496C), the result being that Clark could only finish fifth overall. The class was won by Frank Gardner in the Willment Lotus-Cortina.

Happily it all came good at Goodwood nine days later, when there was continuous rain and the Sussex track was extremely slippery; there was even a hailstorm before the start of the BTCC race. For once the power of the Mustangs counted for nothing, and because the entire event schedule was slipping the race distance was shortened to five laps.

*A very thin field at Crystal Palace in 1964, with Jim Clark (BJH 417B) and Peter Arundell (BJH 418B) on the front row. That is David Haynes (DBH 250) in his own Lotus-Cortina behind them. Clark went on to win the race outright, with Arundell second.*

*Situation normal? Sir John Whitmore in JTW 497C just yards ahead of Jack Sears in JTW 496C at Silverstone in July 1965, where they finished in a dead heat for third place.*

Both Team Lotus cars (Jack Sears was also present in 496C) shot away at the start and were never headed, the result being Jim Clark's first Cortina victory of the season.

With Jim Clark needed to drive an F1 Lotus in the main race at Silverstone in May, Mike Spence stood in for him, settled in immediately, and finished second in the 'Lotus-Cortina' class behind Jack Sears's sister car. The following month, with victory in the Indianapolis 500 race just accomplished, Clark was back in 'his' Lotus-Cortina at the Crystal Palace race. After flinging the car about enthusiastically he ended up second overall behind Roy Pierpoint's AMR-prepared Mustang.

Once again, at Silverstone in the non-BTCC race, Jim Clark had to lend his usual driving place to Sir John Whitmore. At least he had a good excuse, as this was also British F1 GP day and he was committed to driving a Lotus 33, with the result was that he won the race outright, putting him well on the way to winning his second World F1 Championship. In his place Sir John Whitmore enjoyed himself as usual and finished exactly equal third alongside Jack Sears's sister car.

Six weeks later it was almost the same story at Brands Hatch when two Mustangs won the race and Lotus-Cortinas followed them, but Jim Clark's car suffered a blown tyre, had the wheel replaced outside the pit-lane and was subsequently disqualified.

In the last race of the 1965 BTCC season, at Oulton Park, Jim Clark led the field after a banger-racing incident at the start involving many of his rivals, then ceded the lead to Jack Brabham's Mustang and ended up second overall on the road. After the event, however, the Mustang was disqualified by the scrutineers, who discovered several illegal components in the V8 engine.

JTW 497C's BTCC works career then came to an immediate end as the BTCC was due to take the FIA Group 5 route in 1966 and newly-engineered cars would have to be developed.

## Competition Record

| | | |
|---|---|---|
| 1965 Brands Hatch | Did Not Start following a practice crash. | |
| 1965 Snetterton | Jim Clark | 5th |
| 1965 Goodwood | Jim Clark | 1st |
| 1965 Silverstone | Mike Spence | 4th |
| 1965 Crystal Palace | Jim Clark | 2nd |
| 1965 Silverstone (non-BTCC) | Sir John Whitmore | 3rd= |
| 1965 Brands Hatch | Jim Clark | Disqualified |
| 1965 Oulton Park | Jim Clark | 1st |

| REGISTRATION NUMBER | ENGINE SIZE | MODEL TYPE |
|---|---|---|
| **JTW 498C** | **1558cc 4-cyl DOHC** | **LOTUS-CORTINA MK I** |

This, the third of the 1965 Team Lotus works UK Championship race cars, was rarely called on to race, but it first appeared at Brands Hatch in March, driven by Jim Clark after his usual car, JTW 497C, was rolled heavily in the practice sessions. Although it led the race in the early stages, it had to retire on Lap 9 when it lost a wheel.

It then appeared at Oulton Park in April, driven by Sir John Whitmore. The 'bearded baronet' (as he was known in the National press, if not in the specialist magazines) qualified on the front row of the grid and the car then survived some metal-to-metal contact at Old Hall Corner after the start, yet it battled for the lead until mid-distance when it was forced out with a punctured tyre.

Unless it deputised for either 496C or 497C later in the season (carrying a 'false' registration plate?) it rarely raced again for Team Lotus in 1965.

**Competition Record**

| 1965 Brands Hatch | Jim Clark | DNF |
|---|---|---|
| 1965 Oulton Park | Sir John Whitmore | DNF |

*Jim Clark of course – only he ever seemed to get a Cortina front wheel so far off the deck. Here he is in one of the 1965 Team Lotus cars, JTW 498C, at Brands Hatch, where his car lost a wheel, forcing retirement.*

| REGISTRATION NUMBER | ENGINE SIZE | MODEL TYPE |
|---|---|---|
| **KPU 390C** | **1558cc 4-cyl DOHC** | **LOTUS-CORTINA MK I** |

Although this car seems to have been one of the original batch of leaf-spring Lotus-Cortinas that Ford issued to its works teams in 1965, it was the sister car (KPU 392C) which made most of the headlines in that year (see below), whereas KPU 390C does not appear to have been used at all at this time (except, who knows, 'in disguise'). In 1966, however, it was a different story.

The season started badly for the team at Monza in March 1966 in the four-hour race, where the Italian scrutineers seemed determined to eliminate the AMR car before the start, which would favour the new Alfa Romeo GTAs. Purely because Alan Mann was using 1965 homologation papers for a 1966 race, the scrutineers threatened to ban the cars, but as Alan then threatened to take his European Champion away before the start, which would have been very bad publicity for the organisers, they eventually backed down. Not that it

helped in the end, for the Lotus-Cortina retired at around half distance with reported fuel starvation, leaving the event to be dominated by the Alfa Romeos.

Weeks later there was better fortune when AMR sent two red-and-gold cars to fight on the twisty Aspern circuit in Austria for one hour. It was here that Sir John Whitmore was in his element: he led from the second lap to the end of the hour and thus signalled that neither he nor the Lotus-Cortina was obsolete.

For AMR it was the same story at the next ETCC round, a supporting race for an F2 extravaganza at Zolder in Belgium. Sir John was fastest in practice but it was clear that major race opposition would come from Jochen Rindt in an Autodelta Alfa-Romeo Giulia GTA, especially as Autodelta protested the eligibility of the Lotus-Cortina (a protest which was dismissed after a rigorous post-race examination). Sir

John and Rindt scrapped throughout the race, but in the end it was the smart-as-ever AMR Lotus-Cortina which won outright, and Rindt was later disqualified for an homologation infringement !

Sir John then went out to tackle the demanding Mont Ventoux hillclimb qualifying round in the south of France (this location being close to Carpentras, north of Marseilles), where he not only won outright but recorded a time of 12min 12.6sec – which was considerably quicker than he had achieved in KPU 392C in 1965. Both Sir John and Alan Mann loved this event, for it was too short and too concentrated to wear out expensively prepared cars, and it was also ideally suited to the still-improving works Lotus-Cortina.

This could not be said for the Nurburgring 500km race which followed, where 390C and the sister car 391C both had to retire with what was officially stated to be wheel bearing problems. In his autobiography, however, published many years later, Alan Mann admits that it was due to both cars losing steel wheels, which were failing around their stud mountings. Investigation later confirmed that it was wheels made by Sankey which failed, whereas those made by Dunlop never gave trouble. As Alan succinctly wrote, "We stuck to the Dunlops from then on and had no more trouble."

By this time it was clear that the 1966-model lightweight

Alfa Romeo GTAs were at least as rapid as the Lotus-Cortinas, so the outcome of the Snetterton 500km event, held in July, was rather different from the 1965 race. Conditions were very different from a year earlier as this time it was a wet race. Although 390C led right from the rolling start, almost immediately it encountered fuel starvation problems, which led to an enforced pit-stop and – eventually – to the need to change a fuel pump. Although Sir John then spent more than half the race charging up from the tail, after well over two hours the Lotus-Cortina slid off in the dreadful track conditions, damaging the front suspension and causing retirement.

As noted in more detail in the description of 391C's career, the car was then repaired and re-prepared to tackle the 84-hour Nurburgring-based Marathon de la Route, but although the team was joined on this one occasion by the legendary German rally driver Eugen Bohringer, it all came to naught when the car's engine (which was not de-tuned with 84 hours in mind) failed.

Zandvoort in September, on the other hand, was a much more ordered affair. Sir John Whitmore held the lead for a time before being passed in streaming wet conditions by two works Alfa Romeo Giulia GTAs – and, towards the end of the race, by Frank Gardner in 391C!

Sir John's final appearance in an AMR Lotus-Cortina (he

*Looking just as smart as ever, in its red and gold colour scheme, KPU 390C rests in the grounds of the late Alan Mann's home in Hampshire.*

would retire from motor racing immediately afterwards) came when he contested the ETCC season's final event, the hillclimb at Eigental in Switzerland, where he won outright. This was also KPU 390C's last outing as a works Lotus-Cortina, but it went into very honourable retirement and many years later was seen at the Goodwood Revival and at the International Motorsports Show at the NEC. For this book it was photographed at the British base where AMR has lovingly preserved it and where it shares garaging alongside an equally famous AMR Escort Twin-Cam, XOO 349F.

| Competition Record | | |
|---|---|---|
| 1966 Monza 4 Hours (ETCC) | Sir John Whitmore | DNF |
| 1966 Flugplatz Aspern, Austria (ETCC) | Sir John Whitmore | 1st |
| 1966 Zolder (ETCC) | Sir John Whitmore | 1st |
| 1966 Mont Ventoux hillclimb (ETCC) | Sir John Whitmore | 1st |
| 1966 Nurburgring (ETCC) | Sir John Whitmore/Frank Gardner | DNF |
| 1966 Snetterton 500km (ETCC) | Sir John Whitmore | DNF |
| 1966 Marathon de la Route, Nurburgring | Sir John Whitmore/Eugen Bohringer | DNF |
| 1966 Zandvoort, Holland (ETCC) | Sir John Whitmore | 4th |
| 1966 Eigental Hillclimb, Switzerland (ETCC) | Sir John Whitmore | 1st |

*As raced by AMR, the red/gold Lotus-Cortinas featured four recognition stripes under the front grille.*

The neatly detailed announcement of the entrant tells its own story.

This was the way that AMR ensured the security of the lift-up panels on the Lotus-Cortina race cars.

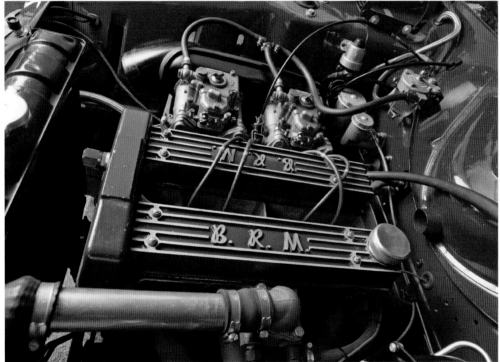

Although AMR tended to prepare their own Lotus engines in the mid-1960s, in more recent 'classic' years, the famous KPU 390C used a BRM-tuned power unit. This shot was taken in 2015.

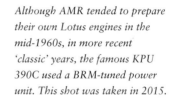

KPU 390C's boot area in later life features a modern-type safety cell fuel tank - and a truly tiny, lightweight, battery.

Rear view of the 1965/1966 AMR Lotus-Cortina race car. No mistaking its purpose, or the team's reputation.

From any angle, the Alan Mann Lotus-Cortina race cars were beautifully profiled and detailed.

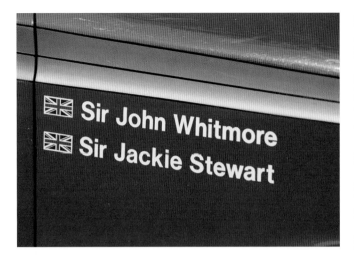

*The truly famous sat here - these being two world champions who drove KPU 390C when it was in being raced by Alan Mann Racing.*

*The cockpit/driving compartment of the Alan Mann race cars was always simple, but effective. KPU 390C as it raced – and as it is in the 2010s.*

| REGISTRATION NUMBER | ENGINE SIZE | MODEL TYPE |
|---|---|---|
| **KPU 391C** | **1558CC 4-CYL DOHC** | **LOTUS-CORTINA MK I** |

Once this car was commissioned, at Zolder in June 1965 (though it seems that it ran with KPU 397C registration plates), it soon settled down to its real job, which was to act as 'rear gunner' to Sir John Whitmore's sister car, whose sights were already set on winning the European Championship. At Zolder, when it was originally painted white with a green spear along the flanks (red/gold would soon follow for future events) Peter Procter used it to finish just inches behind Sir John. Henry Taylor was third fastest up the hillclimb in Austria, and Jackie Stewart was as fast as Sir John in Sweden until the car lost a wheel due to a stud breakage. With Peter Procter at the wheel at Snetterton, 391C stayed with 392C for hours, making only two lengthy planned fuelling stops, but after the second one the engine would not restart and the battery had to be changed, which cost the tough Yorkshireman four laps and four places. Finally, in the last race of the season, a 24-lap sprint at the Dutch Zandvoort circuit, Procter once again finished dutifully behind Sir John's car, in one of Alan Mann's staged near-dead heats.

After a winter rebuild (the author presumes that the 1965 391C was still the same 391C in 1966, not the result of number-plate swapping), its status as the team's back-up car to Sir John Whitmore (for this year in KPU 390C) was resumed. The original master plan was to have the ever reliable Peter

Procter in the car, but a horrifying accident at Goodwood on Easter Monday 1966, which resulted in a Broadspeed Anglia catching fire and badly burning Peter, put paid to that. For the rest of the season no fewer than seven different but very capable drivers took the wheel instead.

Accordingly, this car did not enjoy a settled season. Hubert Hayne retired from the Austrian race, Frank Gardner from the Belgian race at Zolder, while Lucien Bianchi (who drove no fewer than three different makes and types of car on this particular day) finished fourth on the Mont Ventoux hillclimb. Jacky Ickx then shone briefly at the Nurburgring until his car suffered the same wheel failure as did 390C on the same occasion.

Then it was time for Jackie Stewart to be drafted in to race the car in the rain-soaked Snetterton 500km race, which soon claimed Sir John Whitmore's sister car in awful conditions. Jackie led the race for the first hour and thenceforth was always on the leader-board, eventually finishing fourth overall behind the winning Alfa GTA and two BMW 2000TIs.

After this, AMR took on the mad and (as it seemed in advance and was in the event itself) misguided attempt to tackle the Nurburgring-based Marathon de la Route, an 84 hour event, part race/part rally, using the combined Nordschleife and Sudschleife circuits where the cars had to keep going at all costs or be severely penalised. One observer described it as being an endless series of special stages where there were strict penalties for taking too long to do one lap or to stay in the pits. As Alan Mann later wrote, "If our Cortinas had been up to lasting that distance we could have had some real fun in the 1966 Marathon. We had some great drivers there, with a couple of interesting newcomers added to our trusted group of regulars".

Vic Elford shared this car with Ford-Germany competitions boss Jochen Neerpasch, telling the author, "We led all the way, driving triple shifts of three x 2½ hours, up to the 72 hours mark when, guess what? The cylinder head gasket failed."

Rebuilt and re-engined, the car was than entrusted to Frank Gardner for the Zandvoort ETCC qualifier, where he not only finished third overall but actually led his illustrious team-mate Sir John Whitmore across the line, and the season ended three weeks later when Bo Ljungfeldt was second fastest up the Eigental hillclimb in Switzerland.

## Competition Record

| | | |
|---|---|---|
| 1965 Zolder (ETCC) | Peter Procter | 2nd |
| 1965 ASC-Olympia Berg Rennen, Austria (ETCC) | Henry Taylor | 3rd |
| 1965 Karlskoga, Sweden (ETCC) | Jackie Stewart | DNF |
| 1965 Snetterton 500km race (ETCC) | Peter Procter | 6th |
| 1965 Saint Ursanne, Switzerland (ETCC) | Henry Taylor | 5th |
| 1965 Zandvoort, Holland (ETCC) | Peter Procter | 3rd |
| 1966 Flugplatz Aspern, Austria (ETCC) | Hubert Hahne | DNF |
| 1966 Zolder, Belgium (ETCC) | Frank Gardner | DNF |
| 1966 Mont Ventoux hillclimb (ETCC) | Lucien Bianchi | 4th Overall |
| 1966 Nurburgring (ETCC) | Jacky Ickx/Paul Hawkins | DNF |
| 1966 Snetterton 500km (ETCC) | Jackie Stewart | 4th |
| 1966 Marathon de la Route, Nurburgring | Vic Elford/Jochen Neerpasch | DNF |
| 1966 Zandvoort (ETCC) | Frank Gardner | 3rd |
| 1966 Eigental hillclimb, Switzerland (ETCC) | Bo Ljungfeldt | 2nd |

| REGISTRATION NUMBER | ENGINE SIZE | MODEL TYPE |
|---|---|---|
| **KPU 392C** | **1558CC 4-CYL DOHC** | **LOTUS-CORTINA MK I** |

KPU 392C, which took over from BTW 297B as Sir. John Whitmore's 'personal' race car in the Alan Mann team for 1965 (or was it merely a new number on an earlier 1965 car? See BTW 297B above), became outstandingly successful, and for the rest of the 1965 season a sensation was caused not by its winning a race but by losing one! In the end it tackled six events, winning four of them, and finished second twice to another AMR car, Bo Ljungfeldt's 4.7-litre Ford Mustang.

First time out, at Zolder, the white/green new car – the red/gold colour scheme was still to be adopted – ended the one-hour race in a contrived dead heat, with Peter Procter's sister car right behind it. The Austrian hillclimb was run off in heavy rain but Whitmore won in any case, and at Karlskoga in Sweden Sir John was overwhelmed by the 350bhp Ford Mustang which just happened to be prepared and run by the AMR team.

The Snetterton 500km race which followed was a real battle with the newly-homologated Alfa Romeo Giulia GTA

*Alan Mann (left) and Sir John Whitmore both looking tired but happy after winning yet another saloon car race in an AMR Lotus-Cortina in 1965.*

*The two ultra-successful Alan Mann Lotus-Cortinas which dominated European saloon car racing in 1965 prepare to line up on the grid for the Snetterton 500km race of 1965. Sir John Whitmore is at the wheel of KPU 392C and behind it is KPU 391C.*

(coupé body style, aluminium bodywork, and every homologated extra – plus a few more besides – that the inventive Italians could think of). Because it did not start until 6.00pm it was a day/evening race, lasting just under four hours, and Sir John did not have it all his own way. First of all there was the running battle with Bussinello's remarkable GTA, then the fact that his team mate Peter Procter (in KPU 391C) led him narrowly from time to time, and then a burst rear tyre (at the hairpin) on Lap 50. Fortunately Sir John made it back to the pits, where the team not only changed the wheel but also carried out refuelling and the already-planned mid-event pit stop activity at the same time. Returning to the race in third place, by the time darkness fell Sir John had caught and passed the GTA and his team-mate Peter Procter, finally winning by 54.4sec.

The final race of the season was a 24-lap event at Zandvoort circuit in Holland, where AMR not only fielded both the red-and-gold Cortinas but also sent out Bo Ljungfeldt in their Mustang. Predictably the Mustang won, though Sir John finished second to him, utterly confirming that this had been the outstanding car of the 1965 European racing scene.

At this point the car, the 'original' KPU 392C, was retired For a time it was a 'show car' which Ford used to publicise its burgeoning race car programme. As already noted above, for 1966 Sir John Whitmore's 'personal' race car in Europe was KPU 390C, but there is evidence that 392C was later re-born

| Competition Record | | |
|---|---|---|
| 1965 Zolder | Sir John Whitmore | 1st |
| 1965 ASC Olympia Berg-Rennen, Austria | Sir John Whitmore | 1st |
| 1965 Karlskoga, Sweden | Sir John Whitmore | 2nd |
| 1965 Snetterton 500km | Sir John Whitmore | 1st |
| 1965 Saint Ursanne hillclimb, Switzerland | Sir John Whitmore | 1st |
| 1965 Zandvoort trophy, Holland | Sir John Whitmore | 2nd |

Note: Although this car did not race again in Europe, a car carrying that identity later raced in the USA in 1966.

(or perhaps I should say 're-created') and was raced successfully by AMR in the American IMSA Championship, which falls outside the scope of this book.

The 1966 'successor', KPU 390C, need one add, was as successful and looked just as smart as its predecessor.

*Sir John Whitmore and KPU 392C on their way to winning the Snetterton 500km.*

*No rush, no panic, just high-speed routine in this typical AMR pit stop. The extra Marchal driving lamps were fitted because this event at Snetterton was a day/evening affair*

*KPU 392C was, and still is, one of the most famous of all Lotus-Cortina race cars. It always looked, and performed, immaculately.*

*Many years after the 1965 season, Sir John Whitmore was happy to be reunited with the car which had given him so much success in that year.*

*KPU 392C featured at the Goodwood Festival of Speed in the 2010s.*

*The 1965 AMR race cars used self-prepared Lotus-Ford engines, and this example fitted to KPU 392C was of exactly the type it would have used at the time.*

*Alan Mann's team always set their cars up to be as low as possible at the rear.*

*Steel wheels, suitably reinforced, were used throughout the 1965 race season which KPU 392C won so convincingly, and have stayed with the car through its long 'celebrity' career.*

*The cockpit of KPU 392C was very simply equipped, complete with lightweight seats, and is still in 'as original' condition.*

163

| REGISTRATION NUMBER | ENGINE SIZE | MODEL TYPE |
|---|---|---|
| **KPU 396C** | **1558CC 4-CYL DOHC** | **LOTUS-CORTINA MK I** |

This car apparently started what might have been an anonymous and utterly blameless career as Colin Chapman's own road car but was then involved in an accident on a public road close to the Lotus factory. Never one to waste anything, Chapman then had it restored, and turned into a BTCC car, where it acted as back-up/practice/test car to the regular 1966 BTCC cars, PHK 614D and PHK 615D.

We know that it appeared several times at BTCC circuits in 1966 but did not start many races. Peter Arundell ran it at Crystal Palace, where it was apparently the first Team Lotus car to start with a BRM fuel-injected engine – but that blew. It was then apparently damaged in a fire during practice at the British F1 GP meeting at Brands Hatch, but at Oulton Park in September it won a race which featured a running battle with Jackie Oliver's Mustang and Brian Muir's Galaxie before both the American cars broke under the strain.

Finally, Jacky Ickx drove the car in the last race of the season (Brands Hatch at the end of October), this being the only occasion in 1966 when all three Team Lotus cars appeared in the same race. Unhappily for Jacky he crashed the car, which brought its rather on/off career as a race car to a close.

*The driving compartment of KPU 396C.*

*No, not a BRM engine, but a Team Lotus twin-cam race-tuned by that company in 1966 for use in KPU 396C.*

### Competition Record

| | | |
|---|---|---|
| 1966 Crystal Palace | Peter Arundell | DNF |
| 1966 Oulton Park | Jim Clark | 1st |
| 1966 Brands Hatch (October) | Jacky Ickx | DNF |

| REGISTRATION NUMBER | ENGINE SIZE | MODEL TYPE |
|---|---|---|
| **KPU 397C** | **1558CC 4-CYL DOHC** | **LOTUS-CORTINA MK I** |

This race car started life in rather complicated circumstances. According to the registration number (*this* registration number, KPU 397C) it first appeared at Zolder in June 1965, where Peter Procter finished one car's length behind team mate Sir John Whitmore (in KPU 392C), but all the other information indicates that it was actually KPU391C, in which Procter finished the rest of the season. At Zolder, this 'disguised' car ran in white-with-green-spear colours, yet when the definitive car appeared it was always liveried in red-and-gold. But, among friends, who's counting?

**Competition Record**

| 1965 Zolder (ETCC) | Peter Procter | 2nd |
|---|---|---|

| REGISTRATION NUMBER | ENGINE SIZE | MODEL TYPE |
|---|---|---|
| **PHK 614D** | **1558CC 4-CYL DOHC** | **LOTUS-CORTINA MK I** |

The British Touring Car Championship of 1966 was run for FIA Group 5 cars, a category which allowed considerably more technical freedom than the Group 2 rules had done, and this meant that the original Lotus-Cortinas would no longer have been competitive. Team Lotus accordingly built up two brand new cars, PHK 614D and PHK 615D, which were joined later in the season by KPU 496C (which started its life as Lotus founder Colin Chapman's personal road car and only became a race car in its second year of existence).

Although the new cars looked superficially like the old (except that they ran without bumpers, as allowed, to save weight), they were very different under the skin, and took every advantage of the new technical freedoms. To minimise their original three-wheeling habits, the MacPherson strut independent front suspension was abandoned, and although the original lower wishbone mounting points were used, more compact coil spring units were employed, installed at a much more pronounced angle from the vertical and giving different operating geometry; the units were adjustable for length, and the whole suspension had adjustable-length links too. Lotus-designed 6.5in magnesium alloy road wheels were used, with Firestone race tyres.

Early in the season the cars were still using 160bhp Weber-carburetted engines, but from Crystal Palace on Whit Monday these were replaced by new engines having Lucas fuel injection, 12.0:1 compression ratios, forged crankshafts, dry sump lubrication and a claimed peak of 180bhp at 7000rpm. Throughout the year, engines were prepared and maintained by BRM at Bourne. Peter Arundell, now recovered from his awful F2 accident, but still demonstrably more frail than before, was the usual driver of this car, which started seven races in 1966 and finished all of them.

The season began as it was destined to go on, with Team Lotus's 1.6-litre-engined cars battling to stay competitive with the massively powerful V8-engined Ford Mustangs, Falcons and Galaxies, so Peter Arundell had to settle for fifth place at Snetterton on Good Friday, and the same again at Goodwood three days later.

Four weeks later, at Silverstone, with Jim Clark away in the USA on Indianapolis 500 qualifying duty, Arundell became de facto team leader for the weekend, and drove PHK 615D. His usual car, therefore, was taken over by Jacky Ickx, who finished fourth, close behind him, in spite of making a super-rapid pit stop to check that his steering had not been deranged in a nudge with another competitor.

At the end of the month there was something of a switch round. With Jim Clark still at Indianapolis, Arundell ran in KPU 396C and thoroughly enjoyed battling for the lead with Roy Pierpoint's Falcon until the newly fuel-injected Team Lotus car blew a cylinder head gasket. Then, for the support race at the British F1 GP meeting at Brands Hatch, it was John Whitmore's turn to drive 614D, which he did in splendid fashion, leading off the start line until swamped by American V8 power, and finishing fourth with a big smile on his face.

Peter Arundell then got his seat back again for the last three races of the season, finishing third, sixth and second (this one, on aggregate in the last of the season's events, at Brands Hatch, but it involved him and Jim Clark driving both cars!). Peter then left the team, and for 1967 was replaced initially by John Miles.

Like his 'senior partner' Graham Hill in the other 1966 team car, new recruit John Miles was obliged to use the old car for the first races of the 1967 season until the Mk II Lotus-Cortina could be made ready. Unhappily the car blew its engine spectacularly on the second lap of the first heat of the first event (at Brands Hatch), after which Team Lotus decided not to repair it in a hurry, so Miles was obliged to sit out the next two races altogether. It was no way for a successful machine to approach the end of its BTCC career, which was prolonged until mid-season.

### Competition Record

| | | |
|---|---|---|
| 1966 Snetterton | Peter Arundell | 5th |
| 1966 Goodwood | Peter Arundell | 5th |
| 1966 Silverstone | Jacky Ickx | 4th |
| 1966 Brands Hatch (British F1 GP support race) | Sir John Whitmore | 4th |
| 1966 Brands Hatch August) | Peter Arundell | 3rd |
| 1966 Oulton Park | Peter Arundell | 6th |
| 1966 Brands Hatch (October) | Peter Arundell/Jim Clark | 3rd in Class |
| 1967 Brands Hatch | John Miles | DNF |
| 1967 Mallory Park | John Miles | DNF |
| 1967 Silverstone (May) | John Miles | 6th |
| 1967 Silverstone (July, British F1 GP support race) | John Miles | 6th |

| REGISTRATION NUMBER | ENGINE SIZE | MODEL TYPE |
|---|---|---|
| **PHK 615D** | **1558CC 4-CYL DOHC** | **LOTUS-CORTINA MK I** |

The second of the brand-new-for-1966 BTCC Team Lotus cars was reserved for Jim Clark whenever he could spare time from his F1 and F2 commitments, and had the same mechanical specification as the sister car. At Snetterton, to open his account, he finished third overall behind a Mustang and a Galaxie, while at Goodwood on Easter Monday he was fourth, behind a Galaxie and two Mustangs. It was, it seemed, all set to be that sort of a season.

With Jim Clark at the Indianapolis 500 race instead of competing at Silverstone in May, Peter Arundell took over the job of team leader in PHK 615D, and spent much time scrapping for second place overall, but in the end could only take third behind Sir John Whitmore's AMR-prepared Ford Falcon and Sir Gawaine Baillie's supercharged Falcon. There was no substitute, it seemed, for cubic inches.

Jacky Ickx then took his turn to drive 615D at Crystal Palace, where he thoroughly enjoyed getting into third place behind two big V8-engined Fords, and at Brands Hatch (the venue for the British F1 GP) he finished closely behind Sir John Whitmore's sister car, both the cars now having fuel-

*PHK 615D was Jim Clark's regular Lotus-Cortina in 1967, though his financial arrangements (he was a 'tax exile' in that season and could not always be in the UK) meant that he did not take part in every BTCC race.*

*How could the Porsche 911 ever be approved as a 'Touring Car'? Somehow Porsche achieved that for 1967, which had Vic Elford battling head-to-head with Group 5 Team Lotus Lotus-Cortinas. Graham Hill drove PHK 615D three times in 1967 and is seen here at Snetterton in March on his way to finishing fourth overall.*

injected engines.

Six weeks later Jim Clark was back in town, making one of his fleeting visits to the UK, where he raced the fuel-injected Team Lotus Lotus-Cortina for the first time at Brands Hatch in August. The fact that it had been a wet morning and that Jim got off the line to lead into the first corner helped a lot, for he was never caught, and ended up recording the only racing victory that this particular Lotus-Cortina ever enjoyed.

The last race of the year was held at Motor Show time at Brands Hatch in October, where there were two heats and different drivers were allowed in each heat. Confused? Jim Clark drove the car in the first heat and won it, while Peter Arundell

drove the same car in the second heat and finished second.

Although there was going to be massive change as the 1967 season progressed – new drivers, new Mk II cars and new 16-valve engines – the 1966 works cars had to be retained until homologation of the new cars was achieved. Since Jim Clark was currently living outside Britain in Paris and Bermuda as a tax exile, he could not drive the Lotus-Cortinas, which meant that the new recruit to the Lotus ranks, Graham Hill, automatically became team leader.

Hill drove Jim's old car three times early in the season in March, at Brands Hatch, Snetterton and Silverstone, and was thoroughly competitive though always just outpaced by the same Ford Falcons as had made life so hard for Clark in 1966.

## Competition Record

| | | |
|---|---|---|
| 1966 Snetterton | Jim Clark | 3rd |
| 1966 Goodwood | Jim Clark | 4th |
| 1966 Silverstone | Peter Arundell | 3rd |
| 1966 Crystal Palace | Jacky Ickx | 3rd |
| 1966 Brands Hatch (British F1 GP support race) | Jacky Ickx | 5th |
| 1966 Brands Hatch (August) | Jim Clark | 1st |
| 1966 Brands Hatch (October) | Jim Clark/Peter Arundell | 2nd |
| 1967 Brands Hatch | Graham Hill | 2nd |
| 1967 Snetterton | Graham Hill | 4th |
| 1967 Silverstone (Easter Monday) | Graham Hill | 4th |

# CHAPTER 8:
# LOTUS-CORTINA MK II IN RACING

In March 1967 Ford launched the Lotus-Cortina Mk II, which used the same basic steel platform, chassis, engine and running gear as the final type of Mk I but had an all-new two-door body shell, all steel, though aluminium panels were optional extras (which were never actually fitted on the production line examples). The new model was therefore a little heavier but apparently just as aerodynamically efficient as the Mk I, but (as far as the dealer chain was concerned) the important advance was that the Mk II was to be built on the same assembly line as all other Cortinas in the massive Ford factory at Dagenham in Essex. Lotus insisted that this was because they had just moved their manufacturing base from Cheshunt to Hethel Airfield, a few miles south-west of Norwich. Ford, on the other hand, never denied that the move was made so that they could ensure better build quality of the production cars.

As far as the factory and factory-sponsored teams were concerned, the Mk II could look forward to a very active life in motorsport. The rally team worked hard at producing more optional equipment, especially TJ fuel injection (as already detailed in Chapter 5), while the race teams took advantage of a British interpretation of FIA Group 5 regulations allowing alternative cylinder heads to be used. This meant that the new Ford-Cosworth FVA F2 engine, which was built up around the Lotus-Cortina cylinder block/bottom end but featured a 16-valve twin-cam cylinder head and Lucas fuel injection, could be fitted instead.

At this time supplies of the FVA engine were very restricted, as it was originally meant to be a Formula Two engine for use in state-of-the-art single-seater race cars. There were few such units going spare in 1967, especially as the cost was high, and F2 teams like Lotus and Brabham were happy to take as many as were available. When Ford pulled rank with Cosworth and made sure that a few – a *very* few – FVAs would be made available to their favoured saloon car racing teams (one understands, on a lend-lease arrangement), as far as the opposition

*Ford emphasised the Lotus-Cortina Mk II's connection with motor racing by placing a press car alongside a Ford/Cosworth engined single seater. UEV 629E was a road car never otherwise used in motor sport.*

was concerned it was virtually game over.

Other events, however, rapidly caught up with all the teams. As far as Lotus was concerned, 1967 was also the year in which the Cosworth DFV-engined Type 49 F1 car appeared (it started racing, and winning, in June), while Ford began development of a new rally car, the Escort Twin-Cam, of which prototypes started running in the autumn, and which would go on sale in January 1968. What this meant that was that all the works-sponsored teams had more pressing projects to think about.

For 1967 Team Lotus made some big changes. They would use the new Lotus-Cortina Mk II in Touring Car racing, and the cars would be powered by the Cosworth-Ford FVA unit This meant that the saloons would have 205bhp – a very peaky 205bhp, it must be accepted, later rising to 220bhp – but undoubtedly effective.

After a tentative start to the year, when the upgraded old-shape 1966 Mk I cars had to be used (the Mk II road car models were not revealed until March 1967), a new pair of Lotus-Cortina Mk IIs – CTC 14E and CTC 24E – first appeared at the Silverstone meeting in April, where Lotus's new Formula One recruit Graham Hill drove one car. During the season Hill was joined at various times by John Miles, Paul Hawkins and Jacky Ickx, the main class opposition coming from Vic Elford's newly-homologated Porsche 911, which in spite of its cramped cabin had somehow managed to be homologated as a four-seater 'touring car'; it was not only the British who were good at reading regulations!

Class wins were one thing, but in 1967 not even the FVA-engined Lotus-Cortinas could overcome the 4.7-litre and 5.3-litre V8-engined Ford Falcons and Mustangs which were also taking every advantage of the Group 5 regulations in the British series. During the year a works Lotus-Cortina usually won its capacity class, but this was a season in which it could never finish higher than third overall.

As with the rally programme, so with the racing programme. In 1968 Ford knew that the Lotus-Cortina was about to become obsolete, as the new, smaller, lighter and more promising Escort Twin-Cam would be announced in January 1968, and the factory intended to concentrate on those cars in future. Accordingly, after five flamboyant racing seasons, the official Team Lotus Lotus-Cortina racing programme was quietly laid to rest.

Ford, on the other hand, who were never willing to miss a publicity trick in those days, provided a Boreham-built FVA-engined race car (UVX 565E) for *Motor* magazine to test at the end of the 1967 season. Even though it was tested two-up, plus test measuring gear, it still recorded 0-60mph in 6.3sec, 0-100mph in 15.2sec, and went on to a top speed of 130mph – quite remarkable by the standards of the mid-1960s. This, incidentally, was with an engine warning label in large letters fixed to the dashboard which stated: 'DO NOT EXCEED 9,000RPM'!

There was thereafter a short-lived reprieve for these cars. As an interim measure the Frank Gardner/Alan Mann Racing team campaigned two different red-and-gold FVA-engined Mk II Lotus-Cortinas (one of them the UVX 565E car already mentioned) at the very start of the 1968 season before they switched to an Escort Twin-Cam, while Brian Robinson's ex-works machine (CTC 14E) took second place in its class behind one or other of Gardner's Fords on seven occasions.

In racing and rallying the works Lotus-Cortina Mk II motorsport programme was very short-lived. Team Lotus. which retained the contract to contest the British Touring Car Championship, only raced the cars in 1967 (actually only from April to September, just five months), and never again entered the BTCC after that. At the end of the year the entire Team Lotus stock – three 'mothballed' Mk Is and the two Mk IIs, but without their FVA engines, which were Ford property and had been returned to the factory – were sold off to the Brian Robinson team, which campaigned some of them with honour in the next two seasons.

Alan Mann Racing, for their part, chose to run a privately-developed 5-litre Ford Falcon in the 1967 Championship (in fact the red-and-gold car won the 1967 series convincingly, taking seven outright victories in the process), and did not race a single Lotus-Cortina Mk II in the UK, or indeed in Europe, in the whole of 1967. In 1968, however, they raced Mk IIs just a few times in the early months (in the British and the European Championships) while they waited for the new Escort Twin-Cam to be homologated.

So the Lotus-Cortina's works racing career ended as abruptly as it had begun. In September 1963 two Mk I cars first appeared at Oulton Park and were instantly competitive. Its successor, the Escort Twin-Cam, was homologated in May 1968, and the Mk IIs were instantly made obsolete. For five years, though, it had been a very exciting ride.

*Alan Mann Racing was deservedly famous by the late 1960s when this Mk II saloon car was prepared.*

| REGISTRATION NUMBER | ENGINE SIZE | MODEL TYPE |
|---|---|---|
| **CTC 14E** | **1598CC 4-CYL 16V DOHC** | **LOTUS-CORTINA MK II** |

The first of the 205bhp FVA-engined Mk IIs (CTC 24E was the other one) was finally homologated and made ready to race for the late-April *Daily Express* International Trophy weekend at Silverstone. Graham Hill, who had only recently joined Lotus to drive the new Type 49 DFV F1 car, had already done some private testing in the car, and was expecting great things of it.

There was a pre-start drama for Hill in this car, for although it arrived on the grid after the one positioning lap its engine then fell silent, and it was only after minutes of frantic

effort that the mechanics discovered a faulty ignition system, pushed and pulled everything, and persuaded it to fire up; no-one doubted that the start would have been diplomatically delayed if more time had been required! Even so, it was all no avail, for although Hill was immediately fourth behind the Mustangs and Falcons, the ignition system died again after just one lap, and that was that for the day.

Two weeks later, in the short confines of Mallory Park, there was better luck for the team. Graham Hill was otherwise detained so his car was driven by Jacky Ickx, and in a rain-soaked event he held on closely to the usual Falcon and Mustang leaders, set fastest lap in the race, and finally took third place.

It was not until August, at the Guards International meeting at Brands Hatch, that Graham Hill was reintroduced to the FVA-engined Lotus-Cortina race car, and it was not a happy occasion. Having got away from the start with some spirit in and among the assorted V8-engined American cars, he saw rival Frank Gardner's AMR Falcon spin at Westfield Bend and, to quote *Autosport*, "Hill's Cortina did a very good job of entering the Falcon via the driver's door. Both cars drove round to the pits for a quick inspection and then carried on, but Hill was soon out with deranged steering."

Hill had no more luck at Oulton Park in September. He had settled into fifth place when, on the very last lap, the brakes on the Cortina-FVA failed completely at Esso Bend and the car plunged off the road and entered a small lake. Happily, neither Hill nor the car were injured, and as far as Team Lotus was concerned the car's career was over, for it was then sold off to the Brian Robinson team and therefore leaves this story.

*In February 1967 CTC 14E served as a press car for photographs of the new Lotus-Cortina Mk II, but within weeks the self-same identity appeared on a Team Lotus race car which started its life in April. Same number, different cars, or same car re-prepared? Those lions, incidentally, were at Longleat and were very real; the author understands that the driver had the engine running and first gear already selected, just in case.*

### Competition Record

| | | |
|---|---|---|
| 1967 Silverstone | Graham Hill | DNF |
| 1967 Mallory Park | Jacky Ickx | 3rd |
| 1967 Silverstone (May) | John Miles | 6th |
| 1967 Silverstone (July, British F1 GP support race) | John Miles | 6th |
| 1967 Brands Hatch | Graham Hill | DNF |
| 1967 Oulton Park | Graham Hill | DNF |

| REGISTRATION NUMBER | ENGINE SIZE | MODEL TYPE |
|---|---|---|
| CTC 24E | 1598CC 4-CYL 16V DOHC | LOTUS-CORTINA MK II |

Although it lined up on the starting grid at Silverstone in April 1967, alongside Graham Hill in CTC 14E, to John Miles' distress the second of the Team Lotus MK IIs had to be pushed off the track before the race began because oil was seen to be seeping on to the ground under the engine.

This still relatively fresh car finally re-appeared at Silverstone at the British GP meeting in July, when Graham Hill was due to drive a Lotus 49 DFV in the F1 race, so Paul Hawkins stood in happily instead. On this 20-lap race, in a magnificent battle with two Falcons and Jackie Oliver's Mustang, Hawkins set a new class fastest lap and finished fourth overall; not even Vic Elford in a Porsche 911 could keep up with that.

Jacky Ickx then came back into the team for the last two events of the season, using CTC 24E on both occasions. At Brands Hatch in August he benefitted from Graham Hill's shunt with Frank Gardner's Falcon, settled down into third place, steadily reeled in Vic Elford's Porsche 911, and went through into second place just two laps from the end. It was one of those stirring days when the driver seemed to be inspired, for he threw the car around in a way no-one had seen since Jim Clark and Sir John Whitmore in Mk I cars.

The last event of the Championship took place at Oulton Park in September, but any thoughts Ickx might have had about repeating his heroics from Brands Hatch lasted only until Lap Six, when the car went off the road (at Esso Bend, as had CTC 14E) and was eliminated. It was then sold off to Brian Robinson and therefore (everyone thought) left this story.

But it did not. Once Alan Mann concluded that the ex-Boreham race car (UVX 565E) which he had acquired for early 1968 was not up to his standards, and that he needed a better stop-gap until the Escort Twin-Cam was homologated, he approached Ford again –- and by hook and by crook CTC 24E suddenly became available to him after a very short stay in Robinson's hands. What was once a works car, then an ex-works car, became a works car again.

After another midnight-oil exercise, the car was made ready for the Snetterton round of the 1968 European Touring Car Championship, and it would tackle five events in the next four weeks. At Snetterton it used a 175bhp Vegantune-prepared Lotus-Ford 8-valve twin-cam featuring Lucas fuel injection (the 16-valve FVA engine installation was not authorised for ETCC Group 5 racing). The front suspension was like that used in 1967 Team Lotus form but the rear axle was located, Boreham/Len Bailey style, by radius arms and a Watts linkage.

Frank Gardner put the car on the second row of the rolling-start grid and began to settle into third place overall (be-

hind a Mustang and Vic Elford's Porsche 911), but after only six laps the engine began to overheat and retirement was inevitable. That was on Good Friday, but only three days later, on Easter Monday, the team tackled the first BTCC race to be held on the just-completed Thruxton circuit, using an FVA engine, and the car took third place behind two 4.7-litre Ford Falcons.

There was no time for a breather, however. On the following Sunday (just six days later), the car had to get to Belgrade in Yugoslavia (now Serbia) for the Four-Hour race, once again using an 8-valve engine. As it happened, the rush was all a waste of time as a fuel injection pipe broke during practice, causing an engine bay fire, the car broke another petrol pipe in specially-arranged official practice, and after only ten laps of racing the engine once again overheated.

After a rushed return to base, and the insertion of the 16-valve FVA engine instead of the Vegantune unit, six days later the same hard-working machine contested the British Championship race at Silverstone, where Frank Gardner held third place behind two squabbling Falcons, then settled to second place behind Brian Muir's Falcon, but only five laps from the end an oil leak developed in the engine, pressure dropped away, and the car had to be nursed to the finish in fourth place.

It was still not quite the end of the rush for this amazingly durable car, for only a week afterwards (having once again had an engine change, this time a return to a Lotus-Ford 8-valve twin-cam to meet the regulations) it had to make the

*CTC 24E was the second of the FVA-engined Lotus-Cortina Mk IIs prepared by Team Lotus in 1967, here being urged into fourth place at Silverstone by Paul Hawkins.*

trek to Belgium for the fifth round of the European Touring Car Championship, where the AMR Escort Twin-Cam was also set to race for the first time.

With Frank Gardner engaged to drive the Escort, the Lotus-Cortina was entrusted to Richard Attwood and, as far as everyone at Ford was concerned, this was a real demonstration. Attwood took second fastest to Gardner in qualifying, led the entire race at first, soon let the Escort go by, and maintained second place to the finish, only 10.9 seconds adrift.,

It was an excellent way for this stop-gap car to end its career, which it did, there and then.

*CTC 24E had started as white/ green Team Lotus works Mk II race car in 1967, but as a stopgap for Alan Mann Racing it was also used in red/gold guise in the early months of 1968. This was Frank Gardner on his way to fourth place overall (behind a fleet of Mustangs and Falcons) at Silverstone in May 1968.*

## Competition Record

| | | |
|---|---|---|
| Silverstone (April) | John Miles | Did Not Start |
| 1967 Silverstone (May) | Paul Hawkins | 4th |
| 1967 Silverstone (British F1 GP meeting, support race) | Paul Hawkins | 4th |
| 1967 Brands Hatch | Jacky Ickx | 2nd |
| 1967 Oulton Park | Jacky Ickx | DNF |
| Then, after a short sojourn as an ex-works car with Brian Robinson, and henceforth in Alan Mann Racing's hands: | | |
| 1968 Snetterton 500km (ETCC) | Frank Gardner (for AMR) | DNF |
| 1968 Thruxton | Frank Gardner (for AMR) | 3rd |
| 1968 Belgrade (ETCC) | Frank Gardner (for AMR) | DNF |
| 1968 Silverstone | Frank Gardner (for AMR) | 4th, 2nd in Class |
| 1968 Zolder (ETCC) | Richard Attwood (for AMR) | 2nd |

### CTC 24E – A personal memory
*Many years after the car's active career had ended, the author participated in a photoshoot of one of the very last works Lotus-Cortina race cars, CTC 24E, and the impressions I recorded on that day tell an enthralling story.*

It's the colour scheme of that car, no question, that makes everyone grin. No-one else ever raced cars painted like this, in red with gold striping. Not just any red, either, and certainly not just any gold. When AMR raced them there was genuine gold dust in the paint mix – not much, for sure, but enough to bring out the lustre (Alan bought the paint from a metal-flake company in London) – so it's not surprising that today's owners can't quite afford to match it.

CTC 24E is a car with two characters. Posing for pictures, gleaming in the evening sunshine, and very carefully liveried, it is elegant and purposeful. When fired up, and driven hard, it is a rough-riding, raucous, elbows-out monster. The driving seat is hard, the instruments – well, er, basic – and there isn't an inch of surplus trim or decoration. But in 1968 it was a winner – for a few months, the months that mattered.

The story started in 1967 when Colin Chapman's Team Lo-tus built new Mk II Lotus-Cortina race cars for the BRSCC Saloon Car Championship. CTC 24E (CTC = Cortina Twin Cam, Geddit?) was memorable for it always raced with the 205bhp Cosworth-Ford FVA engine. Rapid? Damn right – for the only saloons which could beat it regularly were all vast, V8-engined, American Fords.

Owner Ian Perrett now takes up the story:

"I bought it just about three years ago – but that was for the second time. In 1970 I was working for a Ford dealer, and it was through him that I bought it from Alan Mann. As far as I know, he had put the car away when the Escorts started racing, and except for the odd FordSport Day it hadn't moved again.

"When I bought it, it had a Vegantune Twin-Cam engine on Lucas fuel injection with a dry sump and the oil tank in the boot, and I kept it for about three years. I used it in club races and hillclimbs.

"I sold it on in 1973, and lost touch for a long time – then about 15 years ago a friend called me and asked if I had kept the original log book. I told him I had it, he wanted to buy it, but I never let it go. Anyway, years later Andy Middlehurst, who has two Team Lotus Mk Is, came down to me, buying works parts. Andy had a look through my scrap book, saw CTC 24E, and loved it.

"A few months later he called me and said there was guy in the north who owned it – but it had a V6 engine in, and he was sprinting it. He then sold it on to Andy, who started restoring it but then decided that his allegiance was to Mk Is. Trevor Pritchard then bought it from him, restored it very nicely – and eventually it came to me.

"We're not going to talk money, but it cost me a lot more the second time round that it had done in 1970.

"Now that Trevor has restored it, except for the engine – and we all know why it can't have that – it's an absolute 'time warp' machine, for no-one crashed it and no-one gave it a nasty butchering at any time It's just like it was in 1968 when Frank Gardner raced it. It still has the original bodyshell which AMR had modified from the 1967 Team Lotus shell."

Alan Mann Racing only used this car as a stop-gap. AMR was all set to use Escort Twin-Cams throughout 1968 but homologation was delayed. Only two weeks before the first event of the year, Mann had to make a decision – to miss the first few races, or to find another car to use instead. Ford couldn't be seen to lose face. In the first place they let him have an ex-Boreham Mk II, UVX 565E, a race car originally built by the rally team and also previously used in 1967. With only 10 days to do the job, Alan hastily prepared it for Brands Hatch in March, but Frank Gardner hated the way it handled and the team was in despair.

At this point, even more desperate for a credible car to race, Mann approached the north-country racer Brian Robinson. At the end of 1967 Team Lotus sold five Lotus-Cortina race cars – three Mk Is and two Mk IIs (CTC 14E and CTC 24E) – to Robinson, who had a thriving privately-financed team. Brian raced some of them and found the Mk Is quicker, and CTC 24E hung around for some time.

It was then that AMR, helped along by a bit of subtle arm-twisting from Ford, bought CTC 24E and set about re-preparing it, in another tearing hurry. This, now, is where the wheel turns full circle. Mann and Len Bailey had already engineered a new chassis for the first of their Escort Twin-Cams (the cars were built, but not able to race) so they installed much the same layout under the Lotus-Cortina. It worked, and it worked well !

OK, it looks right, it sits low, and it has those fat slick tyres to give grip. AMR ran 9in rim magnesium wheels at the front and 11in rims at the rear. We know that in 1968 it also ran with the FVA engine. But was that enough to make it so fast? You only find that out when you peer underneath and see

what Len Bailey's design engineering and AMR's preparation skills had achieved.

First of all, a massive fabricated box-section front cross-member was welded up between the chassis legs, which not only stiffened up the shell but was also a perfect base for the complex front suspension. Instead of the standard MacPherson strut, AMR/Bailey engineered a new system with large, wide-based lower wishbones, their inner pivots being near the centre-line of the car.

To meet the Group 5 regulations (which stated that the original suspension pick-ups should be used) dummy struts were retained, but inboard of them, and canted well over, inboard, at the top, were combined coil-over-shocks. A modified, very

*CTC 24E started its racing life as a 1967 Team Lotus car, but was then used (in this beautifully detailed livery) by Alan Mann Racing.*

*Perhaps not as neat and tidy in later life as it would have been when Alan Mann Racing was using it, this was the driving compartment of CTC 24E, which was raced in 1967 and 1968.*

*CTC 24E was the ultimate works-supported Lotus-Cortina Mk II race car. In 1968 it was replaced by the first of the AMR Escort Twin-Cams.*

Suicidal? Not at all, for in 1968 cages were not required – only five years earlier, don't forget, the original Willment Ford Galaxie had been disqualified from several races because it actually had a cage fitted. Don't times change?

Ian Perrett notes, "What AMR used to do, was to weld a square box-section in the roof panel – which is still there – underneath the roof lining. The cage had to be used in recent years, before I bought it."

The front cross-member, welded up to the chassis rails, helped stiffen up the shell considerably, but AMR saved as much weight as possible by fitting aluminium bonnet, boot and doors. These were optional equipment on the Mk II, though every Dagenham-built road car had all-steel body-work. Official option lists can be very useful at times...

Cortina road cars had the fuel tank under the boot floor, but on this race car the tank was an aluminium box, mounted inside the boot, with a big snap-action filler neck which would have been useful for accepting funnels for fuel churns. As far as I know, this car's only long-distance race was the Snetterton 500km race – where it retired before the first fuelling stop!

Ian is so proud of this one-off that he was determined to keep it as original as possible: "I've tried not to mess with it at all. It came to me with a four-speed box in 1970, and I put a five-speed Hewland in it which was based on the 2000E casing. This time round it has the five-speed Trannix gearbox (straight cut gears and all), and I haven't changed that.

"For what I use the car for these days – hillclimbs, sprints and stuff – I have Minilite-lookalike wheels, 8.5in rims at the front and 10in at the rear. Not quite as wide as AMR used to use, but I'm comfortable with that. Those are low-profile slicks, by the way, to keep the gearing well down, because I'm using a 4.4:1 axle, with a Salisbury limited-slip diff. in it. And a single-piece prop shaft, by the way – most people say I should use a split prop, and I've got all the bits needed to convert it back. But it works as it is.

"Although I know how to replicate the exact gold colour – I've actually got a small can of the real thing at home – I can't afford to do the whole thing, so that's the nearest to the actual shade of gold that I could arrange.

"For safety reasons, incidentally, the fuel and oil lines are now braided, not plain rubber, and the oil lines now run through the car, whereas the original AMR spec saw them running in aluminium tubes underneath the floor pan, close to the prop shafts."

Honesty time now. This precious old car no longer has its FVA engine fitted. These were always very rare, and these particular Ford-owned engines were fitted to Alan Mann's own Escorts and were later returned to the company. When it was eventually sold off, CTC 24E got a Twin-Cam engine instead – and the one fitted today is a 200bhp 1.6-litre BDA type, backed by a five-speed gearbox. Maybe it's not strictly origi-nal, and maybe the engine doesn't look quite the same – but the performance, and the noises, are just as good. It impressed

high-geared, rack-and-pinion steering gear was arranged to fit inside the cross-member itself, and the anti-roll bar no longer had any locating function.

At the back end Mann 'accidentally' arranged for the chassis legs to have some 'accident repair' damage. Along with some extra wide inner wheelarches – obvious from pictures of the boot arrangements – these quite coincidentally (nudge nudge, wink wink) allowed him to run 11in rear rims. Axle linkage was by coil-over-shocks, with twin forward-facing radius arms on each side, and with sideways location by a Watts linkage mounted underneath the axle casing (not be-hind, as is more normally provided on cars like this).

Although CTC 24E now has a very simple roll-cage in-stalled, if you look at the period pictures of this car in action in 1968 you'll notice that it raced without a cage of any sort!

*Although the auxiliary instrument binnacle was that of a standard Mk II car, in CT24E the instru-ments themselves were all special.*

the hell out of me, for sure, especially as there isn't any rubber, anywhere, in the engine mountings. Someone mentioned the phrase 'bucket of bolts' and I won't argue with that.

Driving it, by the way, is for masochists. My first problem was actually fitting into the narrow-hipped, moulded Team Lotus seat – Lotus used that in all manner of models of this period. The clutch – well, let's say I stalled the car at least twice before remembering what my RS200 had once been like: in or out, with no half measures. The engine – well, we all know about 1.6-litre BDAs, right? I knew how far it would rev – and I also knew how big a bill I would get from Ian Perrett if I missed a gear.

What was that phrase Ian had used to describe this magnificent old race car? 'A time-warp racer', he said. He was right. It's 36 years old, but time could just have stood still. Great car, great performance, great evening...

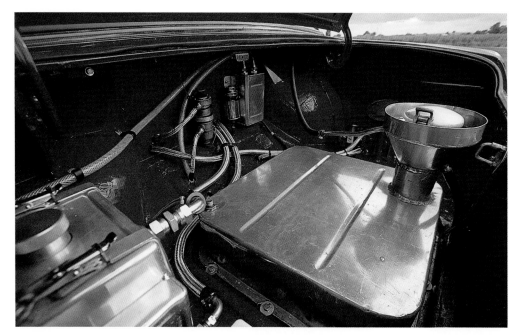

*Neatly installed, as expected, were the dry sump oil tank (left) and alloy fuel tank of CTC 24E.*

| REGISTRATION NUMBER | ENGINE SIZE | MODEL TYPE |
| --- | --- | --- |
| **UVX 565E** | **1598CC 4-CYL 16V DOHC** | **LOTUS-CORTINA MK II** |

One must admit in fairness that this particular car was never quite as pure a race car as Ford (or, later Alan Mann Racing) would have wished, as it was built by a rally team with little state-of-the-art racing experience. Built at Boreham in the spring of 1967 by the rally team mechanics, using a rare FVA 16-valve engine, it was not backed by the detailed circuit-racing knowledge that both Team Lotus and Alan Mann Racing had assembled.

It was only raced twice in 1967, first when the amiable Belgian, Lucien Bianchi, was asked to contest the Team Lotus FVA-powered Mk IIs in the support race held at Silverstone at British F1 GP time. That was a disappointment as the car lasted only six laps before stopping out on the circuit with terminal fuel-injection problems.

The second appearance was at Oulton Park in September, where Roger Clark (not Jim, who was still a tax exile, basing himself on Paris or Bermuda at this time) tried to make sense of it.

We now know more about this car than originally we did, which helps to explain why pure racers like Alan Mann and Frank Gardner were not at all impressed by the handling

*UVX 565E, was originally built by Ford Motorsport at Boreham with a 16-valve FVA engine and occasionally appeared in saloon car races. Lucien Bianchi is driving it at Silverstone in the spring of 1967.*

Taking on UVX 565E on the beggars-can't-be-choosers basis, and fitting it with a rare 225bhp FVA engine, AMR spent just 10 days rebuilding the car to their standards, painting it in true red/gold AMR colours. Against all the odds, driver Frank Gardner then put the car on the front row of the grid at Brands Hatch between a 5.3-litre supercharged Ford Falcon and Vic Elford's Porsche 911. The race was held in two 20-lap heats, with times aggregated afterwards. Gardner was third in the first race and was running second in the second heat until his car suddenly suffered a broken driveshaft, after which he limped home in fifth place, but his aggregate times left him third behind the Falcon and the Porsche.

Although neither Gardner nor Alan Mann himself were happy with the way the car handled (and were already working hard on preparing a replacement for it – CTC 24E, as already described), they refurbished it and sent it out to tackle their first European Championship round of 1968 at Aspern, near Vienna. To everyone's delight and the team's great relief, Gardner romped home ahead of Teodoro Zeccoli's works Alfa Romeo Giulia GTA to win this stop-gap car's final event.

*New generation leads old: this is Silverstone in 1967 and Bianchi in UVX 565E is leading the 1966 Team Lotus car driven by John Miles.*

when they came to use it in 1968. As Ford later revealed, the front suspension used standard lower wishbones instead of Lotus Elan-type struts, while the rear suspension employed upper and lower radius arms to further locate the leaf springs, attached by rollers to the springs themselves. Four-wheel disc brakes were also used.

This all looked very promising, and rally-driver Roger instantly found himself ahead of Hill and Ickx (clearly he had enjoyed the argy-bargy which was always a feature of the starts at Oulton Park), but only two laps into the event the differential began to give trouble, and retirement was inevitable.

Ford then lent the car to Alan Mann Racing, who had originally planned to contest the entire 1968 season in new Escort Twin-Cams, but as these were not to be homologated into Group 2 (which made an upgrade to Group 5 possible) until May 1968 they were left floundering.

*Originally built by Boreham in 1967, UVX 565E was allocated to Alan Mann Racing early in 1968 (while he waited, impatiently, for the Escort Twin-Cam to be homologated). Frank Gardner drove it into third place at Brands Hatch in March 1968, but soon swapped it for a different machine.*

## Competition Record

| | | |
|---|---|---|
| 1967 Silverstone (July, British F1 GP support race) | Lucien Bianchi (for Boreham) | DNF |
| 1967 Oulton Park (for Boreham) | Roger Clark (for Boreham) | DNF |
| Then, in AMR's hands: | | |
| 1968 Brands Hatch | Frank Gardner | 3rd, 2nd in Class |
| 1968 Flugplatz Aspern, Austria (ETCC) | Frank Gardner | 1st |

## FVA-ENGINED LOTUS-CORTINA
## UVX 565E –A REAL BOREHAM RARITY

As the main text relates, Boreham built up a Cosworth FVA-engined Lotus-Cortina race car, UVX 565E, in 1967, raced it twice, unfortunately without any success, and then put it away while they began to concentrate on the development of the new Escort Twin-Cam. FVA-engined Lotus-Cortinas were extremely rare (Team Lotus had a pair), so *Motor* magazine was extremely fortunate to be allowed to use UVX 565E for a time at end of the year. Roger Bell (soon to become a well-respected saloon car race driver as well as being an excellent writer and photographer) wrote all about this car, at length, in the Christmas issue of *Motor*, published on 23 December 1967.

Because it was not judged to be completely road-legal (excessive exhaust noise and the use of race tyres were among the problems), Bell only drove the car at MIRA, the industry's proving ground, and later in the same day at Silverstone, but came away with a full set of performance figures which included an astonishing 0-100mph sprint in 15.2sec, and a top speed of at least 130mph.

The car had been conceived on the 'back-of-a-cigarette-packet' basis by team boss Henry Taylor and his senior engineers, Bill Meade and Mick Jones, with all the expected chassis modifications (including the use of upper-and-lower-link rear axle location and four-wheel disc brakes), and featured the ultra-modern 16-valve Ford-Cosworth FVA 1.6-litre F2 engine, which produced at least 205bhp and could be revved to 9000rpm and more. The axle ratio used was not quoted, the gearbox was the ultra-close-ratio Lotus-Ford four-speeder, and there were Goodyear racing tyres on Minilite wheels.

Bell made much of the rigmarole needed to fire up the engine from cold but was also clearly astonished by the performance it liberated, noting that the engine was twice as powerful as the one normally fitted to standard road cars. This is a summary of the figures published in *Motor* at the time:

| | FVA-engined race car (UVX 565E) | Standard road car (CTC 17E) |
|---|---|---|
| Maximum speed (mph) | 130 | 105 |
| | | |
| Acceleration from rest (secs) to | | |
| 30mph | 2.8 | 3.6 |
| 40mph | 3.7 | 5.3 |
| 50mph | 4.7 | 6.9 |
| 60mph | 6.3 | 9.9 |
| 70mph | 7.8 | 13.5 |
| 80mph | 9.5 | 17.7 |
| 90mph | 12.5 | 25.2 |
| 100mph | 15.2 | 38.7 |
| 110mph | 20.0 | N/A |
| 120mph | 27.5 | N/A |
| | | |
| Top gear acceleration (secs) | | |
| 30-50mph | 10.2 | 9.2 |
| 40-60mph | 9.1 | 9.4 |
| 50-70mph | 9.1 | 9.7 |
| 60-80mph | 8.8 | 10.3 |
| 70-90mph | 8.7 | 12.9 |
| 80-100mph | 8.5 | N/A |
| 90-110mph | 9.5 | N/A |
| 100-120mph | 13.1 | N/A |

# CHAPTER 9:
# CAPRI: RACING, RALLYING AND RALLYCROSS

The Capri was rarely central to any long-term motorsport programme which Ford-of-Europe was carrying out, but there were times during the 1970s when much works Capri success was gained on the racetracks of Britain and Europe. For clarity, I have covered each programme in separate sections and, to keep the story as simple as possible, I have barely touched on the private-owner activity which kept the Capri's image afloat for a time.

*Jochen Neerpasch was the original Ford-of-Germany Competitions Manager (the equivalent of Stuart Turner), who astonished the company by jumping ship to join BMW in 1972.*

## Capris in European Motor Racing
## 2300GT and RS2600 1969-1973

Way back in 1968 Ford of Germany opened up a new Motorsport Department in Cologne with big ambitions. Led by Jochen Neerpasch, with Mike Kranefuss as his deputy and the talented young engineer Martin Braungart, they began by trying everything – Escorts for racing, Taunus saloons for long-distance rallying, and Capris for racing and rallying.

By 1969 Neerpasch's team had started to concentrate on the Capri range in motor racing, at first by using the most powerful German-built model then available, which was the 125bhp V6-engined 2300GT. At the same time (by taking lessons from their UK associates at Boreham) they also inspired the development of an ultra-lightweight version of the Capri. The new model, the RS2600, was a rough-and-ready road car in some ways, but it had great potential in motorsport – as a 'saloon' car.

First of all, however, Cologne needed to convince the FIA that a Capri *was* a 'saloon' car - that it had the necessary four seats and the appropriate minimum dimensions inside the cabin to qualify. Now, those of us who like the author have owned early-type Capris will surely remember how cramped the original car actually was. No matter. If Porsche could get the 911 homologated as a saloon (have you ever tried to sit in the rear 'seats' of an early 911?), Cologne thought the Capri should qualify. A bit of guile helped. Quite by accident, some used to say with a smile, the car presented for FIA inspection had rather saggy rear seat cushions, had clearly been put on a diet, and had miraculously 'enhanced' shoulder-room and rear-seat legroom – the trick was done. Was it totally honest? Porsche thought so with the 911, so Ford had followed suit.

Because the Capri's chassis was really an amalgam and an update of Cortina Mk II/Corsair and Escort thinking, there was no problem in making the cars handle. Right from the start, therefore, most of the effort went into developing the V6 engines. Weslake (of Rye, in England) were hired to carry out much of the power-tuning, which included designing optional light-alloy cylinder heads; this was essential as the standard production heads were positively asthmatic. In the end, though, a mountain of practical input from Boreham's ace engine-builder, Peter Ashcroft, would be needed to make the power units reliable and race-worthy.

As the race cars were often not road-registered (sometimes they carried plates at the rear, but almost never at the front), and the individual factory records of this period do not seem to have survived, it has been difficult to work out how many cars were works prepared, and indeed how many were used for more than one season. What follows, therefore, covers the RS2600 factory effort on a season-by-season rather than car-by-car basis:

## 1969

The very first works Capris were a pair of non-homologated V6-engined 2.3-litre 2300GTs registered in Cologne with KHX... identities. In March 1969 they started the Lyons-Charbonnières International rally, a wintry open-road event in France which used special stages close to the Riviera, entrusted to Dieter Glemser and Jean-Francois Piot. The cars had Weslake-developed engines fitted with three twin-choke Zenith-Solex downdraught carburettors and producing 170bhp, with Minilite magnesium alloy wheels and Bilstein dampers. It was an encouraging start, Glemser taking fourth and Piot taking seventh place; Piot's co-driver, incidentally, was Jean Todt.

Development and motorsport entries from Ford-of-Germany then got under way, and it was significant that this started immediately after German-prepared Taunus saloons had unexpectedly triumphed in the gruelling East African Safari rally. If the team could win in such a high-profile event, it was thought, surely it would be straightforward enough to produce a good Capri track car?

It all started with a single entry in the technically complex 84-Hour Marathon de la Route, which was held under what might be described as high-speed/regularity conditions around the old Nurburgring race circuit, but not even the distinguished duo of Dieter Glemser and Tim Schenken could keep the 2300GT going for long, for it eventually retired with cylinder head gasket failure.

That was in August 1969, and a month later there came an ambitious three-car entry in the ten-day Tour de France, this being the first time that a team of works Capris was seen on

*One of the earliest works Capri race cars was this 2300GT, which finished sixth in the 1969 Tour de France, driven by Jean-Francois Piot and Jean-Francois Behra.*

*By comparison with what was to follow, the original works Capri race cars, built in Cologne, were not as fast and not as powerful. This car competed successfully in the Tour de France of 1969 but had only about 150bhp from its 2.3-litre V6 engine.*

the racetracks of Europe. Fortunately, the Tour de France was one of those wonderful events which allowed non-homologated cars to take part, for which Ford was grateful as the type of Capri they finally intended to use (we would know it as

| The 1969 season's record (2300GT) | | |
|---|---|---|
| Lyons-Charbonnières rally | Dieter Glemser | 4th |
| | J-F Piot | 7th |
| 84 Hour Marathon de la Route (Nurburgring) | Dieter Glemser/Tim Schenken/J-F Piot | DNF |
| Tour de France | J-F Piot/J-F Behra | 6th/1st in Class |
| | D Glemser/K Kaiser | DNF |
| | T Schenken/G Klapproth | DNF |
| Tour de Corse (in a 2.6-litre engined car) | J-F Piot/J Todt | 3rd |

the RS2600) was not yet available for sale. Accordingly, three evolved versions of the Lyons-Charbonnières cars were built in Cologne, but only one of them was fit enough and rugged enough to finish. It was a prototype Group 5 version (running in green-and-yellow BP fuel colours, in a category where Group 2 homologation was not appropriate) which finished sixth in the hands of Jean Francois Piot/J-F.Behra. The two other cars retired, one with fuel injection problems, the other after an accident.

That, in a way, was encouraging enough, but what followed weeks later was even more so. The Tour de Corse was a demanding all-tarmac rally held on the serpentine public roads of Corsica, where vehicle agility (allied to driver bravery) was as important as outright power. Experience, too, counted for a lot, which explains why it was a French crew (Jean-Francois Piot and Jean Todt) who were handed the drive, and they pleased everyone by taking a 2.6-litre engined 2300GT into a

storming third place overall, with Gerard Larousse winning outright in a rear-engined Porsche 911R and Orsini's fragile little Alpine-Renault A110 in second place. All in all, the Capri was less than three minutes behind the 911R at the finish of the weekend-long event.

## 1970

The results achieved in 1969 had been so encouraging that a major International race car programme was envisaged for 1970. This was the year in which what would eventually become a short-lived Ford Advanced Vehicle Operation (AVO) was set up in Europe, with Ford-of-Britain concentrating on Ford Escorts and rallying, while Ford-of-Germany worked hard to get a new light-weight and more powerful Capri RS2600 on to the market. This, though, would take a little time. For 1970, therefore, the Ford-of-Germany works

### The 1970 season's record (2.4-litre/2300GT))

| | | |
|---|---|---|
| Monza 4-Hour race (ETCC) | M Mohr, H Werner | 2nd, 1st in Class |
| | D Glemser/F Mazet | DNF |
| | Yvette Fontaine/ | DNF |
| East African Safari rally | R Aaltonen/P Huth | DNF |
| | D Glemser/K Kaiser | DNF |
| | R Hillyar/J Aird | DNF |
| Austria Trophy race (ETCC) | D Glemser | DNF |
| | M Mohr | DNF |
| | H Werner | DNF |
| Grand Prix of Budapest (ETCC) | D Glemser | 2nd/1st in Class |
| | M Mohr | DNF |
| Brno 4-Hour (ETCC) | D Glemser | 5th |
| | M Mohr | DNF |
| Mont Cenis (EHCC) | J Mass | DNF |
| Mont Ventoux (EHCC) | J Mass | 3rd/2nd in Class |
| Tourist Trophy, Silverstone (ETCC) | D Glemser/M Mohr | 5th |
| | R Stommelen | DNF |
| | R Aaltonen | DNF |
| Trento Bordone (EHCC) | J Mass | 10th/1st Class |
| Sestriere Hillclimb (EHCC) | J Mass | 10th/2nd Class |
| Nurburgring 6-Hours (ETCC) | M Mohr/R Aaltonen | DNF |
| | D Glemser/R Stommelen | DNF |
| | H Werner/Yvette Fontaine | DNF |
| ADAC Bergpreis (EHCC) | J Mass | 4th/4th in Class |
| Monte Dore (EHCC) | J Mass | 3rd/3rd Class |
| Zandvoort Trophy race (ETCC) | D Glemser/J Mass | 7th |
| Jarama 4-Hour race (ETCC) | D Glemser/M Mohr | DNF |
| | J-F Piot | DNF |
| Tour de France (using 2.6-litre engines) | R Aaltonen/F Mazet | DNF |
| | D Glemser/K Kaiser | DNF |
| | J-F Piot//Rabate | DNF |
| Osterreich Dobratch (EHCC) | J Mass | 11th/2nd in Class. |

*Jochen Mass, who is still an important personality in the German 'classic' racing scene, was one of the works Capri stars in the early 1970s.*

*Works Ford-of-Germany Capri RS2600s used new cylinder heads developed by Weslake, with fuel injection, which helped to extract 300bhp from the 3.0-litre V6 engines.*

team was unleashed to tackle the prestigious European Touring Car Championship, which comprised 11 long-distance saloon car races across the continent. Until the RS2600 was homologated – which would not be achieved until the end of the year – the programme would have to be undertaken with 2.4-litre versions of the V6 engined 2300GTs, allied to the new German ZF five-speed gearbox which would soon find its way into many other Ford competition cars in the 1970s and 1980s. It was an ambitious but disappointing effort. As Mike Kranefuss later admitted, "1970 was a complete disaster for us."

The first race cars looked purposeful but crude: wheel-arch flares were still bolted on, the spoilers were tacked on, and the detailing in the engine bays was messy. With Kugelfischer fuel injection early engines produced a little over 200bhp, though the ever-optimistic Weslake test-bed showed 230bhp (Ford would learn to live with the figures produced using 'Sussex air', and became quite vocally cynical about it).

From October 1970, with the RS2600 homologated, things looked up. Ford somehow got approval for all the lightweight panels and other limited-production features of the prototype cars. The RS2600's homologated weight was only 1985lb/900kg, though the lightest race cars rarely weighed under 2095lb/950kg. As roll cages became ever more complex, and wheels/tyres larger, that weight would creep up over

the years.

In 1970, the season was littered with 2300GTs which retired with engine problems of one type or another, yet even so there was a class win at Monza and a second overall in Budapest to celebrate.

## 1971

For 1971, and with the possibility of glass-fibre panelled 2873cc (later 2933cc) RS2600s coming along, something had to be done. Against Weslake's wishes, and even with some resistance from Ford-of-Germany, Ford-UK's Boreham-based engine specialist, Peter Ashcroft, was sent over to Cologne to sort out the mess. To quote my fellow author Jeremy Walton: "Ashcroft's six-month spell at Cologne... was the stuff of which legends are created. He spoke not a word of German. He was English and meant to sort out the problems the Germans felt had been created by an English company [Weslake]..."

Ashcroft found that at 7000rpm the engines were suffering from severe internal vibrations – "They were literally shaking themselves apart". Although he could not do the sums required to prove a point, he concluded that the crankshaft design was wrong. A long phone conversation with Keith Duckworth of Cosworth – from his workbench, with an offending component in front of him as he spoke – and a

## The 1971 season's record (2.8-litre/RS2600s, becoming 2.9-litres from Nurburgring)

| | | |
|---|---|---|
| Monza 4-Hours (ETCC) | D Glemser/A Soler-Roig | DNF |
| | F Mazet/H Marko | 10th/3rd in Class |
| Austria Trophy (ETCC) | D Glemser | 1st |
| | H Marko | 2nd |
| | A Soler-Roig | 3rd |
| Brno Grand Prix, 4-Hours (ETCC) | D Glemser | 1st |
| | K Ahrens | 4th |
| Nurburgring 6-Hours (ETCC) | D Glemser/H Marko | 1st |
| | R Stommelen/A Soler-Roig | DNF |
| Spa 24 Hours Race (ETCC) | D Glemser/A Soler-Roig | 1st |
| | J Mass/G Birrell | DNF |
| Zandvoort Trophy, Holland (ETCC) | D Glemser | 2nd |
| | H Marko | 3rd |
| | A Soler-Roig | 4th |
| 12 Hours (2 x 6 Hours) Paul Ricard (ETCC) | D Glemser/A Soler-Roig | 1st |
| | R Stommelen/G Birrell | 2nd |
| | G Hill/J Surtees | 4th |
| Jarama (Spain) 4-Hours (ETCC) | D Glemser/A Soler-Roig | 3rd, 1st in Class |
| | F Mazet/J-P Jabouille | 4th |
| | J-F Piot | Disqualified |
| Tour de France | D Glemser/K Kaiser | DNF |
| | J-F Piot/J Porter | 7th/1st in Class |
| Kyalami 9-Hours, South Africa (Springbok Series) | D Glemser/J Mass | 7th/1st in Class |
| Capetown 3-Hours, SA | J Mass | DNF |
| Laurenco Marques 3-Hours, SA | J Mass | 1st |
| Bulawayo 3-Hours, SA | J Mass | DNF |
| Goldfields Welkom 3-Hours, SA | J Mass | 5th, 1st in Class |
| Pietermaritzburg, 3 Hours, SA | J Mass | 5th, 1st in Class |
| Macau saloons | D Glemser | 1st |

Plus eight appearances in German Championship events, which included six victories for Jochen Mass.

masterclass in crankshaft design and balancing were needed. In 1970/71 Ashcroft's recommended solutions – to fit a new design of steel crankshaft, with steel rods, to dry-sump the engine, and to beef up the cylinder block – were all adopted: "We started off with around 260bhp," Peter later recalled, "for the season, and ran a variety of Mahle piston compression ratios, maybe down to 10.5:1 for a long race like Spa, but 11:1 and more by the time we were searching for the target of over 300bhp." By mid-season 275bhp was always available, and by the end of the year the latest 2933cc engines were revving to 7500rpm and producing 280/285bhp. All this and a more thoughtful, integrated approach to chassis and aerodynamic engineering made the 1971 cars look much more purposeful.

The difference between 1970 and 1971 was chalk-and-cheese. The cars were now RS2600s, lighter, more powerful, much more reliable, and they handled a lot better. What had almost become the 'corporate' layout of racing rear suspension was adopted – the beam located by upper and lower radius arms, with a Watts linkage pivoting on the rear of the axle casing. Although leaf 'springs' had to be retained, they were in soft and quite useless plastic. The *real* springs were coils wrapped around Bilstein dampers, forming sturdy-looking rear struts. If you think this looked similar to systems already seen on British Escort race cars, you are correct. Four-wheel disc brakes, wider alloy wheels from Limmer (by 1973 these would grow to 16in diameter and 14in wide at the rear), and ever-widening glass-fibre wheel-arch extensions, were added. Front under-bumper spoilers were also developed, but the regulations banned a transverse rear spoiler, which was desperately needed.

Even so, in 1971 in the high-profile European Touring Car Championship the RS2600s almost always led races, often won events, and usually had the beating of the best that major rivals BMW could produce. The works Capris took their first-ever victory in the Austrian Salzburgring event with Dieter Glemser at the wheel.

Throughout the season, the works RS2600s were fast,

*On its way to victory at Monza during the 1972 European series, this is the Mass/Larrousse Capri RS2600.*

*Early in the six-hour race at the old long Nurburgring circuit in 1972, the Mass/Larrousse RS2600 was on its way to second overall.*

stable and very reliable, winning six of the eight long endurance races outright; they also led the other races before hitting engine problems, and notched up a load of seconds and thirds. Team leader Dieter Glemser won the Drivers' Championship. Amazingly, because of a quirk in the Championship regulations, this was not quite enough to give Ford the Manufacturers' Championship, which actually went to 1.3-litre Alfa Romeos in another class.

Famous victories came in the Spa 24 Hour race (where Dieter Glemser/Alex Soler-Roig averaged 113.51mph), and in the double-six-hour race (a total of 12 hours on two successive days) at Paul Ricard in France, when Glemser and Soler-Roig again shared the driving. All of which made victory in the Nurburgring 6-Hour race (Glemser and Helmut Marko) look positively routine.

At the end of the season, and just to rub in the point, Jochen Mass flew out to South Africa with one of the cars and just one mechanic, plus some spares, entered all six events in the Springbok Championship, won one of the six races and finished well up in several others – and gave Ford the Manufacturers' title in that series too!

## 1972

Even though Jochen Neerpasch and Martin Braungart both left the team early in the year (they were head-hunted by BMW), in 1972 the RS2600s were even more successful. An extra winter's development, with Boreham's Peter Ashcroft was once again much involved in the work in Cologne, saw the 2.9-litre engines pumped up to 285/290bhp at 7500rpm. There were more purposeful-looking wheelarch flares, a more sturdy roll cage, and wide-rim 15in wheels. Even so, continuing success was now as much down to immaculate preparation and perfect racecraft as to having a fast car and a team of very talented drivers. Jochen Mass and Hans-Joachim Stuck were the regular stars, but there was even time for a one-off appearance (in the French Paul Ricard Six-Hour race) by F1 heroes Jackie Stewart and Francois Cevert.

In 1972 the Capris won seven of the nine European Championship qualifying rounds, a privately-owned British RS2600 won at Paul Ricard, and a works car finished second in the other event (the Nurburgring 6-Hour race, when a lengthy pit stop was needed to cure brake problems). Once again the team won the Spa 24 Hour race, this time at 116.39mph. Jochen Mass shared a winning drive five times, and Dieter Glemser three times. This helped Mass to become European Touring Car Champion. Hans Stuck also won the German Championship in an RS2600.

In the French 6-Hour race the entire works team was beaten by the privately-prepared British RS2600 of Brian Muir/John Miles. The car was no faster but had a slightly modified engine, with a different inlet manifold and fuel-injection supply arrangements. This gave noticeably better fuel economy. This meant that the British car was just as fast as the works cars but needed one less time-consuming pit stop to

### The 1972 season's record (2.9-litre V6-engined cars used throughout)

| Event | Driver(s) | Result |
|---|---|---|
| Le Mans 4-Hours | Hans Stuck | DNF |
| Monza 4-Hours (ETCC) | J Mass/G Larrousse | 1st |
| | D Glemser/A Soler-Roig | DNF |
| Austria Trophy (ETCC | D Glemser | 1st |
| | H Stuck | 2nd |
| Brno GP (ETCC) | D Glemser | 1st |
| | J Mass | 3rd |
| Nurburgring 1000km (World Championship) | D Glemser/J Mass | 7th, 1st in Class |
| | H Stuck/A Soler-Roig | 8th |
| Le Mans 24 Hours (World Championship) | G Birrell/C Bourgoignie | 10th, 1st in Class |
| | D Glemser/A Soler-Roig | 8th |
| | J Mass/H Stuck | DNF |
| Nurburgring 6-Hours | J Mass/G Larrousse | 2nd |
| | D Glemser/H Stuck | DNF |
| | A Soler-Roig/G Birrell/C Bourgoignie | DNF |
| Spa 24-Hours, Belgium (ETCC) | H Stuck/J Mass | 1st |
| | G Birrell/C Bourgoignie | 2nd |
| | D Glemser/A Soler-Roig | 3rd |
| Zandvoort Trophy, Holland (ETCC) | J Mass/G Larrousse | 1st |
| | B Muir/J Miles | 2nd |
| | D Glemser/A Soler-Roig | DNF |
| Paul Ricard 6-Hours, France (ETCC) | B Muir/J Miles | 1st |
| | J Stewart/F Cevert | 2nd |
| | J Mass/G Larrousse/A Soler-Roig | 3rd |
| | J Mass/D Glemser | DNF |
| Tour de France | G Larrousse/J Rives | DNF |
| Tourist Trophy Race, UK (ETCC) | J Mass/D Glemser | 1st |
| | D Glemser | DNF |
| Jarama 4-Hours, Spain (ETCC) | J Mass/A Soler-Roig/G Larrousse | 1st |
| | H Heyer/G Birrell/D Glemser | 2nd |
| | J Mass/D Glemser | 5th |

Plus many appearances in German events, including eight victories out of ten appearances for Hans Stuck.

*In the ETCC in 1971-72 this was a familiar sight, with the works Capri RS2600s ahead of the pack. The two leading Capris had already swept past the camera at Monza in 1972, as the rest of the field entered the legendary Parabolica curve.*

complete the six hours.

All in all, the Capris were dominant in 1972. They also performed well at the Nurburgring 1000km (for Group 5 sports cars!) and in the Le Mans 24 Hour sports car race, and were rarely troubled. Mike Kranefuss, however, thought BMW would be a problem in 1973. His fears were justified.

## 1973

This was a year when two problems to be faced – one financial, the other an FIA-imposed barrier against further homologation tweaks. There was no solution to the budget cuts imposed on Kranefuss by Walter Hayes (though Hayes found ways of attracting F1 drivers to 'guest' on occasion). Technically, the team now had handling problems. At high speeds the tail of the car felt very light and would oversteer. At Le Mans, the drivers experienced wheelspin at maximum speed on the Mulsanne Straight! If a large transverse rear spoiler could have been added (Ford-Cologne had already developed one) the problem would have been solved, but homologation was only possible if Ford put the necessary spoilers into production, which they never did. BMW, on the other hand, did, and with their super-powerful 3.5-litre BMW engine, provided an opposition with which the RS2600s would struggle.

Looking far ahead, Ford was already preparing a response but that would have to wait until 1974 when the RS3100 appeared. For 1973, and only as an interim measure, the Cologne V6 block was stretched to its limit of 2995cc, where it developed 325bhp at 7600rpm; there was no more to come.

*Brian Muir and John Miles caused a major upset in the Paul Ricard 6-Hour race of 1972 by outpacing the official RS2600s in their own British-prepared Capri RS2600 and winning the race outright.*

Once again there was a revised aerodynamic package, with a new drag-reducing front spoiler and wheelarch extensions. The cooling radiator and its ducting were repositioned and there were yet more changes to the roll cage. A 'ducktail' spoiler would undoubtedly have helped, as Kranefuss later admitted: "It was worth about 10 seconds a lap at the Nurburgring, almost exactly the amount we would have needed to stay ahead of BMW".

To reduce the gap on BMW, they enlisted amazing driving talent. Jackie Stewart, Emerson Fittipaldi, Gerry Birrell, Jody Scheckter, Jochen Mass, Hans Heyer and John Fitzpatrick all figured in the line-up of drivers of what was now known to be an ill-handling beast.

BMW's regulations-busting aerodynamic package, the 3.0 CSL 'Batmobile', appeared in mid-season, but early-1973 cars were already very fast and the balance tipped just far enough to favour them. At the end of the eight-event Championship the RS2600s had won only two races (both of them early in the season), and taken three second places, while Heyer/Fritzringer finished second in the Nurburgring 24

*Ford even entered three RS2600s at Le Mans in 1972, where two of the cars finished the 24-hour race first and second in their capacity class.*

## The 1973 season's record (2.9-litre V6-engined cars used throughout)

| | | |
|---|---|---|
| Monza 4-Hours, Italy (ETCC) | D Glemser/J Mass | 2nd |
| | G Birrell/J Fitzpatrick | DNF |
| | J Stewart/J Scheckter | DNF |
| Le Mans 4-Hours | G Birrell/H Heyer | DNF |
| Spa Cup, Belgium | J Mass | DNF |
| Austria Trophy 4-Hours (ETCC) | D Glemser/J Fitzpatrick | 1st |
| Mantorp Park, Sweden (ETCC) | D Glemser/J Mass | 1st |
| Le Mans 24-Hours (World Championship) | D Glemser/J Fitzpatrick | DNF |
| | J Vinatier/H Koinigg | DNF |
| | G Birrell/H Heyer | DNF |
| Nurburgring 24-Hours, Germany | H Heyer/K Fritzinger | 2nd |
| Nurburgring 6-Hours, Germany (ETCC) | D Glemser/J Mass | DNF |
| | J Fitzpatrick/G Larrousse | DNF |
| | E Fittipaldi/J Stewart | DNF |
| Spa 24-Hours, Belgium (ETCC) | J Mass/J Fitzpatrick | 2nd |
| | H Heyer/H Koinigg | DNF |
| Zandvoort 4-Hours, Holland (ETCC) | J Fitzpatrick/G Larrousse | 3rd |
| | J Mass/D Glemser | DNF |
| Nurburgring 500km. Germany | H Heyer | 2nd |
| Paul Ricard 6-Hours, France (ETCC) 5th | J Fitzpatrick/G Larrousse | |
| | J Mass/J Stewart | DNF |
| Tourist Trophy race, UK (ETCC) | J Mass | 2nd |
| | D Glemser | DNF |
| | J Fitzpatrick | DNF |
| Fuji International, Japan | T Hezemans/J Mass/D Glemser | 1st |
| | T Hezemanns/A Moffat | DNF |
| Macau saloons | A Moffat | 1st |

Plus three victories and three second places in seven races in the German Championship

*By 1973 the works RS2600 had reached the limits of its development and was widely criticised by the drivers for its evil handling. The major opposition, from BMW, now featured the 'Batmobiles' with their newly homologated 'Aero' kit.*

Hour event and Mass/Hezemans won the non-Championship Fuji race in Japan.

This, though, was an expensive season, for the Capris' at-the-limit engines gave a great deal of trouble, and five cars were badly damaged in accidents. The problem was that the RS2600's handling seemed to have got worse, not better: the faster they went, the lighter they seemed to get at the rear. This often meant that the cars were seen to lift *both* inside wheels on dry corners; they looked, and felt, quite unsafe. John Fitzpatrick, as brave as any Ford driver of his day, once commented that "The 1973 Capri was the worst handling racing car I have ever driven". F1 World Champion Emerson Fittpaldi sometimes thought that the car was going to turn over on him. Even Jackie Stewart, that most analytical of racing drivers, found it difficult to wring any more out of what had become a brute of a car.

A quick resumé of the RS2600s' ETCC season is significant. Early in the year there were two wins and a second place for the 3.0-litre RS2600, at Monza, the Salzburgring and in Sweden. BMW then homologated the bewinged and bespoiled 3.0CSL Batmobile, after which the RS2600 did not win again: Nurburgring 6-Hour no finishes, Spa 24-Hours 2nd, Zandvoort 3rd, Paul Ricard 6-Hour 5th, and the TT (Silverstone) 2nd. Before July, competition between Ford and BMW was close. Afterwards, the new BMW 'aero' package proved to be worth 15 seconds per lap around the long 'old' Nurburgring circuit, and more than eight seconds per lap at Spa.

It was really Game Over. Quite suddenly the RS2600s were no longer competitive, and Ford's bosses thought they were no longer battling like with like. Spectators at Silverstone for the TT saw just how hard the rival teams of drivers were trying – and to just what extreme angles they got their cars – but Jochen Mass could only manage second place, three laps (nearly nine miles) behind the winning BMW, which proved a point. Would it be a different story in 1974?

*This excellent cutaway drawing shows the layout of the ultimate works Capri RS2600 race cars of 1973, complete with 3-litre fuel-injected engine, five-speed XF gearbox, four-wheel disc brakes, ultra-wide magnesium alloy wheels, and much-modified suspension linkages.*

*By 1973 the ETCC series featured race after race of close combat between the works RS2600s and the BMW 3.0CSLs. John Fitzpatrick was at the wheel of the Capri at Silverstone on this occasion.*

*This impressive front view shows how the RS2600s were set up to be low and purposeful.*

*As they developed in the early 1970s, the Cologne Capris gradually took on wider and wider flared wheel arches, and wider-rim wheels.*

*BBS split-rim alloy wheels featured on many of the Cologne Capris of the early 1970s.*

*The boot of the works race cars included the big filler for the fuel tank, and the dry sump oil tank.*

The front suspension struts were adjustable, to help trim the handling for different circuits.

The rear view is dominated by the vast petrol filler cap and surrounding recess.

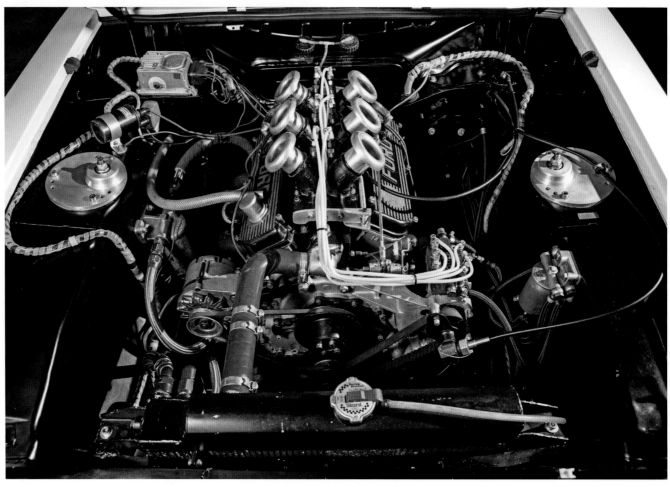

This was the neat and purposeful installation of the 2.9-litre race-tuned engine of a works Cologne Capri RS2600.

*This was early days for electronic engine management systems, which explains the bulk of the Bosch ECU.*

*The driving compartment was starkly trimmed but purposeful. Note this early example of a side reinforcement bar on the roll cage installation.*

*The works RS2600s had a sturdy roll cage, which helped stiffen the bodyshell.*

*Like the works Escorts of the period, the underside of the RS2600 bodyshell featured sturdy boxes to support and surround the radius arms that had been added to the rear suspension.*

*For 1974 Ford produced an even more extreme works Capri, the RS3100, complete with a four-cam 3.4-litre V6 engine developed by Cosworth which had well over 420bhp. It was a race winner.*

## Capri RS3100 and 3-litre in Europe

Well before BMW started beating the RS2600s in 1973, Mike Kranefuss knew that the game was up. If he could not a get a new aerodynamic package homologated a lot more power was needed to match the BMW 3.0CSL, for the RS2600s were now struggling to stay ahead.

Ford, however, was already preparing a response. Existing Group 2 regulations allowed alternative heads to be used if homologated after 100 car sets had been put on sale. Ford asked Cosworth to evolve the GA, which was a twin-cam, four-valves-per-cylinder 3.4-litre derivative of the British (*not* the German) V6. This was to be ready for the 1974 season. The engine was a big step forward. The 'Essex'-based GA V6 produced 420bhp (later 455bhp) instead of 320bhp, which made a colossal improvement. In addition there would be bigger brakes, better aerodynamics and more.

To keep the legislators happy and to get FIA approval Ford needed to sell a new Capri derivative, however short-lived. Accordingly, the RS3100 was a typical 'why don't we?' project cooked up between Stuart Turner and AVO Product Planner Mike Moreton. The RS3100 road car evolved from the Capri 3000GT, with an enlarged 3091cc version of the V6 engine and a much larger rear spoiler. Ford would only need to build 1000 cars to gain homologation. The bigger engine squeezed the car into the 'Over 3-litre' category, and allowed Cosworth to enlarge it as far as modified cylinder blocks would allow.

The RS3100 was launched in November 1973 (in the same week as the world-wide Energy Crisis struck), and Ford built the road cars at Halewood, among the last of the original-shape Capris. As we now know, only about 250 such cars were ever produced, though homologation ('We've built 1000 RS3100s, honest, Guv.') was duly achieved from 1 January 1974.

Cosworth's four-cam GA engine used the classic twin-cam per bank, narrow-valve-angle layout of earlier units such as the four-cylinder BDA, and Lucas fuel injection and ignition were chosen. These engines were certainly not hand-built one-offs. 100 engines (or kits of parts) had to be built to qualify for homologation, and they were all produced by Cosworth in Northampton. About 30 complete engines were delivered to Ford-Cologne (who needed a new high-capacity test bed to check them out), the balance going into stock at Boreham. At £4000 for a kit of parts and an extra £750 for assembly, these were never likely to be quick sellers and in the end many were scrapped.

Although the Energy Crisis and a temporary disruption in Middle East oil supplies disrupted motor racing confidence during the winter, Ford-Germany pressed on with RS3100 race-car development for 1974, no matter how truncated that season might be. As with the RS2600, much of the engineering work was credited to Thomas Ammerschlager, and the RS3100 race cars were very different from the last RS2600s. The engine, and many other fittings including body panels, were more substantial than before, so the cars' dry weight was about 2315lb/1050kg. The suspension layout was much as before, as was the four-wheel disc brake installation – 12in ventilated types at the front and 10.5in at the rear. The works team was contracted to Dunlop for its tyres.

The new 3.4-litre GA engine was mated to the ZF five-speed transmission, but to improve the weight distribution the engine cooling radiators were relocated to the boot, at each side of the luggage container, and fed by air intakes ahead of the rear wheels. This moved a 26lb/12kg mass back from the nose to the boot. At the same time, the axle cooler was repositioned behind the right rear wheel, the gearbox oil cooler behind the left rear wheel. The fuel tank was lower and further back, and the new car had a very large transverse spoiler.

To quote Mike Kranefuss: "On the RS2600 the rear end was always very light, while the front end stuck like hell. It was a difficult car to drive, and the star drivers we employed were very surprised to find the job which the regulars like Mass and Glemser had to do."

*When fully developed the Cosworth GA 3.4-litre engine of the works Capri RS3100s produced up to 455bhp.*

| REGISTRATION NUMBER | ENGINE SIZE | MODEL TYPE |
|---|---|---|
| **NOT REGISTERED** | **3412CC V6 24V DOHC** | **CAPRI RS3100** |

Perhaps the RS3100's success in 1974 and 1975 seemed slightly muted because the works BMWs had been withdrawn – but why did the rival Bavarian cars drop out? They had been race-winners, in 1973 with 370bhp cars, but BMW now realised that they could do little more for 1974. Having seen the potential of the 3.4-litre RS3100s, they might have 'retired' as a precaution. However, to keep up appearances, the very latest cars were made available to 'private' teams, which explains why BMW beat Ford in the first three races, but not thereafter.

Except for early-season problems in 1974 (in fact they missed the first race, at Monza), the works RS3100s were extremely successful. In two shortened seasons they started in 17 long-distance races, winning eight times, finishing second six times and third once. Not bad for a car whose engine was total unproven before its first race, and for a department which was suffering seriously from budget and manpower constraints!

The programme started badly at Monza, with no RS3100s ready, and with only one 1973-spec. ex-works RS2600, driven by Hans Akersloot and Toine Hezemans. That car started well but retired before the end of the afternoon. Things looked up at the second race of the 1974 season, at the Salzburgring in Austria, when Mike Kranefuss sent two new RS3100s to do battle with one 24-valve 400bhp BMW. On the fast sweeping sections of the 'Ring, the Capris were geared to attain 178mph, and reached it with great aplomb; the new aerodynamic aids proved to be remarkably effective. Unhappily, al-

*Although it still lifted a front wheel under extreme cornering stress, the RS3100 of 1974 was a formidable race car which had the beating of anything else in the European Touring Car Challenge.*

Glemser and Toine Hezemans won their Group 2 class and took a storming 11th place overall against full Group 6 prototypes from Matra, Alfa Romeo, Gulf and Porsche. Four seaters competing against two-seater prototypes? Whatever next?

Then came the Nurburgring 6-Hour race, the fourth ETCC qualifier of the year, and an obvious showcase for the Ford-Cologne cars. According to Kranefuss's script the RS3100s should have defeated the BMWs but things did not quite work out that way. One car retired with a broken axle and the other was actually outpaced by the amazing works-backed 2-litre Zakspeed Ford Escort RS1600!

Things improved in the last events of the year, with Jochen Mass/Rolf Stommelen winning outright at Zandvoort (Holland) in a wet race, while the Ludwig/Hezemans/Heyer RS3100 repeated that feat in Jarama (Spain) at the end of the season. The factory was embarrassed to be beaten on two occasions in 1974 by the Zakspeed Escorts (the Radio Luxembourg-sponsored RS1600 also won the non-Championship 9-hour race at Kyalami, South Africa in November), but considering all the budget cuts it had been a satisfactory season. Ford had taken maximum points in three of the six rounds and finished second overall in its division.

This, though, was really the end of Ford's serious involvement at European Championship level, for neither Ford nor their big rival BMW took much interest in the 1975 ETCC, which sank to a very low, 'private-owners' level.

In the aftermath of the Energy Crisis and in the series of cutbacks which saw the AVO factory in Essex also closed down, Ford-Cologne's works team operation suffered brutal near-closure at the hands of the number-crunchers. Somehow, Kranefuss's workshops kept one or two of its RS3100 cars alive, entering Jochen Mass for the Norisring event in the German Championship, which he won. Another RS3100 was loaned to Team General Anzeiger of Bonn, where Klaus Ludwig won two out of three races (both of them at Hockenheim) also in the same German Championship. But that was that, the remaining cars were dispersed, and Cologne was never again to be directly involved in Touring Car racing.

though the RS3100s soon got in to the lead, and stayed there, both cars retired with broken (literally, for one car suffered a split cylinder block) engines. Cosworth's gloomy forecast, that *their* pieces would do the job but that they were not happy about the strength of Ford's own V6 cylinder block casting, came true. It was not until some strengthening was made to the casting cores at Dagenham that reliability was assured.

Ford then missed the Vallelunga (Italy) round of the ETCC, preferring to choose some local motor racing (and publicity), in the Nurburgring 750km sports car race instead. Dieter

| The 1974 season's record | | |
|---|---|---|
| Austria Trophy 4-Hours (ETCC) | J Mass/N Lauda | DNF |
| | T Hezemanns/D Glemser | DNF |
| Nurburgring 1000km (World Championship) | D Glemser/T Hezemanns | 11th |
| | J Mass/N Lauda | DNF |
| Nurburgring 6-Hours (ETCC) | T Hezemanns/D Glemser | 2nd |
| | J Mass/N Lauda | DNF |
| Zandvoort 4-Hours, Holland (ETCC) | J Mass/R Stommelen | 1st |
| | D Glemser/T Hezemanns | 6th |
| Jarama 4-Hours, Spain (ETCC) | K Ludwig/T Hezemanns/H Heyer | 1st |
| Kyalami 9-Hours, South Africa | J Mass/T Hezemanns | 5th |
| Plus three victories and five second places in seven races in the German Championship. | | |

## The 1975 season's record

There were no entries in the European Touring Car Championship, which had become moribund. Instead, works RS3100s started four German Championship events and won three times, with Jochen Mass and Klaus Ludwig sharing the driving honours.

The final appearance of the works RS3100 was at:

Wynns 1000km race, South Africa       J Mass/K Ludwig       DNF

## Capri 3-litre in the UK and in Europe

In Britain, apart from spending much time and a great deal of money on trying to make sense of four-wheel-drive Capris for rallycross use (described later in this section), Ford was not really interested in developing the cars for works competition, though there was a period when a fleet of very lightly modified cars was produced for use in 'celebrity' races on various British circuits.

It was not until 1973 that Capri 3000s, using near-standard engines, were prepared for the inaugural Avon-Motor Tour of Britain, where FIA Group 1 regulations were enforced, along with a limited choice of road tyres. Even this event only held Ford's interest for a single year, as the more suitable Escort RS2000 took over in 1974 and subsequently won the Tour three times in succession (1974-76). No fewer than three factory-blessed cars and eight other privately-prepared Capri 3000s competed in the 1973 event, where Capris took second, fourth, fifth, seventh and eighth. It was, however, the last time that Ford-UK officially entered Capri Is in motorsport.

For many years the most gruelling saloon car race of all was the 24-hour race held at Spa, Belgium, in July – on the original, classic 8.76-mile/14.1km public road until 1978, then on the truncated but still spectacular new F1 circuit. This race offered a unique challenge and required cars which were not only fast but also durable. As already noted, works RS2600s from Ford-Cologne raced there from 1971 to 1973 – winning in 1971 and 1972 and finishing second in 1973 – though the RS3100s which succeeded them never got the chance to tackle the Belgian circuit.

For 1974, the Spa organisers imposed their own special 'Group 1¾' regulations, which automatically disqualified the fully-modified Group 2 Capri RS3100s from taking part. Instead, Ford-UK, with cars built in Britain at Boreham not at Ford-Cologne, sent two newly-built triple-Weber 200bhp Capri IIs (the first and last works Capri IIs ever built), with big fat wing extensions and 8in wide rear wheels. The Walkinshaw/Fitzpatrick car led the Belgian race in the early hours – it had a top speed of more than 135mph –- but it eventually retired with a broken driveshaft. The other car never figured in the top positions before it blew a cylinder head gasket.

Thereafter, Capri entries in the Spa 24-Hour race were all privately built, and driven by notable Touring Car heroes such as Gordon Spice. Later in the 1970s, they won in 1978 (Gordon Spice/Teddy Pilette), 1979 (Jean-Michel and Philippe Martin), and 1980 (Jean-Michel and Philippe Martin), helped by the very resourceful and inventive homologation of special engine and chassis parts that was carried out for the Capris by John Griffiths at Boreham.

*One of the two works Capri 3000 Mk IIs that started the Belgian Spa 24-Hour race in 1974, with the special three-Weber carburetted engine about to be installed.*

*Very few modifications were allowed, though ultra-wide wheel-arch extensions (seen here) were authorised.*

| REGISTRATION NUMBER | ENGINE SIZE | MODEL TYPE |
|---|---|---|
| **XWC 712L** | **2994cc V6 OHV** | **Capri 3000GXL Mk I** |

Among the 11 FIA Group 1 Capri 3000s which started the 1973 Tour of Britain (a three-day event involving 1000 road miles and an eclectic mixture of special stages and circuit races), three were prepared by the works rally team at Boreham. Because they were Group 1 cars, their specification was recognisably close to those of the 138bhp road cars which

*Roger Clark drove this near-standard Capri 3000GXL in the 1973 Tour of Britain and would certainly have won the event if an engine problem had not delayed him at Oulton Park. This was Roger in full cry at Brands Hatch.*

sold so well in the UK. The British V6 engines, however, were 'blueprinted', producing a reputed 160bhp, and after a pre-event dispute over eligible 'road car' tyres had been resolved, the Capris were among the favourites. Ford had wanted to run on rather special soft-compound Dunlops but these were rejected by the scrutineers so they ran on Michelins instead.

Roger Clark shared this car with Tony Mason, and in an event which made all the best sort of headlines, was in the lead after being very fast on the initial special stages. Unhappily, his problems had already begun at the Llandow race circuit when a front wheel bearing collapsed, but this was quickly repaired. Then on the second day, during the race at Oulton Park, the engine's electrical system gave trouble, the distributor failed, the master cut-out switch failed, and the car coasted to a halt, where it lay, picking up a maximum penalty. Although it was eventually repaired in the post-race paddock, apparently it restarted in 90th place, the balance of the event being completed without major problems, and fast too, but it could do more than drag itself back up to 24th place, a massive 12 minutes behind James Hunt's winning Chevrolet Camaro Z28. The car did not figure in any further works-backed outings but was sold off to Adlards, the London-based RS dealership. Its principal claim to fame in the first year of private ownership (1974) came in the next Tour of Britain, where F1 driver Jody Scheckter crashed it at Oulton Park.

**Competition record**

| | | |
|---|---|---|
| 1973 Tour of Britain | Roger Clark | 24th |

| REGISTRATION NUMBER | ENGINE SIZE | MODEL TYPE |
|---|---|---|
| **XWC 713L** | **2994cc V6 OHV** | **Capri 3000GXL Mk I** |

The second of three works Capri 3000s started the 1973 Tour of Britain in the care of HRH Prince Michael of Kent and Nigel Clarkson, and although it was not expected to be among the front runners the attendant publicity of having a Royal in a factory car was bound to figure strongly. Prince Michael and Nigel Clarkson both drove the car at different stages of the event, made sure that they kept out of the way of the more aggressive driving tactics which seemed to occur up front, and finished steadily in 16th place.

Only two weeks later the same car, hastily returned to Boreham and lightly modified for what was to be a 24-hour event on the legendary Spa (Belgium) circuit, which was still running

to its traditional long circuit format, was fitted with Dunlop tyres and was driven by Nigel Clarkson and Ford motorsport press officer Jeremy Walton. As Walton later wrote, "The Capri finished 13th having no trouble at all, save ripping those [Dunlop] tyres to shreds on the Masta straight with monotonous regularity". In summary, although Jeremy seems to have been somewhat disappointed with his finishing position, the car completed 2322 miles/3739km and therefore averaged nearly 97mph for the full 24 hours – a remarkable performance by what was a very basically specified car. By comparison, the full-house works Cologne Capri of Jochen Mass/John Fitzpatrick, which finished second, averaged 109mph.

This car did not figure in any further Boreham-based works entries in 1973, and was shortly put back into store at the workshops in Essex. However, following the scares of the Energy Crisis which occupied the winter of 1973/74, it was brought out to compete in the British Touring Car Championship of 1974, which was to be run under FIA Group 1 regulations, which suited the Capri 3000GXL's specification quite well.

This was the year in which a relatively unknown young Scot called Tom Walkinshaw battled long and hard against the Opel Commodore GS/E and BMW 3.0CSi coupés in its capacity class, and it always put up a brave show, running in the latest Boreham corporate colours of blue and white, with substantial sponsorship from Shell. Early in the year the problem was that very few performance-raising items were homologated, and even with a bit of judicious work on the engine and its carburation the 3-litre power unit produced a mere 175bhp. The gear ratios too were not at all suitable for circuit racing, and it was not until the following year (after which Boreham's direct involvement in touring car racing had ended) that a more suitable Hewland gear cluster became available.

All in all it was to be a frenetic, not to say exhausting, season for the Walkinshaw Capri, for there were 13 events in the calendar. Nonetheless, Tom won one race outright (Ingliston in his native Scotland), took second place once, three third places and three fourth places, the outcome being that he won the 2.5–4.0-litre capacity class outright. Outright victories were usually out of the question because of the phalanx of vast American V8-powered Chevrolet Camaros which dominated the scene in this and future seasons.

No fewer than eight Capri 3000s, Walkinshaw's being directly backed by Boreham, were entered for the first event at Mallory Park, but they had to line up behind nine Chevrolet Camaros. This was the first but not the last time that the Capri suffered a deranged transmission, but a week later at Brands Hatch it finished third overall behind a Camaro and a BMW 3.0CSi. Having finished seventh at Silverstone, the car was subjected to a great deal of tyre and suspension development testing at Boreham and then took fifth place at Oulton Park on Good Friday before making the Easter weekend journey to Thruxton for what turned out to be an incident-packed event. Here the engine suddenly sprung an engine oil leak when already in the collecting area before the race grid assembled (Mick Jones and Peter Ashcroft made a hasty repair), and during the race Walkinshaw suddenly finding himself holding a broken gear lever, causing him to lose more than a lap to all his rivals.

There was an unrelated oil leakage problem at Silverstone in May, when the oil contaminated the Capri's tyres, leading Walkinshaw to spin twice and lose several places, but things then started to get better. At the second Thruxton meeting, in May, the works Capri was the fastest of the Ford bunch in

*In the 1973 Tour of Britain, works Capri 3000GXL XWC 713L was shared between HRH Prince Michael of Kent and Nigel Clarkson. This is Clarkson at the wheel at the Welsh Llandow circuit.*

qualifying, and soon settled into third place in the race (behind a Camaro and a Broadspeed Dolomite Sprint), before swooping past Andy Rouse's Dolomite on the very last lap to take second place overall.

Soon after this, with newly-homologated components in the cylinder heads of the Dagenham-built V6 engine, and having qualified on the second row of the grid at the Brands Hatch support race for the British GP meeting, Walkinshaw battled strongly with two 5.7-litre Camaros (driven by Stuart Graham and Richard Lloyd) to take a sturdy third place overall.

Held in mid-September, the Silverstone-based Tourist Trophy was certainly the biggest and most important Group 1 saloon car race of the season. It attracted no fewer than 40 starters, was run over 107 laps of the full F1 circuit, and took more than three hours to unfold. Boreham rebuilt the hard-working Capri which Tom Walkinshaw had been racing all season, fitting a larger fuel tank to cut down on the number of pit stops the Capri would have to make, and successfully sorted out a fuel starvation problem they discovered in the qualifying period. Even though this was to be a long race, the field settled down in its usual way, with Camaros leading and the Capri scrapping with Opel Commodores and BMWs immediately behind them. Just one pit stop for fuel should have been enough, but it was during that halt that a wheel and tyre had to be replaced. This too was unsatisfactory, so another halt was needed to change to yet another wheel, which dropped the Scot from fourth to eighth, with only about an hour's racing left in which to claw something back. This he did, but not by his own demanding standards, and eventually he took sixth overall.

Two weeks later the penultimate Championship round was held in very wet conditions at Snetterton where the results, as headlined in *Autosport*, proclaimed, 'The Same Old Story'. For Walkinshaw. however, there was disappointment, for although he was holding a strong third place (behind – guess what – two Camaros), a slow puncture in a rear tyre meant that on the very last lap he lost a position.

The final race of the Championship, at Brands Hatch in October, was almost farcical, for there were a number of crashes, on-track bullying, and incidents to spoil what should have been a perfect end to a close-fought year. Thirty-five cars started on a dry track, with two Camaros at the front of the grid and Walkinshaw's Capri on the third row, 32 seconds

*Prince Michael of Kent (left) and Nigel Clarkson (centre) discuss detail while their Capri 3000GXL is being serviced during the Tour of Britain.*

slower. Towards the end of the race there were several car-on-car accidents (even Walkinshaw spun once but did not make contact with anyone), and so much near-carnage and blockage on the track that the organisers hung out the red flag with two laps still to go. In the event Walkinshaw finished behind the two leading Camaros, took third place overall, and easily won his capacity class.

The final result in the Championship was that Walkinshaw not only won his capacity class but finished fourth overall. This had been a fascinating season which, above all, confirmed that in races where big-engined American cars were present, British machines did not stand much of a chance. The RAC recognised this and hastened to rewrite the regulations to restrict eligible cars to 3-litres from 1976. By then, however, Ford had lost interest in any further works participation, and left stalwarts like Gordon Spice to win on their behalf.

## Competition record

| | | |
|---|---|---|
| 1973 Tour of Britain | HRH Prince Michael of Kent | 16th |
| 1973 Spa 24 Hours | Nigel Clarkson/Jeremy Walton | 13th |
| | | |
| then in the 1974 British Touring Car Championship | | |
| 1974 Mallory Park | Tom Walkinshaw | DNF |
| 1974 Brands Hatch | Tom Walkinshaw | 3rd |
| 1974 Silverstone | Tom Walkinshaw | 7th |
| 1974 Oulton Park (Good Friday) | Tom Walkinshaw | 5th |
| 1974 Thruxton | Tom Walkinshaw | 3rd in 4-litre Class |
| 1974 Silverstone | Tom Walkinshaw | 4th in 4-litre Class |
| 1974 Thruxton (May meeting) | Tom Walkinshaw | 2nd |
| 1974 Brands Hatch (British F1 GP meeting) | Tom Walkinshaw | 3rd |
| 1974 Ingliston | Tom Walkinshaw | 1st |
| 1974 Brands Hatch | Tom Walkinshaw | 4th |
| 1974 Oulton Park | Tom Walkinshaw | 4th |
| 1974 Silverstone (Tourist Trophy) | Tom Walkinshaw | 6th |
| 1974 Snetterton | Tom Walkinshaw | 4th |
| 1974 Brands Hatch | Tom Walkinshaw | 3rd |

| REGISTRATION NUMBER | ENGINE SIZE | MODEL TYPE |
|---|---|---|
| **XWC 718L** | **2994cc V6 OHV** | **Capri 3000GXL Mk I** |

The third of the trio of new Capri 3000s prepared at Boreham for the 1973 Tour of Britain was entrusted to the increasingly successful saloon car race driver Dave Matthews, his co-driver being Charles Reynolds of the Fordsport Club (who would go on to become Boreham competition manager Peter Ashcroft's deputy later in the 1970s). Matthews had more circuit experience than colleague Roger Clark, and was expected to be very competitive if the car did not let him down.

He performed well, if not spectacularly, throughout the three-day event, and although beaten to the finish by the privately-prepared Capri of Gordon Spice, who was thoroughly used to racing Capris by this time and who finished second to Hunt's Camaro Z28, Matthews was only 1min 46sec behind the flying Camaro and took an excellent fifth place. Matthews would have used this car again but was badly injured in a crash at Silverstone just after this event (in another car) and was not seen in a competitive race car again.

*Dave Matthews in full flow in the 1973 Tour of Britain in the Boreham-built Group 1 Capri 3000GXL, XWC 718L. Along with co-driver Charles Reynolds, he finished fifth overall.*

**Competition record**

| 1973 Tour of Britain | Dave Matthews | 5th |
| --- | --- | --- |

| REGISTRATION NUMBER | ENGINE SIZE | MODEL TYPE |
| --- | --- | --- |
| TWO CARS, NEITHER REGISTERED | 2994CC V6 OHV | CAPRI 3000GXL MK II |

Somehow, in the middle of a frantically busy 1974 rally season, and the effort of keeping Tom Walkinshaw's British Touring Car Championship Capri competitive, Boreham found time to prepare two rather special Capri II (hatchback) types to compete in the famous Spa 24 Hour race in Belgium. One car, extensively backed by Shell and painted black, was shared by Tom Walkinshaw and John Fitzpatrick, while the other car, in yellow-based (sponsored by BP) livery, was for the Belgian duo of Claude Bourgoignie and Yvette Fontaine.

These brand-new cars were lovingly prepared to what was whimsically called 'FIA Group 1¾' regulations (the Belgian organisers would no longer allow full Group 2 cars, like the Cologne Capri RS3100s, to take part). These among other details meant that they ran with extensively expanded wheel-arch extensions to cover 8in rim (front) and 10in (rear)

Minilite alloy wheels, along with removed bumpers and extended front spoilers.

Under the bonnet, the 3-litre V6 engine was fed by three downdraught twin-choke Weber carburettors, which were only authorised for this particular event. At least 200bhp was claimed for this state of tune, and the cars were said to achieve 135mph on Spa's fastest sections. More than one driver suggested that this sort of car found almost the entire circuit to be flat out, with brakes only being used for a newly-installed 'temporary' chicane at Malmedy, and at the La Source hairpin (which in those days before the pits complex was extended for the 'new' F1 circuit was the last, rather than the first, corner of the entire lap).

Although the cars were only completed a day before they were due to leave Essex for Belgium (and, consequently, had completed no pre-event testing), they were clearly competitive, as Walkinshaw put his Shell-backed car on pole with a lap time of 4min 27.9sec. Amazingly, Walkinshaw led the entire field in the very early stages after a 3pm start, though soon overtaken by a 7-litre 1969 Mustang, but he led again after a couple of hours during which the engine seemed to loosen off a little, making the car even faster than it had been in qualifying.

Unhappily, the BP-sponsored sister car expired at an early stage with a blown cylinder head gasket and was abandoned at the side of the track part way around the lap. This then led to a pantomime later in the event when the Walkinshaw/Fitz-

patrick car began to have problems of its own. As reported by my colleague Ray Hutton of *Autocar*, "The Walkinshaw/Fitzpatrick car lost the lead when an exhaust manifold cracked and took nearly 30 minutes to replace. It retired at 10.30pm when a half-shaft broke and a rear wheel rolled away, the car coming to rest next to its team-mate beyond Stavelot. Walkinshaw attempted to fit a shaft assembly from the abandoned Belgian car (which he had to break into) but the fittings were not the same and all he got was a badly cut finger for his trouble".

So that was the end of a brave effort, on which Ford never officially tried to improve. For the next few years, all their Capri cars were raced by enterprising, experienced and ultimately extremely successful drivers like Gordon Spice, and although Boreham backed them thoroughly with a whole series of homologation improvements, they never again tried to build race cars of their own.

## Competition record

| 1974 Spa 24 Hour race, Belgium | Tom Walkinshaw/John Fitzpatrick | DNF |
| | Claude Bourgoignie/Yvette Fontaine | DNF |

## Silhouette Racer – the Zakspeed Capris (1978-1982)

| REGISTRATION NUMBER | ENGINE SIZE | MODEL TYPE |
|---|---|---|
| NOT REGISTERED | 1427CC/1746CC 4-CYL 16V DOHC | CAPRI MK III |

It was almost as if Zakspeed's body designers had been sampling mind-expanding chemicals, or fiercely potent booze. In their sober moments they must have studied a Capri or two, but none of them could ever have looked like this. Wider, lower, faster and more powerful – you've never seen this sort of Capri before. And neither, in 1978 when they appeared, had anyone else! Zakspeed, like UK specialist companies such

as Broadspeed and Alan Mann Racing, had firm links with Ford, their products really qualifying as works cars.

It's difficult to know where to start when describing Zakspeed's near-unique Capris of the late 1970s. Capris, or not? Saloons or racing sports cars? Modified production cars or race cars with familiar styling? One thing was certain: no-one but Zakspeed ever built faster or more successful cars carrying the Capri name.

In the 1970s, International motorsport was run according to a long list of FIA categories – from Group 1 (showroom standard machinery) to Group 7 (two-seat racing sports cars). In Britain in the late 1960s, when Alan Mann's Escort Twin Cams ran with Ford-Cosworth FVA engines, and Ralph Broad's 1-litre 105E Anglias had 115bhp, we saw just how exciting Group 5 racing could be. Ten years later, when the technology, and the regulations, had moved on a lot, the Germans embraced Group 5 for their own national sporting categories.

One must start with a standard bodyshell, Group 5 regulations stated, but feel free to alter almost everything else. Which explains why non-original fittings like engine transplants, massively reinforced monocoques, turbocharged engines, composite bodywork and extrovert aerodynamics all faced up to the scrutineers without challenge.

In Germany, BMW and Porsche had Group 5 racing all to

*Mike Kranefuss (right) was Ford-of-Germany's Competitions Manager in the mid-1970s. Here he is in deep conversation with Erich Zakowski, the founder of the Zakspeed team.*

themselves at first, as Ford and Zakspeed were still committed to Touring Car racing, in which more restrictive Group 2 regulations still applied. By the mid-1970s Ford's works Capris RS3100s were fastest of all, though it was Zakspeed's Escort RS1800s which had won the European and German Championships. Until 1977, that is, by which time the European Championship had died the death.

One morning, it seems, Erich Zakowski woke up, decided that he was bored with Group B, that Group 5 racing was spectacular, and that he wanted a part of it. Ford-Germany, who had been curiously somnolent since their own Capri RS3100s had retired, offered technical, material and moral support. The result, unveiled in mid-1978, was effectively a works machine, the most astonishing 'Capri' that the world had ever seen. The Capri elements which survived were the front-engine/rear-drive layout, and some features of the styling, plus the much-improved MacPherson strut front suspension, but that was about all. Chassis, engine and other components were all vastly different. Vastly wider and longer than the road car, stuffed with an aluminium roll cage which did more for the chassis that the bodyshell had ever done, and with a turbocharged version of the BDA engine, this package made a mockery even of the lax regulations which applied.

Those were the days, incidentally, when turbocharged engines were allowed, the regulations then multiplying their actual capacity by a factor of 1.4:1, which in effect limited a turbo engine to 1428cc to compete in the 2-litre class. Zakspeed, like Porsche and BMW before them, concluded that they could produce better than 1.4 times the power by turbocharging an engine, decided that this really was 'power for nothing', and chose to do it. Capri 3000GT road cars had just 138bhp, but even the very first of the 1.4-litre Zakspeed cars boasted 380bhp; these engines had bore and stroke dimensions of 80mm x 71mm. By 1980, when a larger 1.75-litre BDA had been installed (with bore and stroke dimensions of 87.4 x 72.755mm), there was no less than 560-600bhp – four times the power of the road car, in a lighter machine which handled like a thoroughbred!

They won races, lots of them, of course. For the 1.4-litre car, the first victories came in 1978, Hans Heyer using one to win its 2-litre Championship division in 1979, and in 1980 it was Klaus Ludwig who won no fewer than six races in the larger division in the latest 1.7-litre machine. 1.4-litre cars could reach 174mph and 1.7-litre cars 186mph.

Then came 1981 and the most emphatic victory of all, when Klaus Ludwig used the 1.4-litre-engined car to dominate the 2-litre division, going on to win the German Championship overall. Since this was to be the last season of Germany silhouette racing, it was the right time for the extrovert machines to bow out.

So how was it done? The original secret was that engineer Thomas Ammerschlager read the regulations extremely carefully, proposed a truly radical solution, and persuaded

*Although the Zakspeed Capri Turbo looked superficially like a normal Capri when completely clothed, under the skin everything was different. Some Capri panels were retained, but much of the strength came from this multi-tube spaceframe structure.*

Zakowski, Ford-Germany and a raft of enthusiastic sponsors to back a truly radical restatement of the Capri theme. The whole design was based on the hugely complex roll cage which doubled as a multi-tube chassis frame. According to Zakspeed's own data, no less than 80 metres of tubing – some round-section, some square-section – were involved, augmented by some (but not much) of the original Capri sheet steel panelling. The screen and side glass were standard Capri, and there was a near-standard bulkhead/front firewall, but much of the rest of the bodyshell was in composite material.

Wider than standard and lower – no less than 10 inches wider and eight inches lower – this was also a car with much-extended rear wings (as on the RS3100s the cooling ra-

*This was the head-on view of the original Zakspeed Turbo race car of 1978, Capri-based but only just.*

evolve these to their ultimate limit. Not that the detailing of these cars ever stood still, for by 1980 they had also grown longitudinal air-smoothing strakes along the bonnet (rather like the BMW 3.0CSLs of 1973 which had given the old Capri RS3100s such a hard time), and the front splitter had also become adjustable for length. This, don't forget, was still nominally a Capri!

As for power, right from the start Zakspeed chose to develop their own turbocharged versions of the famous four-cylinder Ford-Cosworth BDA rather than using the RS3100's normally-aspirated 3.4-litre GA. And why? Because Zakspeed knew that the GA could only achieve 455bhp and was heavy, while they had every hope of beating that figure with the smaller, lighter turbo-BDA. And so they did. Not all alone, but with help from the German engine specialist Dr Schrick, and with many rugged and reliable pieces from Cosworth of Northampton. By modern standards, not much boost was used – only 1.1 Bar at first and 1.5 Bar later – but these were always meant to be high-revving, high-output engines.

The motorsport development of these cars (there were only four chassis, none being written off or sold off while the programme was running) was of course intense. Early 1.4s produced 380bhp, yet by 1980 that figure had been pushed up to 460bhp and it finally rose to 500bhp. Then, for 1980, a 1.7-litre derivative was produced, giving no less than 560bhp at first and up to 600bhp when evolution was finally complete. These, let's not forget, were 'sprint' engines which needed a rebuild after every outing, but by any standards these were remarkable figures.

Dispersing all that heat from conventional front-mounted water-cooling radiators would have produced blasts of hot air both through the engine bay and into the cockpit, so Zakspeed's decision to mount the radiators behind the cabin was very wise indeed. Even in a Capri road car engine bay there would have been space, and to spare, but in this larger, wider, 'look-alike' machine the engineers could make all their own decisions. The squat BDA engine – based, incidentally, on a 1.3-litre iron block – sat vertically, and well back towards the bulkhead. Long inlet tracts were on the right side, stainless steel exhaust manifolding was on the left, and the bulky KKK turbocharger was towards the front left of the compartment, feeding pressured air to the largest air/air intercooler that Zakspeed could find, which was up front where a water radiator might normally be located. By 1980 not one but two intercoolers were fitted.

The ubiquitous ZF gearbox and the broad-beamed live axle were familiar Capri stuff, as was the general layout of the suspension – MacPherson strut at the front, and a live axle located by radius arms and a Watts linkage at the rear, along with the adjustable height Bilstein strut and damper bodies which every serious Ford competition car seemed to use in the 1970s and 1980s – yet almost every component of every installation was updated, made more specialised, and 'tuned'

*Sleek, fast and ultra-special, the Zakspeed-designed Capri Turbo race cars were astonishingly successful in German motorsport at the end of the 1970s.*

diators were located ahead of the rear wheels, with oil coolers nearby), as well as a massive snowplough front spoiler and a colossal rear spoiler. The spoilers were not there merely for effect (or just to provide somewhere for the sponsors' logos to be located), but were diligently and carefully tested on wind-tunnel models. The rear spoiler was so effective that in 1980 the authorities found an excuse to ban it, and a narrower spoiler then took its place.

The size and shape of the front 'splitter' was critical, and the high transverse rear aerofoil had an adjustable blade. Although the regulations would have allowed full underbody 'ground effect' channels, there never seemed to be time to

*Have you ever seen an engine like this in a Capri road car? No, thought not – for this was the turbocharged BDA power unit that powered the Zakspeed racers.*

for the occasion.

The cast alloy wheels – centrally-locked Germany BBS as on the earlier works RS2600s and RS3100s —were colossal. Fronts were of 16in diameter with 10.5in wide rims, while at the rear they were of no less than 19in.diameter with 14in rims. Goodyear, who supplied the tyres, had a hard time, not in dealing with roadholding demands but in coping with up to 600bhp.

The brakes were disc all round and originally evolved by ATE for use on the Porsche 917s of the early 1970s, using four pistons per caliper. Brake water cooling was used at some of the high-speed circuits where hauling the car down from high speed for slow corners was regularly needed.

High speeds? Oh yes! Even with the 'small' 1.4-litre engine there was so much power, with such good aerodynamics, that this Zakspeed monster could be geared to reach more than 170mph. Later, when the 600bhp 1.7-litre version of the engine was employed, top speed could be well over 180mph. And where in Germany could these cars even approach such speeds? Think of the extremely long straights at the Hockenheim circuit (where contemporary F1 cars could reach over 200mph) and at the Norisring, and this becomes clear.

They were incredibly quick in all conditions, of course. Everyone interested in the Super Touring championships which followed in the 1980s knew the detail of the Rouse/ Trackstar/Eggenberger level of Sierra RS500 Cosworths – yet the 1.7-litre Zakspeed Capri had at least 50bhp more power, weighed about 660lb/300kg less, had effective front and rear aerodynamic aids *and* had a much lower drag coefficient. Around the old Nurburgring circuit, all 14 miles of it, the ultimate development of the 1.7-litre Zakspeed was 51 seconds faster *per lap* than a works RS3100 had ever been.

Yet a bare description of the mechanical layout doesn't tell the whole story, for these were machines which were almost alive and definitely had a character of their own. So much more powerful than any race car that Zakspeed had ever produced, they needed to be tamed and mastered to give of their best.

Heroes who regularly drove them to their flame-spitting limits included Harald Ertl, Hans Heyer, Klaus Ludwig, Klaus Niedzwiedz and Manfred Winkelhock. Since it was the two Klauses who later got together to make the Eggenberger Sierra RS500 Cosworths into such formidable saloon car racers, perhaps we now know where they got their high-power-output training!

600bhp Capris! Have you ever seen faster ones? You certainly had not seen such outstandingly different ones. This is how the Zakspeed Capris originally compared with a normal 3.0-litre Capri III of the period :

|  | Zakspeed race car | Capri 3.0 road car |
|---|---|---|
| Length (inches) | 197.34 | 172.2 |
| Width (inches) | 78 | 66.9 |
| Height (inches) | 44.85 | 53.2 |
| Weight, 1.4-litre (lb/kg) | 1740/790 | 2578/1,169 |

## Capri in Rallycross – a British diversion, with four-wheel-drive monsters

Do you remember those monstrous works rallycross Capris of the early 1970s? The ones which always beat the opposition off the line but which struggled to get round the first corner? And did you ever wonder how they evolved? Henry Taylor takes most of the credit. Like all the best petrolheads, he was always looking for a way to beat the opposition, and the organisers. Although the original Escort Twin-Cams had made such a splash in 1968, on muddy tracks they were often beaten by powerful front-wheel-drive Minis. Traction, not outright power, was the solution. The ever-observant Taylor had already identified the problem. Although four-wheel-drive was still specifically banned from rallies, he wanted, at least, to start working out what it could do for him. In rallycross, where millions of people were currently watching ITV's *World of Sport* event, there were no restrictions at all. Ford's marketing people loved the idea of seeing works cars on TV – but only if they were winning.

"I'm not a qualified engineer," Henry once said, "but I was Mr Fixit who always tried to get things done. One of our bright ideas was to put the V6 3-litre engine into a Capri, and another was to try out the Ferguson four-wheel-drive system." Well before the end of 1968 – and this was before the general public even knew that the Capri was soon to be put on sale —- Taylor somehow got his hands on a pre-production Capri 1600GT, 'just for a look-see.' This new model would be launched in January 1969, though sales were not due to begin for weeks after that. "I knew Tony Rolt very well," Henry recalls, "he was the managing director of Harry Ferguson Research, so I arranged for the Capri to be sent to him in Coventry. Although we knew that his four-wheel-drive system, with Dunlop Maxaret anti-lock braking, was bulky, and too heavy, we wanted to see what it would do for us."

By this time Harry Ferguson Research had already built about 30 Zephyrs with a 4WD conversion, and had also supplied Ford's engineers at Dunton with two prototype Capris, complete with V6 engines and 4WD (at a piece price, they say, of around £2,000 for the conversion job). During the winter of 1968/69, therefore, the very first competition V6 3-litre engined Capri took shape in Coventry, and in January it was returned to Boreham. There, the ever-resourceful mechanics completed preparation of a car which would be eligible for rallycross, the engine having Weslake-modified cylinder heads, a different camshaft, and about 160bhp though still running only on a single twin-choke Weber carburettor.

Like the four-wheel-drive Sierras and Escorts which were to follow in the 1980s, these Capris used the 'classic' Ferguson Formula/FF layout. Behind the main gearbox, a step-off/transfer chain case moved the drive sideways to a centre differential, from which the rear propshaft pointed backwards as normal, the front prop shaft leading alongside the right of the engine to a front differential mounted beside the sump.

Curiously, the front and rear final drive ratios were slightly different, the one at the rear being 4.63:1 and the front one an Escort crown-wheel-and-pinion set of 4.71:1. For its motorsport purpose the difference, actually of 1.7 per cent, did not seem to matter at all, especially on loose surfaces where there was wheelspin all the time. Although several different torque splits could be used, Ford eventually settled on a 40%:60% split front to rear as providing the best balance. This was at the drivers' request, because it allowed them to start spinning the rear wheels before the front end broke traction – all the better for getting a Capri sideways on loose stuff.

The installation was heavy – Ferguson reckoned that there was an extra 171lb of clobber – and Boreham's mechanics had to design new front suspension subframes to hold everything together. They also had to carve away at the floor-pan between the front seats to make space for the bulky centre transmission.

On 8 February 1969, just days after the new Capri range had been unveiled, and only then in 1.3, 1.6 and 2.0-litre four-cylinder form, Boreham sent Roger Clark to contest a televised rallycross meeting at Croft, near Darlington. A year earlier, Roger had shown off the original Escort Twin-Cam at Croft. Now he would do the same with the Capri. Quite simply, this appearance caused a sensation. Not only did the Clark/Capri 4WD combination win all three races that it started, but it set fastest time of the day overall. Where there was good traction, this monstrous Capri was no quicker than its rivals, but on muddy going, where traction mattered, it was uncatchable.

Apart from the four-wheel-drive installation this was still a very simple machine. Specification details included

*Boreham built three special four-wheel-drive Capri 3000GTs between 1969 and 1971 for rallycross use. Stan Clark, Roger's brother, was one of the regular drivers.*

rough-treaded Goodyear tyres (as used by the works Escorts on the recent Monte Carlo rally) on 7in-wide Minilite wheels, plastic side and rear windows, and a glass-fibre bonnet, plus Ford Taunus front-wheel-drive type front struts. Taunus? This was because the Taunus was then the only front-wheel-drive Ford in existence. The engine was only tuned a little – by no means as much as the cars which would follow in 1970 – not only because Ford didn't trust the ability of the new four-wheel-drive transmission to deal with more torque, but because they had not yet had much time to work on the engine.

Four weeks later two Capri 4x4s turned out at two different events. Ove Andersson drove the original Clark-mobile at Croft (where he couldn't match the pace of a white-hot works Mini-Cooper S), while at Lydden Hill Barry Lee was entrusted with a brand-new car with automatic transmission. It was unfair to ask much of Barry, who had not driven the car before he met it in the paddock before practice. Unhappily, he crashed it when the automatic transmission system kicked-down at an inappropriate moment !

After the original success everything then went very quiet at Boreham. Roger Clark complained loud and long about the car's handling and its brakes, demanding that the crude anti-lock mechanism be disconnected. Henry Taylor soon accepted that the performance of the much-vaunted Dunlop Maxaret braking system, which was being used on aircraft landing gear, could easily be beaten by skilled drivers. Henry personally proved this point on the Dunlop skid pan in Erdington, Birmingham, when driving his own Ford-USA Mustang Shelby Cobra.

But in early 1969, time was against any further progress. Rallycross was essentially a bad-weather, winter activity, which meant that this very special Capri would not be able to shine again before the end of the year. By then Henry Taylor had moved on, Stuart Turner had taken his place as Competition Manager, and at Boreham the World Cup Rally effort took precedence over everything.

In the meantime, prototype Capris shown to the world's press had also previewed Cosworth's all-new 16-valve 1.6-litre BDA engine. At that stage Boreham had had little to do with the evolution of the BDA, and Walter Hayes's original hope was to see it used in the Capri in due course. Initially, in fact, there were absolutely no plans to put this magnificent little power unit into an Escort of any sort. Within months, however, it became clear that a 3-litre V6-engined Capri would not only be more powerful than a BDA-Capri, but also more flexible and cheaper to produce, so no such car was ever put on sale, and the Capri 3-litre took prominence. When the time came, Hayes and Turner thought, Capri rallycross cars might be an ideal showcase for these cars, so the three existing cars went into storage for the time being.

By the autumn of 1970, with the *Daily Mirror* (London-Mexico) World Cup Rally won, the Capri 4WD rally-cross cars were made ready for use again. During the winter of 1970/71, three four-wheel-drive Capris were prepared and further developed for use in the ITV/Castrol rallycross series and at Lydden Hill. One of these was the car which had appeared briefly in February 1969, after which it had been stored at Boreham. All three cars used fuel-injected Essex V6 engines on which a lot of power-raising development work had been carried out; both Lucas and TJ systems were employed. Two cars, for Stan Clark and Rod Chapman to drive, had about 212bhp (later massaged up to nearer 230bhp), while Roger Clark's ferocious machine – the original 1969 car, by all accounts – used specially designed aluminium cylinder heads and straight-tube Lucas fuel injection to produce a very healthy 252bhp. This car needed a massive 'tower' on top of the bonnet to hide the inlet trumpets, which rather spoilt the car's looks.

Ford (and this was a typical Stuart Turner ploy, to ensure maximum publicity) arranged different media sponsorship for each car – the *Daily Express* for Roger Clark, the *Telegraph Magazine* for his brother Stan, and for Rod Chapman. Rod's car was not ready for the first meeting of the winter but joined in shortly afterwards.

The ever-inventive Mick Jones (who had taken over from Bill Meade as Boreham's Rally Engineer) would eventually have many rude things to say about these cars (no, let's be honest, very rude things), but did a great job with what was still a very crude four-wheel-drive installation, which by this time had been mated to an early version of the ZF five-speed main gearbox recently adopted on the works Escorts.

Interestingly enough, these were apparently the first 4WD systems ever to use an FF viscous coupling limited-slip device. Nothing was ever admitted about this at the time (not even Jeremy Walton's seminal book about the Capri mentions it), and such a diff would not finally be unveiled until the early 1980s. The V6 Capris, by the way, were the first works cars from Boreham to use Dunlop tyres for some years; this was a separate Stuart Turner-inspired contract, as the rally team's contract with Goodyear was still in force.

What followed was a rather troublesome campaign. Cars were entered in two different TV series, which ran to rather different sets of rules. In the six-round Castrol-sponsored ITV series based at Cadwell Park, in Lincolnshire, the Capris usually won if they did not hit mechanical trouble, because their 4WD system was not handicapped by the regulations. If they could harness their superior traction off the line (and this was usually possible) they could arrive at the first corner in the lead, then control the races. In this Championship the result was a perfect 1-2-3 in the standings, with Roger Clark leading the list narrowly from Rod Chapman, and Stan Clark (to quote Roger, 'my fat little brother') bringing up the tail.

At Lydden Hill, in the TEAC series, the Capris were obliged to start five seconds behind their two-wheel-drive rivals, which was a grave handicap. This meant that there was always an unseemly overtaking battle to be tackled. Not easy,

particularly in awful visibility! This, along with the fact that all three cars were still unreliable and were difficult to drive, meant that they struggled. In the end, Rod Chapman's car could only finish fifth in the Championship, with Roger eighth and Stan tenth.

The records, therefore, show that if there was no unfair attempt by the organisers to cut away at their advantage, then the cars did what they were asked to do, but none of the drivers really enjoyed them and there were many mechanical dramas to cope with. If it wasn't overheating due to mud blocking up the radiators, it was a tendency to break front driveshaft joints, and all the engines suffered repeatedly from fuel injection problems. Those were the days when, in spite of their cast iron bulk, the Essex V6 cylinder blocks were none too strong (Mick Jones once described the material as 'f*****g black-painted Weetabix'), and when revved very high several units lunched themselves.

After one very hectic winter the Capris (and their drivers!) were virtually worn out, and Ford sold off the remains to Stan Clark and Rod Chapman during 1971. As Roger Clark later wrote in his autobiography. "Basically, we ditched them because they were an enormous amount of trouble, not just in reliability, which was dreadful enough, but because they were absolute pigs to handle". Jeremy Walton once asked Roger for his comments. He replied, "It's vital to get the car into the right attitude way before a corner. If you can get that right, it's perfect, but more often it'll be wrong and you'd just wind up with more and more understeer lock". In addition the cars were heavy and there was a lot of friction in the transmission system, so they were not as fast as the original forecasts had suggested. Monsters? Oh yes, and like all monsters they became extinct.

*The most brutally powerful Capri 4x4 rallycross Capri of all was specially developed for Roger Clark to use in 1971. In its final form it had a 252bhp engine featuring Lucas fuel injection.*

# APPENDICES

## Appendix 1: Henry Taylor – Ford Competitions Manager 1965-69

As far as the works Cortinas and the evolution of the increasingly professional HQ at Boreham were concerned, Henry Taylor was a pivotal figure. The following is an edited version of the profile the author built up of Henry Taylor in a series of interviews.

In 1961 Ford's works rally team was using standard cars and amateur drivers. Ten years later they were using 16-valve Escort RS1600s and a highly-ranked squad of professionals. The transformation was complete, and much of the credit goes to Henry Taylor. First as a guest driver, then as *de facto* team leader, and finally as Competitions Manager, Taylor pushed through the changes which made Ford rally cars competitive.

"I lost the sight of an eye in F1 racing so I'd finished racing – my sight eventually came back, but not for some time. Then I met someone from Ford at a cocktail party," Henry Taylor recalls, "who asked me if I would do the Monte Carlo rally in an Anglia 105E. But I still knew nothing about rallying. I said OK, but only if I had a good co-driver, and could practice to find out what rallying was all about".

An easy to way to get a works drive? Maybe, but those were different days. Way back, and well before Boreham was even thought about, Ford's works team was running 105Es and Zephyrs, from the Lincoln Cars workshops in Brentford. Main Ford dealer T.C. 'Cuth' Harrison was the senior driver, with his chums and other 'good types' alongside him. Except for the year when Jeff Uren ran the team, the word professionalism was unknown.

Henry admits that he thought it would be easy: "In practice I was getting the Anglia sideways and really enjoying myself on ice, and I thought I could win the rally easily. Suddenly my co-driver [Dick Bensted-Smith of *Motor* magazine] said 'Stop!' So I did, and he said: 'If you don't get your finger out you will not get into the last 60'. That was the treatment I needed".

Not that he won anything that year, as the Monte handicap favoured the French Panhards. "I remember passing one of them, and taking about five minutes out of it on one long stage …but it still beat us on the formula". Ford, though, was impressed, and immediately hired him to do the full season. "They paid me a lot of money. All this time, by the way, I didn't tell them I had lost the sight of one eye".

### Developing the Cortina

This was the start of Ford's transformation. First they appointed a new Manager (Syd Henson), then the Cortina arrived, and shortly after that the new centre at Boreham was completed. Even for Henry, though, there would be no real successes until 1963: "Ford had lagged behind in preparation. The cars simply wouldn't go, they were still too heavy, and preparation was poor.

I started criticising the rally engineer, Jack Welch – I thought he was past it. He was a nice man but from the old school and he really didn't know what was going on".

Change came rapidly and in 1963 Alan Platt replaced Syd Henson. Platt was an able manager but no rallying expert, and – as so often – the team relied heavily on Bill Barnett for its know-how. Henry and Bill had managed to ease out the 'Old Lags' from the driving team, and in 1963 they were joined by the formidable Pat Moss along with David Seigle-Morris and Peter Riley.

Things began to look up, especially after Henry quite unofficially took his Cortina GT rally car, all ready to tackle the Alpine rally, to Alan Mann, who spent two days power-tuning it, stripping out weight, and improving the brakes by removing the stone guards behind the front discs. "After Alan had worked on it, it went like s\*\*t off a shovel – much faster than the other team cars. Alan also welded up the exhaust system – previously they hadn't been welded and kept falling off. Jack Welch was furious about this but I didn't care as my car did some great times. Unfortunately later on I got diarrhoea, and on the Entrevaux stage I told my co-driver I just had to stop. I stopped, did what I had to do, rushed back to the car – and all Brian said was, 'You've lost 28 seconds' – and I lost my Coupe des Alpes by 11 seconds".

Even so, in 1963 Henry took fourth on the Acropolis, third on the Alpine, fourth on the Spa-Sofia-Liège (in a Twin-Cam engined Cortina GT) – and sixth in the RAC rally, in a Lotus-Cortina. The works team had turned the corner, and Henry was leading it.

In the next two years Henry drove the cars, harried the engineers to make them faster, and even found time to win a race or two in one of the Alan Mann Racing Lotus-Cortinas. Although Pat Moss left the team, Vic Elford arrived, the Cortina GTs won the Safari, and the Lotus-Cortina shone in the Tour de France. Maybe Henry wasn't the fastest of all the drivers – which shows just how far Ford had progressed in a very little time – but he always had the ear of management. And a good thing too, especially after the post-1964 Safari shindig on the ballroom floor for the prizegiving: "On the event, Erik Carlsson had rolled his Saab sideways to get it out of a mud-hole. When we heard of this, the whole team did it to the winning Cortina, which was on the dance floor – and all the oil, petrol and battery acid went on to the polished floor and ruined it. Ford got a big bill".

Then there was the occasion when Walter Hayes invited the drivers and the media to an end-of-season party in Cortina, in the Italian Dolomites: "All the national champions were invited along, but Walter couldn't decide what to do with the journalists on one particular day. So, as I had been in England's bobsleigh team, he asked me to see if a Cortina would go down the bob run!

There wasn't much snow so I said I would have a look. Jim Clark was sitting next to me when we drove down the run. It was very narrow but maybe *just* wide enough. We actually pranged three cars trying this out. The first one was my fault. Jim then had a go, got too high on a corner, turned it over, and slid down the track on the roof. With the third car, I drove the car all the way down but damaged both front corners just keeping it between the walls".

Quite suddenly in mid-1965 Alan Platt was promoted and therefore recalled to Ford's central office, after which Walter Hayes made a phone call and Henry Taylor became Competitions Manager: "That meant big changes. First of all I had to sell the family farm in Bedfordshire, Peggy and I had to find a house near Boreham, and then I had to retire from driving – you couldn't do both jobs. Because I'd been driving for four years I could already see the problems. Not only did I get Bill Meade to take over from Jack Welch, but I got Peter Ashcroft in to run our engine programme."

Earlier, Henry had worked out ways of getting new gearbox ratios for the Cortina GT: "I went to see Jack Reece, the Ford dealer in Liverpool, and we went to see the plant manager at Halewood. The manager told me not to worry, he would do them on the night shift and would 100 sets be enough?" It was Henry's pressure which allowed Brian Melia to work at Boreham. Officially his job title was 'Navigator', but he spent much time assisting Bill Barnett and also looked after parts sales to private owners.

Enormous changes followed at Boreham, and it helped that Henry always had the ear of Walter Hayes. In any case, he stamped his authority on the workforce from his very first morning as Manager: "When I arrived the office and the workshops were still empty. Being a farmer I was always early – I was probably there by 7.30, and I understood the workshops started up at 8.00. That time came and went, and I hadn't seen anyone arrive. Suddenly I could hear the timing clock machine rattling away, and when I went into the workshop I found just one bloke clocking all the cards. No-one else had arrived". One chat with the union representative meant that this would never happen again. The workforce, though, must have cursed the farmer's background which always brought Henry into his office before their day had even started".

## Homologation specials

Suddenly the team and its cars began to blossom. Taylor and Barnett had already pushed through homologation of the leaf-spring Lotus-Cortina, and it wasn't long before a youthful Roger Clark joined the team. Bengt Soderstrom and Gunnar Palm soon joined them, which meant that Boreham, and Henry Taylor, seemed to have a 'Dream Team' for the future.

1966 should have been the year when Ford's rally team won everything – except that fate got in the way. Roger Clark's car was disqualified from the Monte (the 'lighting fiasco') and Vic Elford's from the San Remo (a homologation error), but the team fought back, with Soderstrom winning the Acropolis and the RAC. Work progressed with fuel-injected engines, BRM built most of the carburetted twin-cams during the season – and the original-shape Lotus-Cortina then went out of production.

Henry, though, could be quite ruthless. Once Vic Elford started complaining about his Lotus-Cortinas, their reliability, and the team around him, Henry soon decided to ease him out. Which he did, but not before formulating Plan B first. No sooner had Elford been shown the door than Ove Andersson from Sweden arrived. Ove would stay at Ford until after Henry had moved on.

At this time Henry's main racing contractors were Colin Chapman and Alan Mann, who were two entirely different characters: "Colin was the only person in my life where I needed to have a tape recorder fixed to the phone so that I could record what he said. Alan, though, was a very good engineer, a very clever man, far ahead of the rest. Alan would read every line of the Group 2 regulations, he would know them by heart."

It was all Henry's idea that F1 World Champion Jim Clark should drive in the rally team: "I said to Jim one day, 'Come and do the RAC rally for us, for the publicity. We'll train you properly'. It wasn't for the money – he just wanted a bit of fun. We didn't have to persuade him much. He and I were both farmers and we were old chums".

This was the time when Henry was at his most inventive. Although it was Bill Meade who most famously saw a prototype Escort and commented, "Blimey, that wouldn't half go with a twin-cam in it", it was Henry, along with product planner Bob Howe, who spent all of one Sunday at his house in Wickham Bishops, working out the details of it. It was Henry, too, who saw the potential of four-wheel-drive, and who arranged to 'borrow' a pre-production Capri in 1968 and sent it up to Ferguson in Coventry to be converted. Maybe that car didn't work very well at first, but Roger Clark won a rallycross event in it within weeks of the Capri's launch and inspired the building of a team for the 1970/71 series.

Once the Escort Twin-Cam was launched, it was Henry's much practised wide-eyed innocence (an expression which he honed to perfection, especially for dealing with officials) which ensured early homologation for the car. Very few Twin-Cams had been built when Ford approached the FIA to get the car approved to go rallying. As Bob Howe recently told me, "This led to the hilarious situation of the Homologation inspector sitting in Henry's office with Henry, Bill Barnett and, I think, Bill Meade, plus me as a 'proper' company representative whilst most of the fitters walked round and round the office building – past the windows – carrying the few modified wings, which supposedly had been taken from a delivery truck parked in the yard, to support the build. The FIA inspector finally certified that we qualified. Henry was brilliant, and convincing, at some things."

Like all true petrolheads, too, he was always pushing for improvements and for ways of making the cars quicker. Henry got on well with Alan Mann and always encouraged him to get the best out of the racing Escort Twin-Cams. Later, he would make sure that many AMR tweaks (courtesy of his designer Len Bailey) would be added, and homologated, to the works rally cars.

Henry was one of the first to urge Ford to start building special cars. Although he was not in on the ground floor of the AVO project (Bob Howe found the building at Aveley, and Ray Horrocks ran the operation in its early years), Walter Hayes soon found him invaluable in setting up the operation. "I helped to get AVO going. When Walter asked me who should take over from me, I suggested Stuart Turner …the rest you know."

Although Ford seemed to have earmarked Henry for higher-management jobs, he was not at all convinced about that prospect. After AVO he moved to Dagenham, where he ran sections of the assembly plant. A proposal to move him to Genk to run an operation at Ford-Belgium finally made him look around for another life. The result was that in 1972 he bought a large Yachting Park business in Golfe Juan, just down the coast from Nice in the south of France. Selling out in the late 1990s, he lived for many years in the cool house alongside the Park – and was always proud to recall the years in which he helped turn Ford Motorsport into a world-famous operation.

## Appendix 2: Identities – when is a car not a car?

In writing a massive book like this, when even the youngest machine described was already approaching its 50th birthday, I have often agonised over the way in which individual cars should be described.

The main problems are that no company – whether Ford or any of its trusted consultants of the day – has kept full and accurate records for such a lengthy period (and in some cases, never did so), so it has been difficult to work out what car did which events, why and in what state of mechanical tune. It has become normal for historians like myself (and other respected contemporaries) to identify a car by the registration number which it habitually carried. However, in some cases the cars – race cars, mainly – did not carry registration numbers at all. But can that be trusted? As I am sure most enthusiasts now realise, many long-serving cars were re-shelled more than once when in works hands, and have probably been re-shelled at least once since moving into private hands. Not only that, but at times of stress, when a car had been crashed or mechanically damaged in an event, and when an appearance just had to be made at the next outing in the calendar, it often seemed to be easier to move number plates from one car to another than to scratch the entry. This happened, for sure, in the period when Ford was racing or rallying Cortinas of one type of another.

Two examples spring to mind to make this point. In the late 1960s there was a classic case of a race Championship car being shown at the London Motor Show, while the 'same' car – i.e. one carrying the same registration number – was actually raced at Brands Hatch during the same weekend. The 'real' car, it seems, was racing, while the one on show at Earls Court was certainly an authentic sister car but had a borrowed number plate. On another occasion I was in a famous workshop inspecting cars being prepared for a major international rally, and in answer to an innocent query, "Which car is this?", was shown a small sheaf of registration plates and asked, "Which one would you like it to be?"

If, therefore, there is a reader out there who can suggest a better way of working out which car did what events and who drove it at any time, I would be delighted to be corrected in time for the next edition of this book.